THE
NATIONAL
DIALOGUE

A Framework for Sustainable Peace, Economic Growth, and Poverty Eradication in South Sudan.

LUAL A. DENG

Africa
World Books
Pty Ltd

A Note from the Publisher

The publisher wishes to acknowledge and thank Dr Douglas H. Johnson for his invaluable help and support for Africa World Books and its mission of preserving and promoting African cultural and literary traditions and history. Dr Johnson and fellow historians have been instrumental in ensuring that African people remain connected to their past and their identity. Africa World Books is proud to carry on this mission.

ISBN: 978-0-6489698-4-6 (paperback)
ISBN: 978-0-6489291-3-0 (hardback)

DEDICATION

◆

I dedicate this book to the people of South Sudan who have spoken the truth with courage, through the grassroots consultations and the three Regional Conferences, about the root causes of the crises of governance and leadership in our country. Our people have demonstrated beyond doubt their resilience to endogenous and exogenous shocks, a fundamental social capital that reinforces my professional conviction and commitment to serve them with integrity, pride, and dignity.

LIST OF CONTENTS

LIST OF TABLES

LIST OF FIGURES

ACKNOWLEDGEMENTS

◆

I would like to first thank President Salva Kiir Mayardit for appointing the Ebony Center for Strategic Studies as one of the five organizations constituting the Secretariat of the National Dialogue Steering Committee. Secondly, I thank the other four members of the Secretariat – Sudd Institute; Institute of Development, Peace, and Security Studies, University of Juba; South Sudan Council of Churches; and South Sudan Islamic Council – for their confidence in nominating me as the Coordinator of the Secretariat to the Leadership of the National Dialogue Steering Committee. Thirdly, my appreciation goes to the Leadership of the National Dialogue for appointing me as the Coordinator and for their unwavering support to the work of the Secretariat. Fourthly, I am highly indebted to my colleagues in the Secretariat for their commitment to the service of our people; I thank them from the bottom of my heart for enduring the stresses of my constant demand to meet the obligations of the task. Fifthly, Prof. Daniel Bromley assisted me in the reorganization of the chapters of the book and provided a foreword; I thank him for his continued support and for his interest to serve the people of South Sudan. Sixthly, I thank Ms. Alexandra Dominique Gould and Professor Augustino Ting Mayai for their editorial assistance. Finally, my daughter Nyandeng (NuNu) designed the cover of the book; I thank her greatly. I also thank Peter Lual Reec Deng, my publisher, for sharing my thoughts about and experience with the South Sudan's National Dialogue with the world.

FOREWORD

◆

Dr. Lual Deng stands alone in South Sudan. There is not another individual who possesses his comprehensive understanding of the social, economic, and political landscapes that now grip this tragic nation. However, understanding is but the first step in helping others to grasp the intricacies of what is currently impeding improved livelihoods, individual aspirations, and lasting peace. Yet, even when that shared comprehension settles over the land, there remains the Sisyphean task of getting that large boulder up to the eager summit. Here is the challenge of bringing others to your side. The National Dialogue is central to that necessity, and here again Lual Deng is a singular force.

There are many ways to express the wishes of the South Sudanese, and there are many ways to articulate their justified impatience with the "political class." I have listened to a variety of those lamentations. And I understand their frustrations. After all, those who survive by the incessant need to keep their cattle fed and watered do not have the luxury of doing nothing. Their motto, perhaps unspoken, is "… get on with it!" In the face of despair and persistent stasis, the worst thing that governments can do is to do nothing. The cattle keeper knows this all too well. It can keep him awake at night.

The National Dialogue is a promise and a threat. The vision is too grand, the logic too compelling, and the process too enlightened to risk failure. The stakes are now of such a magnitude that failure is not an option. That is the threat—that once again the comfortable ruling elites will continue to find reasons to squabble, dither, stall, argue, posture, and drag it out for show and trivial gains. Perhaps they imagine that doing so makes them look important. Actually, it reveals their defects as leaders.

In this book Lual Deng clarifies that which needs clarity, he gives structure to what remains inchoate, and he shows a clear way forward. This comprehensive work certainly increases the threat of the National Dialogue. After all, how can the political class fail to act when Lual has shown them a clear and inspiring road map?

Daniel W. Bromley
Anderson-Bascom Professor of Applied Economics (Emeritus)
University of Wisconsin-Madison

Acronyms

AAA	Abyei Administrative Area
AfDB	African Development Bank
AFM	Aggregate Financial Management
ARA	Arusha Reunification Agreement
ARCSS	Agreement On the Resolution of Conflict in the Republic of South Sudan
BGR	Bahr el Ghazal Region
BoSS	Bank of South Sudan
CANS	Civil Authority of New Sudan
CBO	Community Based Organizations
COLA	Cost of Living Allowance
CPA	Comprehensive Peace Agreement
DPF	Development Policy Forum
DPO	Development Policy Operations
FDI	Foreign Direct Investment
FDs	Former Political Detainees
FFP	Fund for Peace
FRM	Fiduciary Risk Management
FVP	First Vice President
FY	Fiscal Year
GDF	Growth Diagnostic Framework
GDP	Gross Domestic Product
GER	Greater Equatoria Region
GONU	Sudan Government of National Unity
GoSS	Government of South Sudan
GUNR	Greater Upper Nile Region
HLRF	High Level Revitalization Forum
IBRD	International Bank for Reconstruction and Development
ICT	Information and Communication Technology
IDA	International Development Agency
IDF	Infrastructure Development Fund
IFIs	International Financial Institutions
IGAD	Intergovernmental Authority on Development
IMF	The International Monetary Fund
IRA	Institutional Readiness Assessment
JCE	Jieng Council of Elders

JAM	Joint Assessment Mission
LDF/LDC	Local Dialogue Forum/Conference
M&E	Monitoring & Evaluation
MoFP	Ministry of Finance and Planning
NCP	National Congress Party
ND	National Dialogue
NDC	National Dialogue Conference
NDM	National Democratic Movement
NDS	National Development Strategy
NL	National Legislature
OECD	Organization for Economic Cooperation and Development
OFM	Operational Financial Management
OMB	Office of Management and Budget
PAA	Pibor Administrative Area
PFM	Public Financial Management
PoCs	Protection of Civilian Sites
R-ARCSS	Revitalized Agreement on the Resolution of Conflict in the Republic of South Sudan
RTGoNU	Revitalized Transitional Government of National Unity
RDC	Regional Dialogue Conference
SPLA	Sudan People's Liberation Army
SPLM	Sudan People's Liberation Movement
SSA	Sub-Saharan Africa
SSCC	South Sudan Council of Churches
SSND	South Sudan National Dialogue
SSOMA	South Sudan Opposition Movement Alliance
SSP	South Sudanese Pound
TBs	Treasury Bills
TCI	Technical Committee of Intellectuals
TCoS	Transitional Council of State
TNL	Transitional National Legislation
TNLA	Transitional National Legislative Assembly
TOF	Triangle of Fragility
TOR	Triangle of Resilience
UNDP	United Nations Development Programme
UNMISS	United Nations Mission in South Sudan
VP	Vice President

CHAPTER ONE

INTRODUCTION

◆

National Dialogue is both a forum and a process through which the people of South Sudan shall gather to redefine the basis of their unity as it relates to nationhood, redefine citizenship and belonging, restructure the state and renegotiate social contract and revitalize their aspirations for development and membership in the world of nations.[1]

The central premise of this book is that there comes always a point in the history of nations when leaders transform challenges (i.e. crises) into opportunities for serving their people with dignity and pride. The South Sudan National Dialogue (SSND) would seem to me to be the instrument through which our leaders could undertake such a transformation. However, the question that comes to mind on reading the title of this book is how could a national dialogue be a framework for sustainable peace, economic growth, and poverty eradication? The answer to such an inquiry lies in the above epigraph, which is under-pinned by the objectives of the South Sudan National Dialogue as articulated in the Concept Note.

The people of South Sudan have gathered and have expressed their views through grassroots consultations, which have culminated in three Regional Dialogue Conferences (RDCs) to be followed by a National

---

1   From Concept Note of South Sudan National Dialogue, By President Salva Kiir Mayardit (December 2016)

Dialogue Conference (NDC) as the last phase of the process. Moreover, the elites have gathered and spoken through the Intergovernmental Authority on Development (IGAD) High Level Revitalization Forum (HLRF), which has given birth to the Revitalized Agreement on the Resolution of Conflict in the Republic of South Sudan (R-ARCSS) that was finally signed in Addis Ababa, Ethiopia on 12 September 2018. The two processes – SSND and HLRF – have a strong synergy; a synergy that could be highlighted on how the five main points (5Rs) in the passage at the beginning of this book have been addressed. The people have been consulted with respect to the following:

1. *Redefine the basis of their unity as it relates to nationhood;*
2. *Redefine citizenship and belonging;*
3. *Restructure the state;*
4. *Renegotiate social contract; and*
5. *Revitalize their aspirations for development and membership in the world of nations.*

My focus is on the SSND, which has concluded its second of three phases. The third and final phase – the National Dialogue Conference (NDC) – has been interrupted by the coronavirus (COVID-19) pandemic and there is uncertainty as to when it would be convened. The delay in the convening of NDC does not, however, affect the central premise of this book, for sufficient information has been assembled, analyzed, and compiled in various documentations of the National Dialogue Steering Committee. Hence, putting my thoughts before the end of the process is driven by a sense of duty and obligation to give, as one of the individuals who have been involved in this noble project, an informed view at this point before the start of the third and final phase of the National Dialogue process. The overarching objective of this book is to show how the broader objectives of the national dialogue have been addressed. I would like first to provide the context in which the SSND was launched

South Sudan was born on July 9, 2011 with a "golden spoon" in its mouth and a solid political capital; symbolized on the one hand by monthly oil revenues of USD600 million, and as articulated by a strong international support on the other. There was, nevertheless, no national conversation among the stakeholders on how to govern the new state. Moreover, political dysfunctionality underpinned by weak institutions of governance accelerated the process of squandering these opportunities. Consequently, the new country in the world embarked, within six months of her independence, on series of "man-made" crises, such as the voluntary shutdown of oil production in January 2012; the invasion of Panthou/Heglig in April 2012; and violent conflict that erupted in December 2013. The consequences of the above series of "man-made" crises are manifested in:

1. *A generalized insecurity all over the country, including some areas in Greater Equatoria that were relatively peaceful until September 2016;*
2. *Inter-communal conflicts, e.g. in Greater Jonglei Sate;*
3. *A desperate humanitarian situation characterized by famine in the former Unity State and by about a million people in refugee camps in northern Uganda; and*
4. *An economy whose basic activities have essentially stopped functioning.*

It is by way of getting at the bottom of the root causes of the "man-made" crises that persuaded, in my view, President Salva Kiir Mayardit to initiate, on 14 December 2016, the National Dialogue for South Sudan. This was in his address to the people of South Sudan through the Transitional National Legislative Assembly (TNLA). The President outlined in his speech ten objectives of the SSND. These are to:

1. *End all forms of violence in the country;*
2. *Redefine and re-establish stronger national unity;*
3. *Strengthen social contract between the citizens and their state;*
4. *Address issues of diversity;*
5. *Agree on a mechanism for allocating and sharing of resources;*
6. *Settle historical disputes and sources of conflict among communities;*
7. *Set a stage for an integrated and inclusive national development strategy;*
8. *Agree on steps and guarantees to ensure safe, free, fair and peaceful elections and post transition in 2018;*
9. *Agree on a strategy to return internally displaced persons and refugees to their homes; and*
10. *Develop a framework for national peace, healing, and reconciliation.*

THE NATIONAL DIALOGUE

The call for a National Dialogue was generally welcome by a majority of the stakeholders, though there were some reservations from opposition groups outside the country[2]. It is, therefore, important that the key principles of a National Dialogue are highlighted so as to avoid any ambiguity about how the process was formulated and executed. In this regard, a review of the literature on national dialogues indicates that there are six key principles, which would have to be followed in order to have all the stakeholders on board. The principles are: a) inclusivity; b) transparency and public participation; c) a credible convener; d) an agenda that addresses the root causes of conflict; e) a clear mandate, appropriately tailored structure, rules and procedures; and f) an agreed upon mechanism for the implementation of the outcomes of the dialogue process.

The rest of the book is organized around three themes. Part I is about bringing peace to South Sudan and comprises of two chapters – the imperative of peace is discussed under Chapter 2, while Chapter 3 is on the structure and process of the National Dialogue. Part II is on the economy –its purpose and what makes it grow. There are four chapters – leveraging peace is the topic of Chapter 4, pathways to economic growth is discussed in Chapter 5, the curse of conflict on the economy is the focus of Chapter 6, and Chapter 7 is about corruption and its impact on the economy. Part III is on the revitalization of the economy and consists of three chapters. Chapter 8 highlights the role of the Presidency (i.e. leadership) in the revitalization of the economy, Chapter 9 is on economic policy management, and Chapter 10 is on the imperative of investing in broad capital formation.

---

2   Press statements and positions papers from a number of political parties questioned the choice of members of the Steering Committee and the Secretariat not to be consistent with the basic principles of inclusivity and transparency.

PART I

BRINGING PEACE
TO SOUTH SUDAN

CHAPTER TWO

THE IMPERATIVE
OF SUSTAINABLE PEACE
IN SOUTH SUDAN

◆

The next period will be payback time by the SPLM to the Sudanese people who fought and sacrificed for the last 21 years. The major problems and programs that will require extensive attention by the SPLM-based GOSS and the State Governments of the Nuba Mountains, Southern Blue Nile and Abyei during the Interim Period and beyond fall in the areas of physical infrastructure, good governance, financial infrastructure and viable markets, development and provision of social services and basic necessities: health, education, water, food security, employment opportunities, building the SPLA as an army that will safeguard the agreement, building the SPLM in both North and South to lead the political transformation of Sudan, and above all, dignity rather than elitism.[3]

The National Dialogue has revealed, through grassroots consultations, that sustainable peace is a function of leadership. The above passage from the historic speech of Dr. John Garang de Mabior on 9 January 2005 is an important point of departure for

---

3   From Dr. John Garang de Mabior's Address at the Signing Ceremony of the Comprehensive Peace Agreement (CPA) in Nairobi, Kenya on January 9, 2005

elaborating the critical role of visionary leadership in creating resilient institutions and associated capacities for effective governance. The opening sentence in the cited passage is, in my view, the foundation for sustainable peace. The sentence articulates the underlined professional conviction of Dr. John and his associates that the overarching objective of the liberation struggle was to ensure a *dignified and sustainable livelihoods for ordinary people in the marginalized areas of Sudan in general, and Southern Sudan in particular.*

The inherent logic for starting the next period at the end of the armed struggle with "*payback time by the SPLM to the Sudanese people who fought and sacrificed for the last 21 years,*" was to ensure sustainability of the Comprehensive Peace Agreement (CPA). It was not to immediately reward the liberators by starting the payment with themselves. The new leadership of the Sudan People's Liberation Movement (SPLM) after the tragic and untimely death of Dr. John on 30 July 2005 would seem to have, in my view, misinterpreted that inherent logic for payback time. It was re-interpreted to mean payback time for the ruling elite (or gun class, courtesy of Dr. Majak D'Agoot Atem[4]). The consequence of this misinterpretation was the inability to build "*the SPLM in both North and South to lead the political transformation of Sudan.*" The failure at political transformation was the beginning of the political dysfunctionality of the ruling party, the SPLM. Generalized insecurity and weak institutions of governance all over the country characterize such dysfunctionality.

Hence, the root causes of violent conflict in the land of plenty called the Republic of South Sudan have been identified, by the SSND through grassroots consultations, as injustice, unequal sharing of, and mismanagement of resources, including political power. Inequality, injustice, and mismanagement have appeared in the four clusters of issues that have emerged from the grassroots consultations. They are two faces of the same coin; which is political dysfunctionality. I would therefore think that political dysfunctionality is the key driver of our crises of gover-

---

4   "Taming the Dominant Gun Class in South Sudan." Special Report No. 4: Envisioning A Stable South Sudan (May 29, 2018). See https://africacenter.org/spotlight/taming-the-dominant-gun-class-in-south-sudan

nance and leadership. This calls for a complete political transformation of South Sudan.

I have taken three out of twelve (12) reports of Subcommittees of the Steering Committee of the National Dialogue to be a representative sample of the grassroots' views on governance. These reports are from: 1) Northern Bahr el-Ghazal (representing Greater Bahr el-Ghazal Region); 2) Upper Nile (representing Greater Upper Nile Region); and 3) Central Equatoria (representing Greater Equatoria Region). I have added to these the views of the organized forces ((SPLA, Police, National Security, Fire Brigade, Prison and Wildlife Services).

The Northern Bahr el-Ghazal Subcommittee

The people in Northern Bahr el-Ghazal have identified ten issues that have undermined the effectiveness of governance and subsequently to the eruption of violent conflict. The issues under the Governance Cluster:

1. *Lack of respect for the rule of law and constitutionalism;*
2. *Weak institutions of transparency and accountability;*
3. *Power struggle;*
4. *Loss of vision and unclear priorities;*
5. *Creation of many states, which are not sustainable administratively and financially;*
6. *Political differences, division, and grouping in the SPLM are responsible for the crises in the country;*
7. *SPLM has been hijacked by strangers, i.e. by people who were not part of the liberation struggle;*
8. *Lack of political will to implement treaties the country has signed;*
9. *Weak diplomacy and lack of a well-defined foreign policy, which in turn encourages encroachment of our international borders by neighboring countries; and*
10. *No interest in democracy to conduct timely elections.*

The Upper Nile Subcommittee

The issues under the Governance Cluster:

1. *Power struggle among the politicians;*
2. *Lack of accountability;*
3. *Lack of the rule of law;*
4. *Divisive policies used by the government;*
5. *Administrative failure;*
6. *Tribalism and nepotism practiced by politicians;*
7. *Unfair distribution of national resources;*
8. *Marginalization of some communities;*
9. *Rewarding the rebels with high political and military positions;*
10. *Land and border disputes;*
11. *Creation of more states in the country was one recurring issue in many consultative meetings as the engine of the conflict in the area;*
12. *Cattle rustling/raiding;*
13. *The politicians inciting the citizens against each other; and*
14. *Lack of service delivery to the citizens.*

Table 2.1: Views of the organized forces on root causes of poor governance

SOURCE	CAUSES	EFFECTS	RECOMMEND-ATIONS
Legislative	-Selection/ Appointment of semi-illiterates to the parliament based on mere representation. - Monopoly/ combination of executive and legislative powers in one person. - Ambiguity in the constitution -Information breakdown between MPs and their constituencies.	- Dormant and passive parliament. -Conflict of interest. -Lack of check and balance principles -Absence of effective governance -Lack of parliamentary oversight	-Parliament should impeach any corrupt public official found guilty of misappropriation of public fund or misuse of his/her position in any form. -Develop check-and-balance system by enforcing parliamentary oversight - Constitutional review.

SOURCE	CAUSES	EFFECTS	RECOMMEND- ATIONS
Executive	–Lack of a clear vision and grand strategy –Weak institutions –Appointment based on nepotism and favoritism. –Re-structuring of states without popular consultation –Misinterpretation of decentralized governing system, including localization of government administrators –Weak foreign policy – Lack of Revenue Authority to organize revenue collection	–Loss of sense of direction – Rampant corruption at all levels of government – Lack of service delivery – Weak foreign relations – Wrangling among all levels of government over taxes	–Clear vision, one objective for the nation should be developed – Implementation of laws, rules and regulations that govern the operations at all levels –Review and restructure foreign policy strategy. –Government to review its current policy of appointing senior state officials (Governors, ministers, etc.) within their localities. In other words, avoid localization of Government Administration –Support the implementation of the ARCSS and other agreements entered into by the government –Transformation of civil service –Strengthening the weak government institutions –Eradicate harmful practices (eg. Corruption, nepotism and tribalism) –Nationalism be inculcated in every citizen –Adoption of suitable federal system that suits the interests, cultures and values of South Sudan. –Transparency and accountability –Establishment of Revenue Authority to streamline collection of revenues

THE NATIONAL DIALOGUE

SOURCE	CAUSES	EFFECTS	RECOMMEND-ATIONS
Judiciary	-Weak judiciary system -Interference of the executive in the judiciary system -Weak law enforcement agencies	-Myriads of crimes at alarming rate -Lack of implemen-tation of rule of law	-Restructuring of judiciary system and law enforcement agencies -Strict enforcement of rule of law
Historical (SPLM/A)	-Power struggle of Anya'Anya 2 over the leadership that ended in 1987 which led to the integration of the Anya'Anya 2 into SPLA -Incident of Kerbino Kuanyin Bol in 1987 -Incident of Arok Thon Arok in 1988 -Coup attempt & rebellion of Dr. Riek, Dr. Lam & Gordon Kong, 1991 -Rebellion of William Nyuon, 1992 -The Yei Disagreement (Before signing of CPA), 2004 -Following the death of Dr. John Garang, Salva Kiir was endorsed as successor by the leadership of SPLM/A, which annoyed some elements within the leadership of the SPLM/A e.g. Dr. Riek Machar and Dr. Lam Akol	-All problems mentioned herein during the liberation struggle, had a ripple effect on the ongoing conflicts in South Sudan; for example: i. poor image of South Sudan regionally and internationally ii. Disunity and disharmony among the communities	-National reconciliation and healing -Building the spirit of nationalism and national identity

SOURCE	CAUSES	EFFECTS	RECOMMEND-ATIONS
Political	- SPLM struggle over leadership, and issues of government corruption and lack of accountability -Intentional deviation from the Constitution of the SPLM party and electoral college system guiding rules led to indiscipline in the party. The same scenario occurs in other political parties -The government reshuffle in July 2013 and SPLM National Liberation Council discussion on reform document generated anger among the SPLM members, which led to December 2013 alleged coup attempt and rebellions -SPLM's loss of direction undermines the development of the spirit of nationalism and unity -Weak political parties in the country -Lack of political will to resolve conflicts		

The Central Equatoria Subcommittee

The issues under the Governance Cluster:

1. *Tribalism has become the main source of conflict in South Sudan that has affected the whole country as reflected in: a) tribal army so called Mathiang Anyor, which is seen as the main source of conflict in Yei River State and in other parts of Central Equatoria (e.g. Bongo and Lobonok in Jubek state); and b)* **The *Jieng* Council of Elders** *(JCE) is accused of being the main contributor to all the conflicts in South Sudan.*
2. *Power struggle has also become one of the main sources of conflict in South Sudan.*
3. *Pastoralists are seen as the main source of conflicts in former Central Equatoria State, particularly in Yei River State.*
4. *Corruption: Most government officials are corrupt and steal from public funds, but they are not accountable for their actions.*
5. *Land has become a big problem in former Central Equatoria State and needs serious intervention from the national government.*
6. *State boundaries: Issues of boundaries between Terekeka and Bor, Terekeka and Jubek are seen in Terekeka State as serious enough problems to warrant intervention from Central Government.*

The Subcommittee on the organized forces

The views of the organized forces are presented in a tabular format that was taken from the report of the Subcommittee. I have taken the format, as it is, to illustrate the clear understanding of the organized forces about the crises facing South Sudan as a country.

The views on the root causes of poor governance are consistent with the findings of many policy analysts dealing with South Sudan. These views are also consistent with the general literature on fragile states. They would not have been expressed without a political space that was made available through open and transparent grassroots consultations process. It is this political space, which has led me to conceptualize the National Dialogue as a framework for sustainable peace, economic growth, and poverty eradication. I would rely on my previous work on fragility and economic growth to show how the SSND could be an operational framework for sustainable peace. Lual A Deng et al have, for instance, stated the problem as follows:

> Since 1983, the Sudan People's Liberation Movement (SPLM) has been the vehicle by which the oppression of South Sudanese under several regimes in Khartoum has been vanquished; the instrument by which the long-standing civil war was ended; and the mechanism by which independence was achieved. Yet, over time, particularly since 2005, the SPLM and its leaders have greatly declined in effectiveness, mired in corruption, tribalism, and mismanagement while its unique vision has been forgotten, resulting now in a dysfunctional government despised by many though once the darling of the world. The current violent conflict started in December 2013 is the result of this dysfunctionality, which if not halted will plunge the new nation into the abyss[5].

They farther stated that:

> We can unambiguously conclude, in the light of the preceding paragraph, that there is now a general consensus within the development policy community (local, regional, and international) that the underlying cause of the current violent conflict in South Sudan is the failure of the political system to build resilient institutions and effective governance. That is, political dysfunctionality has in turn led on the one hand to the crisis of governance and leadership, and on the other into a fragility trap[6].

A critical look at the above two passages would indicate that violent conflict could have been avoided if there were in place a political space and/or a system of dialogue both within the SPLM as a ruling party and within all segments of society in the country. It would be recalled that the current crisis of governance in South Sudan was triggered by an

---

5   See "A Conceptual Framework for Resolving the Crisis of Governance and Leadership in South Sudan." A paper presented to the Development Policy Forum (DPF), By: Lual A. Deng, Constantine O. Bartel, Abraham A. Awolich, Augustino Ting Mayai, Census Lo-Liyong, Zechariah Manyok Biar, James Alic Garang, Elias Nyamlell-Wakoson, and Grace Keji. On 19 July 2014: from 10:00 to 13:00 hours, Juba Grand Hotel, Juba, Republic of South Sudan

6   Ibid

internal disagreement within the SPLM Political Bureau (SPLM-PB) when Dr. Riek Machar challenged, in February 2013, the leadership/ chairmanship of President Salva Kiir. Dr. Machar raised the following six issues as clear evidence of leadership failure of Chairman Kiir:

1. *Dysfunctional SPLM;*
2. *Generalized insecurity in the country;*
3. *Economic mismanagement;*
4. *Pervasive corruption;*
5. *Foreign policy failure; and*
6. *Tribalism.*

There were attempts behind the seen by some SPLM policy analysts to persuade Chairman Kiir, First Deputy Chairman, Dr. Machar and Secretary General Mr. Pa'gan Amum to dialogue around the above stated six issues. The First Deputy Chairman and the Secretary General ignored all those efforts by insisting that the Chairman of the SPLM was solely responsible for all the six problems. In fact, the three leaders of the SPLM are equally responsible for the drivers behind the above six (6) symptoms of South Sudan's malady. This is because they were all in the government during the period from August 2005 to July 23, 2013. This is a long period in which they could have resolved these issues amicably and without resorting to the senseless war that has cost the country thousands of human lives and billions of United States dollars in both private and public properties.

The people of South Sudan, through the National Dialogue process, have now confirmed the six issues. The people have identified peace to be a pre-requisite in implementing the proposed solutions for resolving the root causes of the crises with the above-mentioned symptoms. Some of the recommendations for resolving the crises of governance and leadership are contained in the Communiqués of the Regional Dialogue conferences presented in the next chapter (i.e. three) of this book. The challenge then is for President Salva Kiir Mayardit to create an enabling environment for the full and timely implementation of the recommendations and resolutions of the National Dialogue. The President was the one who made the grassroots consultations to succeed by opening a political space for people to express their views freely and without intimidation. Moreover, his decision confirms *"it's leadership, stupid,[7]"* as far as the crises of South Sudan are concerned.

Leadership: In Turbulent Times, by Doris Kearns Goodwin[8], would be a good reference for President Kiir and his associates as they ponder on the ultimate legacy he will leave behind. The President has a golden opportunity to make the SSND one of his enduring legacies and which would be the tenth decision of his leadership in turbulent times. I encourage associates/advisers of President Kiir to carefully study the following long passage from one of the reviews of this timely book:

> Doris Kearns Goodwin demonstrates how leaders are made, not born, as she thoughtfully explores the highs and lows of four U.S. presidents who faced moments of horrific national crisis. Goodwin's clean, assured sentences set the stage as each future president discovers within himself the desire to enter politics, the calamitous blows that knocked each one down, and how they tackled the struggles that tore at the sinews of the country. Most fascinating is Goodwin's revelations about how very differently Abraham Lincoln, Theodore Roosevelt, Franklin D. Roosevelt, and Lyndon B. Johnson approached not only their political careers but how they developed the character traits that helped them see—or make—a path toward a critical response that many others disagreed with. Lincoln's delivery of the Emancipation Proclamation, Theodore Roosevelt's handling of labor strikes, FDR's battle against the Great Depression in his first 100 days, and Johnson's prioritization of civil rights while a nation mourned were actions that could have ripped the country further apart but eventually bound it together and strengthened its democratic foundations. The rare weakness within Leadership: In Turbulent Times is the outlining of specific qualities, such as "Take the measure of the man" and "Set a deadline and drive full-bore to meet it," that are meant to distill leadership wisdom into bullet points, like contemporary business books[9].

I would venture to mention nine decisions of President Kiir, which

---

7   I am re-phrasing James Carville's "The economy, stupid," which he invented when he was a campaign strategist of Bill Clinton's successful 1992 presidential campaign against president George H. W. Bush

8   Doris Kearns Goodwin. 2018. Leadership: In Turbulent Times

9   From Amazon Best Book of September 2018

capture or describe his leadership in turbulent times. The first is the Yei standoff of October 2004 in which a bloody confrontation between the late Chairman Dr. John Garang and his Deputy Salva Kiir was avoided. Commander Kiir accepted the call for dialogue, with Dr. John Garang from various segments of the society, especially leaders from Rumbek. This decision of listening to the advice of the people paved the way for the signing of the Comprehensive Peace Agreement (CPA) on 9 January 2005.

The second decision is when he pushed the SPLM to join the Sudan Government of National Unity (GONU) in September 2005 even though the National Congress Party (NCP) had violated the rules and procedures for selecting cabinet portfolios as stipulated in the CPA. Had the SPLM not joined the GONU, the CPA would have collapsed and South Sudan might have been still struggling until now for its independence.

The third decision is when he ordered in April 2012 the SPLA forces to pull out from **Panthou** (so called Hegilig), which they had pre-maturely taken over without orders from the President. The SPLA leadership didn't know then that the President of the Republic of South Sudan is the only one who could declare war with another sovereign state after the approval of the National Legislature (NL). The decision to withdraw from **Panthou** was not popular with the people of South Sudan, but it was the correct one given the strong opposition then from the international community in general, and friends of South Sudan in particular.

The fourth decision is the signing in February 2015 of the Arusha Reunification Agreement (ARA) of the SPLM. The fifth decision of President Kiir is the signing in August 2015 of the Agreement for the Resolution of Conflict in the Republic of South Sudan (ARCSS).

The sixth decision is the sparing of the life of Dr. Riek Machar at the Presidential Palace (popularly known as J1) on the evening of 8 July 2016. President Kiir ensured the safety of his political rival after what looked like a "dog fight" between their respective guards that left behind dead bodies littering within and around J1. President Kiir, through this humane act, demonstrated beyond doubt, skills of leadership in turbulent times. The seventh decision is the initiation and launching of the South Sudan National Dialogue in December

2016 and May 2017 respectively. The relevant point here is when President Kiir decided not to be a patron of the National Dialogue; a decision, which in turn ensured the independence and credibility of the dialogue process. The eighth decision is the lifting, in 2017, of military barricade around the house of Gen. Paul Malong Awan, former Chief of General Staff of the SPLA. A potential devastating confrontation was thus avoided.

The ninth decision is the signing of the Revitalized ARCSS on 12 September 2018 in Addis Ababa, Ethiopia. The R-ARCSS has created an enabling environment for the pursuit of sustainable peace by all stakeholders, including the political parties as evidenced by the Pretoria Declaration of April 2019. The Declaration was adopted by all the seven grouping of South Sudanese political parties, including SPLM-IO of Dr. Riek Machar. It affirmed that[10]:

> The Retreat offered the participants the opportunity to foster and strengthen their unity of purpose and to engage in cordial and constructive dialogue on the challenges confronting the country and the need for credible mechanisms for the implementation of the recommendations of the National Dialogue. Presentations were made by experts on the experience of South Africa and of other national dialogues, with emphasis on methods of achieving peace and reconciliation, and how they can best be adapted to the specific conditions of South Sudan.

The lack of dialogue and absence of a culture of internal democracy within the SPLM could, in my view, constrain President Kiir from implementing some of the key recommendations of the SSND during these turbulent times in our history. This is because the politics of fear has come to dominate the way the SPLM is managed. It is, therefore, important to reassure those around President Kiir that the call for regime change is no longer a viable agenda in the light of the National Dialogue. Nevertheless, it is important to know the behavior of a leader of any entity, such as country or firm in a conflict environment. For instance, being insecure creates tactical responses that become an

---

10   The Declaration was issued on 12 April 2019 in Pretoria, South Africa by representatives of: SPLM, SPLM-IO, FDs, South Sudan Opposition Alliance (SSOA), National Agenda, National Alliance, and Umbrella

integral part of rational behavior of a leader and accepted by his/her associates overtime.

For instance, leaders (on both sides of the conflict) are not sure if they would be forgiven and protected if they voluntarily and peacefully give up their positions. They would, unless they have a vision and political morality, hang-on to power, until they meet their fate in one way or another! But, there are diminishing returns to the utility of the politics of fear, so our leaders must be prepared for the eventual awakening of the people of South Sudan from their *"induced-long sleep"* since that dark night of July 30, 2005, when Dr. John Garang left us forever.

The work of Alex de Waal on kleptocracy (2014)[11], Daniel Akech Thiong on the politics of fear (2018)[12], and Majak D'Agoôt (2018) on the "gun class," constitute, in my view, important contributions to the empirical literature on the root causes of poor governance in South Sudan as expressed by our people through grassroots consultations and regional dialogue conferences. That is, poor governance seems to be underpinned by fear of the "unknown gunmen!" The potential whistleblowers are afraid to say anything, while the national revolutionaries become prisoners of their own fear as well as the desire for living. D'Agoôt particularly articulates below what seems to be inherent in our political culture:

South Sudan's proclivity for violence and conflict and its inability to acquire institutional depth is broad and deep. In part, this is attributed to age-old militarization of all facets of life and society stretching back to slavery and colonialism. Self-interested elites have held sway because of the utility of violence. In the past, native servicemen provided military clout to the extractive colonial enterprise and plunder. Afterward, similar arrangements were utilized by the indigenes to purge the homeland from

---

11 de Waal, Alex. 2014. "When Kleptocracy Becomes Insolvent: Brute Causes of The Civil War In South Sudan." African Affairs, 113/452, 347–369. Published by Oxford University Press on behalf of Royal African Society

12 Thiong, Daniel Akech. 2018. "How The Politics Of Fear Generated Chaos In South Sudan." African Affairs, 1–23. Published by Oxford University Press on behalf of Royal African Society

foreign occupation—particularly from Sudanese Jalaba colonialism[13].

The people of South Sudan have, however, crossed this point of fear, evidenced by the way they spoke during the grassroots consultations. They are slowly overcoming the *"age-old militarization of all facets of life and society."* Hence, the political elites must draw some lessons from the SSND process and from the following powerful passage by the New York Times Opinion Columnist, Roger Cohen in describing the Lebanese public discontent:

> People are sick of the sectarian manipulation of politics to mask theft, corruption and state capture by oligarchical elites. They are sick of the manipulation of fear. They are sick of the life being sucked out of them[14].

If we substitute "sectarian" with "tribalism," the above citation would perfectly fit the description of what the people of South Sudan have essentially said during the National Dialogue process. People are no longer afraid to express their views openly and without any intimidation. The third Regional Dialogue Conference (RDC) was that of Greater Equatoria, which demonstrated beyond doubt that the National Dialogue has created a political space, which the political leaders of South Sudan must take advantage of. But, how?

I would answer this intriguing question by turning to the idea of a **viable South Sudanese State at peace with itself and with its neighbors**. We must not dwell on the past blaming each other on the failure to create a coherent state by those in charge of our affairs since 2005. We have to focus on sustainable peace as one of the pressing demands of state creation in South Sudan. That is, we need a state that will ensure the pursuit of sustainable peace, economic growth, and poverty eradication. There are two views about the nature of South Sudanese state. The first is by Daniel Bromley, which considers South

---

13 "Taming the Dominant Gun Class in South Sudan." Special Report No. 4: Envisioning A Stable South Sudan (May 29, 2018). See https://africacenter.org/spotlight/taming-the-dominant-gun-class-in-south-sudan/

14 The New Middle East of a Post-Sectarian Generation: America is gone. Regional leaders have concluded Trump is all hat and no camel, a pawn of Saudi Arabia. The New York Times, Opinion November 8, 2019

Sudan to be a notational state:

> The absence of a coherent state in South Sudan is apparent by the lack of essential government services across the full geographic extent of the nation. This absence of essential government services is the reason for—it explains—the persistence of civil conflict.[15]

He farther explains that:

> States have evolved as extensions of historic collections of families and clans. The central purpose of states is to offer a constellation of services that individuals, living in isolation and autarky, are unable to provide for themselves. The survival of the idea of states resides in the obvious economies of scale in the provision of essential services. These services consist of two broad classes: (1) a constellation of necessary goods and services that facilitate sustainable livelihoods; and (2) the necessary institutional architecture that enables individuals to go about their life reasonably secure in their social and economic circumstances[16].

The second view is that South Sudan was born on 9 July 2011 as a fragile state; a characteristic it inherited from Sudan, which was ranked 3rd that year on the list of the most fragile state in the world[17]. This is further articulated by the Fund for Peace (FFP) as follows:

> Instability and violence continue to define Sudan. The southern half of the country voted to secede from the north in January 2011. Though this process has been partially successful, new clashes are now being reported between the North and the South, especially in and around Abyei. The discovery of oil in southern Sudan in 2005 [sic] exacerbated an already complex secession crisis and it remains to be seen how peaceful the planned separation will be. Violence also continues in Darfur, sending refugees into central Sudan and neighboring states, giving the conflict

---

15   South Sudan: Institutional Environment for Service Delivery. Ebony Policy Brief: EPB #2019/2

16   Ibid

17   Sudan was ranked number 3 in the Failed States Index 2011, published by the Fund for Peace (FFP) on June 18, 2011

a regional dimension. Leaders in the North and the South will have to exercise restraint in the use of violence by fringe rebel groups if the fragile peace is to be kept[18].

The International Monetary Fund (IMF) in one of its studies defines fragile states, as "*states in which the government is unable to reliably deliver basic public services to the population — face severe and entrenched obstacles to economic and human development*[19]." The IMF study further explains that: "*While definitions of fragility and country circumstances differ, fragile states generally have a combination of weak and noninclusive institutions, poor governance, and constraints in pursuing a common national interest.*[20]" Moreover, the Organization for Economic Cooperation and Development (OECD[21]) defines a fragile country as one that "*lacks political will and / or capacity to provide basic functions needed for poverty reduction, development and to safeguard the security and human rights of their populations.*"
There is an over-riding commonality from the two views of the ideas of a state and that is the "*necessary institutional architecture that enables individuals to go about their life reasonably secure in their social and economic circumstances.*" This **necessary institutional architecture** is what we should focus on in our determined quest for sustainable peace, economic growth, and poverty eradication. How did we miss to put in place the necessary institutional architecture that would have provided "*basic functions needed for poverty reduction, development and to safeguard the security and human rights*" of our people?

It would seem to me that we did not comprehend the nature and magnitude of the fragility we were in! Hence, I provide at this juncture what I consider to be the drivers of the vicious cycle of fragility in order to deepen our understanding of it. I categorize the key characteristics of a fragile state into two categories. The first category is what I would like to call "*drivers of conflict-induced fragility.*" The report of OECD has identified four drivers of conflict in a fragile state. Three

---

18 Ibid

19 Quoted from Building Resilience in Fragile States in Sub-Saharan Africa, chapter 2 of *Regional Economic Outlook for Sub-Saharan Africa,* African Department, International Monetary Fund, October 2014

20 ibid

21 States of Fragility 2015: Meeting Post-2015 Ambitions, OECD Publishing, Paris, France

of these drivers – injustice, inequality, and ethnic tensions – are more relevant to the South Sudanese situation. The second category constitutes what the same OECD report identifies as dimensions of fragility:

- *Violence dimension;*
- *Justice for all dimension;*
- *Institutions dimension;*
- *Economic foundations dimension; and*
- *Capacity to adapt to shocks and natural disasters dimension.*

I would call OECD's dimensions as symptoms/indicators of fragility or of a notational state, which are manifested in violent conflict on the one hand, and weaknesses in system of justice, institutions, economic foundations, and capacity on the other. Ethnic-based injustice (real or perceived) is likely to create unequal opportunities (inequality) between the various ethnic groups (nationalities/tribes) comprising a multi-ethnic country, such as South Sudan.

That is, when one ethnic group dominates access to political power, resources and wealth creation opportunities, the excluded groups would resist by all means available to them, what they see as injustice and associated inequality. These drivers, in turn, deepen the fragility of the state (i.e. weakening the basic functions) and thereby creating a vicious circle of fragility that is difficult to break, especially where there is a knowledge gap on how these drivers and dimensions interact and reinforce each other.

It is now clear, in my view, that fragility has been a major intervening characteristic in Salva Kiir's leadership in turbulent times. What is equally clear is that the Leadership Council of the SPLM, which elected him unanimously on 1st August 2005 to fill the position of the Chairman upon the tragic death of Dr. John Garang, did not provide the new Chairman with sufficient political space. I would argue that such a political space was necessary, though not sufficient for Chairman Kiir to embark on building the SPLM that would have in turn lead the process of political transformation (or state building) as envisaged by Chairman Garang. The first step in this process of transformation was the creation of resilient institutions and capacities for effective governance. Such a first step was never taken, since the SPLM was, according to the views from the grassroots, hijacked and rendered dysfunctional by the very people who opposed the Movement during the liberation struggle.

I would cite only two cases to illustrate my point on how the new Chairman was not given a space within the Movement/Party to pursue a coherent strategy for achieving political transformation. The first was when the SPLM suspended in September 2007 its participation in the GONU for a period of three months without any tactical or strategic plan. The second is when Chairman Kiir tried during the Second Convention of the SPLM in May 2008 to replace Dr. Machar and Secretary General Pa'gan Amum with those whom he thought could help him in establishing a robust political system in the country through a process of political transformation. He was persuaded by some wise and eminent Southern Sudanese personalities not to do that in the light of the envisaged referendum on self-determination, which required unity of all the people of South Sudan.

The requisite broad-based national conversation on the process of state building (i.e. political transformation of South Sudan) was, therefore, delayed by several years. The consequences of such a delay are manifested by the vicious cycle of fragility that has trapped South Sudan. Hence, the National Dialogue is an important vehicle to enable South Sudan to embark on the state building project. Daniel Bromley reminds us that:

> State building is a process of creating governance across the geographic space of a nation. Specifically, state building requires the construction and maintenance of a transportation and communication infrastructure, the provision of certain public services (schools, electricity, water and sanitation, the national defense, domestic security), and a legal structure that acknowledges and enforces various property regimes, contracts, and judicial protections[22].

The participants of the National Dialogue process, at the three Regional Conferences, came from *"across the geographic space of a nation"* and unani-

---

22   South Sudan: Institutional Environment for Service Delivery. Ebony Policy Brief: EPB #2019/2

mously agreed on the establishment of a federal presidential system of governance for South Sudan. The underlined premise of this unanimity is that establishment of a federal system of governance would in turn eliminate injustice, inequality, and ethnic tension on the one hand, and provide equal access to resources and opportunities for wealth creation on the other.

This unanimity on the system of governance by the people of South Sudan would, however, require the leadership of all political parties to internalize three key concepts – **governance, capacity, and institutions**. These three concepts are, in my view, the pillars of a coherent state that we desire for the people of South Sudan. Stated differently, the desired outcome from the process of political transformation is to create, what Daniel Bromley calls, a coherent state. He states:

> South Sudan became an independent nation on July 9, 2011. Eight years later it is still not a coherent state. Coherent states require two essential attributes—one of which is structural in nature, the second of which concerns processes. When these two necessary conditions are absent, the economy cannot perform its necessary functions, and civil conflict is inevitable. These necessary structural and procedural parameters are institutions.[23]

The challenge then is to fully understand the three pillars of a coherent state. The rest of this chapter is, therefore, devoted to the task of explaining each of these pillars with the main objective of contributing to the debate on the state building project; a debate which has been made possible by the National Dialogue process. Those political leaders and their parties that will not listen to what the people of South Sudan have said during the National Dialogue process will do that at their own peril. The time for "tribal manipulations" is over and gone forever after the broad-based grassroots consultations on what has gone wrong in our country, which has been established through the precious souls of martyrs.

----

23 Daniel W. Bromley (2019). South Sudan: Country Policy and Institutional Environment, Ebony Policy Brief, EPB#2019/1

Effective Governance for a Coherent State

This is the first pillar in our determined quest for a viable South Sudanese state at peace with itself and with its neighbors. But, we must first have a common understanding of the idea of governance. A common understanding of the term governance among all the stakeholders is, in my view, a *sine quo non* for creating a coherent state underpinned by resilient institutions and effective capacities. And there is an emerging body of empirical work on governance that would assist the leaders of South Sudan to internalize this concept.

The Information and Communication Technology (ICT) has now made information easily accessible to analysts. Moreover, the advent of social media has popularized the usage of certain political terms that were inaccessible to ordinary people few years ago. For instance, policy analysts around these leaders could benefit from an empirical body of literature on governance, which is accessible for instance at the World Bank website. Daniel Kaufmann, Aart Kraay, and Massimo Mastruzzi (KKM) give a comprehensive definition of governance.

> [T]he traditions and institutions by which authority in a country is exercised. This includes (1) the process by which governments are selected, monitored and replaced, (2) the capacity of the government to effectively formulate and implement sound policies, and (3) the respect of citizens and the state for the institutions that govern economic and social interactions among them[24].

Governance is underpinned, in my view, by the moral foundations of sustainable livelihoods of the citizenry. In this regard, the people of South Sudan have now chosen a federal system as the tradition through which authority will be exercised. They are also recommending a presidential system be adopted with a two-term limit, and a clear separation of powers between the three branches of government – **executive**, **legislature**, and **judiciary**. What is not clear though, is the type of federal system that is suitable to the objective conditions of South Sudan. It is disappointing to note that discussion within the

---

24   See htt://www.worldbank.org/wbi/governance/Kaufmann

political community in South Sudan, about federalism, has drifted into the number of the states and not the features of such a system.

The KKM's definition essentially tells us that traditions and institutions by which authority is exercised must be inclusive for countries to exit from fragility or avoid it all together. That is, countries must include traditions and moral values of all the stakeholders (e.g. ethnicities/tribes); so as to ensure better governance at all levels relative to the one, which contributed to the violent conflict in the first place. An important point to note here is that institutions are a critical component of governance, but not synonymous with it. That is, governance is an outcome (i.e. output in an economic sense), while institutions and capacity are inputs (factors of production) necessary for its production. Good/effective governance then is to be viewed as a function of quality institutions and robust capacity. Visionary leadership in turn determines quality institutions and capacities. In short, *it's Leadership stupid!*

Indices of Governance

The tenth decision of President Kiir would be well informed if his associates (aides) were to carefully study the attributes of effective governance. They could do this by conducting a situation analysis or institutional readiness assessment (IRA) I have mentioned earlier in this chapter. A situation analysis of the prevailing types of governance in those countries that have successfully exited from fragility would certainly benefit, in my view, from the work of KKM cited in the preceding paragraphs. A comparative analysis of governance would guide these associates (or aides) of the President in prioritizing steps to be taken in the restoration/establishment of effective governance. The sequencing of actions to be taken would in turn avoid overloading the institutional reform/building process that is stipulated in Chapter IV of the R-ARCSS.

President Kiir's policy advisers/aides do not, therefore, need to re-invent the wheel when they could be guided by empirical literature. For instance, KKM have constructed the overall index of governance consisting of the following six indices that a fragile/notational state, such as South Sudan must strive to achieve:

- *Voice and accountability;*
- *Political stability and absence of violence;*
- *Government effectiveness;*
- *Regulatory quality;*
- *Rule of law; and*
- *Control of corruption.*

A brief look at the first index of governance would provide an illustration for comprehending the other five indices. That is, understanding these indices would also help in the identification of capacities and institutions for the establishment of good governance the people of South Sudan have been calling for – by answering the capacity for what and which institutions questions. Policy advisers of the President should not be bogged down with numeric values of the indices, but rather with the qualitative dimensions of governance, so as to appropriately guide them in the identification and design of capacities and institutions as critical inputs in the "production" of effective governance.

Voice and accountability Index

This is a composite index, which is constructed through the following four indicators:

i) The political process: It has to be inclusive through a system of equity in access that is transparent and easily understood by ordinary people in the society. This is a process through which all citizens (stakeholders/actors) participate in the selection (appointment and removal) of governments without resorting to violent or unconstitutional methods[25]. For post-conflict countries the process would seek to incorporate all the systems of various actors (ethnicities/nationalities, etc.) that competed against each other through violent means in an attempt to advance their own visions and agendas. An inclusive political process provides equity in access to resources (political,

---

25   A clear system of checks and balances between the conventional three branches of government
      – legislature, executive, and judiciary – is a critical component of the political process.

economic, social, legal, etc.) for all its inhabitants irrespective of gender, ethnicity, region, religion or political affiliation. In this regard, an inclusive political process would move the country from a triangle of fragility (ToF) to triangle of Resilience (TOR) characterized by justice, equality in opportunities, and peaceful coexistence among all the nationalities comprising the nation sate (see Figure 2.1 below). **The Revitalized Transitional Government of National Unity (R-TGoNU) would be an example of the TOR.**

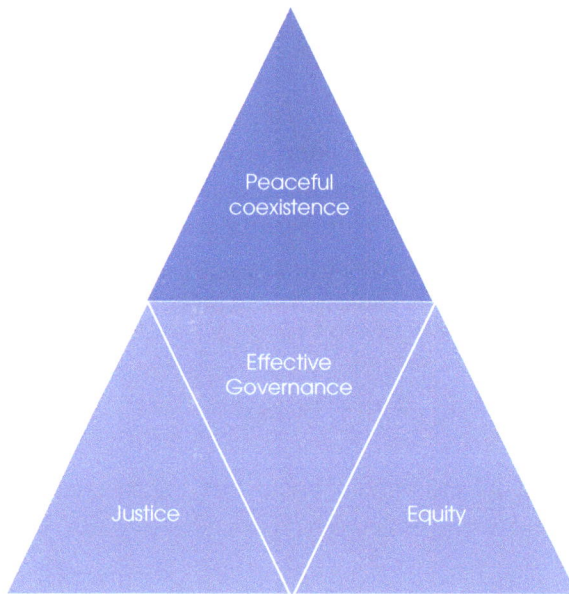

Figure 2.1: Triangle of Tranquility (TOR)

ii) Civil liberties: KKM provide a checklist of 13 questions used by Freedom House in assessing the state of civil liberties in 193 countries (see Box 2.1 below). Here civil liberties are defined as "freedom to develop views, institutions and personal autonomy apart from the state[26]." **The advisory team around President Kiir must answer 13 questions in Box 2.1 below in the affirmative (i.e. put in place mechanisms to ensure civil liberties are exercised without interference or intimidation) to enable South Sudan to leave the fragility trap (i.e. turbulent times) forever.**

---

26   A definition provided by Freedom House in KKM (2003:73).

iii) Political rights: These are "those freedoms that enable people to participate freely in the political process" (KKM 2003:73). **The advisory team around President Kiir should strive to include these rights in the constitution and/or any legal framework governing the rules of political behavior.**

iv) Independence of media: To what extent is the freedom of the press protected by law? **It is to the best interest of a fragile state to guarantee the freedom of the press within the overall framework of democratic governance.** The SSND process has been successful due to the way the press was allowed to cover it.

Capacity-building/strengthening for effective governance of a Coherent State

This is the second pillar of a coherent state. Developing a deeper understanding of the concept of capacity has led me to undertake a quick survey of its various definitions. This in turn provided me with a working definition for this section of the book, which is based on a combination of the UNDP and the World Bank definitions. UNDP defines capacity as "*the ability of individuals and organizations or organizational units to perform functions effectively, efficiently and sustainably.*[27]" An alternative definition provided by the World Bank, defines capacity as "*the ability to access and use knowledge to perform a task.*[28]"

A combination of the above two definitions enabled me to formulate a working definition, where I define capacity as **the ability of individuals or organizations to acquire knowledge and skills and use them to perform a specific task effectively, efficiently, and sustainably**. In deriving this working definition, I have added three key notions: **acquire, skills, and specific**, which would in turn facilitate critical examination of two groups of factors underlying

---

27 UNDP. 1998. Capacity Assessment and Development in a System and Strategic Management Context. Technical Advisory Paper, Management Development and Governance Division, Bureau for Development Policy

28 World Bank. 2002. Building Institutions for Markets. World Development Report 2002, Oxford University Press: New York

Box 2.1: Selected questions for a checklist of rights and freedoms for rating countries

Civil Liberties:

1. *Are there free and independent media, literature and other cultural expressions?*
2. *Is there open public discussion and free private discussion?*
3. *Is there freedom of assembly and demonstration?*
4. *Is there freedom of political or quasi-political organization?*
5. *Are citizens equal under the law, with access to an independent, non-discriminatory judiciary, and are they respected by the security forces?*
6. *Is there protection from political terror, and from unjustified imprisonment, exile or torture, whether by groups that support or oppose the system, and freedom from war or insurgency situations?*
7. *Are there free unions and peasant organizations or equivalents, and is there effective collective bargaining?*
8. *Are there professional and other private organizations?*
9. *Are there free businesses or cooperatives?*
10. *Are there free religious institutions and free private and public religious expressions?*
11. *Are there personal social freedoms, which include such aspects as gender equality, property rights, freedom of movement, choice of residence, and choice of marriage and size of family?*
12. *Is there equality of opportunity, which includes freedom from exploitation by or dependency on landlords, employers, union leaders, bureaucrats or any other type of denigrating obstacle to a share of legitimate economic gains?*
13. *Is there freedom from extreme government indifference and corruption?*

Source: From KKM (2003: 74).

the main features of capacity – **ability** and **performance**. "Acquire knowledge and skills" center, in my view, on inputs that lead to ability (i.e. determinants of ability).

The ability to acquire knowledge, which implies learning, is important in the understanding of this feature of capacity. I view learning as a process of acquiring an asset, which is knowledge. One of the important points of this definition is that we cannot appoint persons with limited technical knowledge and experience and expect them to perform well. A point that has not been fully internalized by many leaders involved with post-conflict reconstruction and development. It is therefore imperative that leadership in turbulent times should be careful about assigning persons with limited capacities to sensitive positions for this could prolong the number of years in fragility trap[29]!

Moreover, to "acquire" knowledge is more critical than to "access" it. A learner can access information but not knowledge; for knowledge is earned (i.e. learnt or acquired). Similarly, a person may have access to knowledge, but without necessarily learning much to enable her/him to undertake a given task that requires a certain level of know-how in order to ensure effectiveness and efficiency. Although interrelated and sometimes used in place of the other, skills and knowledge are quite different. For the purpose of this book, skill is viewed to be the "**art of doing**" things as opposed to the "**know how to do**" things, which is knowledge. Two individuals may have the same knowledge but have different skills. Learning in this sense can then be viewed as a process of acquiring an asset, which is knowledge.

The ability to acquire knowledge at the individual level is a function of economic, social and mental well-being on the one hand, and the learning environment on the other. In this sense, capacity largely depends on a combination of endogenous and exogenous factors. These factors would undoubtedly be different at the meso and macro levels (e.g. organizational unit or entity/state) of analysis. For instance, social and mental well-being for a state emerging out of conflict, such as South Sudan would be described as trust and norms. The lack of

---

29   South Sudan has had nine ministers of finance since 2005 – four during the six years (2005 – 2011) of interim period and five during the first eight years (2011 – 2019) of independence.

trust (i.e. a high degree of mistrust) is one of the contributing factors to most of the conflicts, underpinned by politics of fear. Hence, policy advisers of President Kiir should know that trust is among the key inputs in the ability of an emerging state (government) out of conflict to effectively perform (addressing symptoms/dimensions of fragility) the basic functions of policymaking, implementation of decisions, service delivery, and aid management and coordination.

A second characteristic of capacity is performance and results as articulated by Lee Kuan Yew the founding father of Singapore: "*the acid test of any legal system is not the greatness or the grandeur of its ideal concepts, but whether, in fact, it is able to produce order and justice*[30]." This is of particular interest especially as it relates to the quality of performance (i.e. delivery) – in terms of efficiency, effectiveness and sustainability. The quest for quality is the ultimate objective in the performance of any task by an individual, organization and/or state. But in order to ensure quality performance, a task to be performed must be clearly defined. In turbulent times (i.e. fragility setting), ensuring order and justice would be two of the primary tasks to be performed by the State and its organs. The effectiveness of the exit strategy from fragility would be judged, among other things, on how the overriding objectives of establishing justice and equal access to resources have been addressed.

As captured in the discussions thus far on the concept of capacity, there are multiple levels and numerous dimensions of capacity. A literature review on capacity development pinpoints three levels of capacity – system/state, entity, and individual (UNDP)[31]; and more than 50 dimensions/areas of capacity (VanSant, 2000)[32]. For the sake of clarity, I would not use the terms level and dimension interchangeably. The level refers to a point at which capacity is being assessed (i.e. whose capacity question), while dimension is about the type/category of capacity (i.e. capacity for what?)

---

30 From Lee Kuan Yew: Lessons for leaders from Asia's 'Grand Master', by Graham Allison, Special to CNN Updated 1817 GMT (0217 HKT) March 28, 2015

31 See footnote number 33

32 VanSant, Jerry. 2000. "A Composite Framework for Assessing the Capacity of Development Organizations." USAID

Dimensions of Capacity-building/strengthening: Capacity for what?

The multi-dimensional and multi-level aspects of capacity-building would undoubtedly place an enormous burden on those seeking to identify the most appropriate capacities for managing the exit from fragility (or war-to-peace transition for post-conflict environment). Hence, the point of departure for such search is to reduce the categories/dimensions of capacity to a manageable size by asking the question – "capacity for what?" This critical question of "capacity for what" in the context of post-conflict situations would seem to have been answered by Ian Bannon[33] in stressing four "different, but inter-related dimensions" of capacity. Such a narrow focus would in turn enable countries emerging out of conflict to address the problem of absorptive capacities. The absorptive capacity[34] problem would then center on the following five key dimensions – four of which have been identified by Bannon:

- **Decision-making capacity**: which refers to the ability to make decisions. Poor decision-making systems are often associated with the centralization of decision-making, institutional weakness and capacity deficits, which can in turn be a major constraining factor on absorptive capacity during the transition period. This is a critical area, especially in Africa where traditional African decision-making systems/processes are based on consensus – elders can sit under a tree and debate a single issue the whole day until all those present have spoken. Such a system of decision-making would undoubtedly, in our view, contribute toward the general problem of absorptive capacity within the overall framework of RTGoNU. **Hence, capacity-building**

---

33 I was a consultant with the World Bank Institute (WBI) at that time when Ian Bannon responded on June 18, 2003 to an e-mail message from Markus Kostner (with a copy to me) about a proposed study on institutional reform and capacity development in post-conflict countries, which I was working on. Bannon identifies four dimensions of capacity as policy reform capacity, implementation capacity, service delivery capacity, and aid management capacity

34 Absorptive capacity is being used in a broader sense to include the five dimensions of the capacity for what question in the context of an exit strategy for fragile states

for timely and effective decision-making must be one of the priorities for RTGoNU.

- **Policy formulation capacity**: which refers to the ability of a coherent state to put in place a set of rules, policies and strategies for good governance. These rules, policies and strategies would in turn create or foster an enabling environment for all stakeholders to undertake economic activities at the macro, meso and micro levels of a newly established governance system resulting from a peace agreement. **In this regard, capacity-building for effective policy formulation (e.g. security sector reform) is imperative for RTGoNU.**

- **Implementation capacity**: the ability to translate policies into actions -- implement formulated policies, strategies and associated programs/projects within given resource constraints, including time, human and financial resources. It would also include capacity for monitoring and evaluation of programs being implemented, capacity for budgeting and financial management, and capacity for procurement of goods and services. In the case of South Sudan, the SPLM leadership was aware of this potential constraint; so it decided earlier on (2003) to outsource some critical elements of public financial management (PFM) system to KPMG. **Capacity-building for efficient and timely implementation of government policies and programs is one of the urgent actions required from RTGoNU to embark on**.

- **Service delivery capacity**: the ability of a coherent state to provide basic public services, e.g. security and administration of justice, including human rights protection, education, health, water, and physical infrastructure is one of the imperatives for RTGoNU to **"lay the foundation for a united, peaceful and prosperous society based on justice, equality, respect for human rights and the rule of law.**[35]**"**

---

35 From the preamble of R-ARCSS, page 1

- **Accountability capacity**: the ability for transparent, accountable, and efficient utilization of public resources, including development assistance and effective coordination of donors' support is one of the key pre-requisites for RTGoNU. **This is also one of the priority areas of capacity-building with respect to fighting corruption, auditing, and public financial management, including procurement of goods and services.**

Building Resilient Institutions for Effective Governance of a Coherent State

I have briefly discussed capacities for effective governance in the preceding section. I now look at the third pillar of a coherent state. This pillar consists of resilient institutions, which are critical factors for the production of effective governance of a coherent state. A critical determination in building resilient institutions for effective governance is the decision about "which formal institutions" would enable fragile states, such as South Sudan to exit from fragility. These institutions would normally be required to formulate appropriate policies, implement programs, deliver basic services, and manage public resources efficiently, including external aid.

Reminiscent of "capacity," there are numerous definitions of institutions. However, for the purpose of the discussion on effective governance, only six definitions would suffice. These are:

- *"Working rules of collective action in restraint, liberation, and expansion of individual action"* John R. Commons[36].
- *"Rules and conventions of society that facilitate coordination among people regarding their behavior"*[37]. Vernon Ruttan and Yujiro Hayami
- *"The rules of the game in a society or, more formally, are the humanly devised constraints that shape human interaction*[38]*"* Douglas C. North.

---

36   From 1990 edition

37   Quoted from Daniel Bromley (1989:22)

38   North, D. C. 1990. *Institutions, Institutional Change, and Economic Performance.* New York, NY: Cambridge University Press: Cambridge

- *"Social phenomena which restrict and pattern interactions in society like laws, regulations, rules, norms, established practices and routines"* Klaus Nielsen and Björn Johnson[39].
- *"Rules, enforcement mechanisms, and organizations"* The World Bank[40].
- "Institutions are the *working rules* of a nation. Institutions specify what: **…individuals must or must not do (duty), what they may do without interference from other individuals (privilege), what they can do with the aid of collective power (right), and what they cannot expect the collective power to do in their behalf (no right).**" Daniel Bromley[41].

The term rules is a common denominator among all the six definitions of institutions that I have presented above. Nonetheless, the definitions of institutions given by Commons, Bromley, and Ruttan et al, are most preferable due to the broader considerations of institutional tenets. The other definitions emphasize the constraint/control aspect of institutions and in this sense make them as if they are static. John R. Commons, on the other hand, stresses three tenets – restraint, liberation, and expansion – or aspects of the 'working rules of collective action,' hence, the dynamic feature of institutions is inherent in this definition. And Bromley provides a powerful clarity on the ideas of **duty**, **privilege**, and **rights** of individuals that are determined by the **working rules** of a coherent state. It is also imperative to make a distinction between institutions and organizations as they are quite often used interchangeably.

If institutions are rules of the game, then organizations can be defined or viewed as formal groups of players subject to a common subset of these rules. This interpretation notwithstanding, there are, however, occasions in which the divergence between organizations and institutions is not easily distinguishable. For example, the World Bank Group is widely considered to be an organization and at the same time,

---

39 Nielsen, K. and B. Johnson. 1998. "New Perspectives on Markets, Firms and Technology" in E. Elgar, ed., *Institutions and Economic Change*. London, UK

40 World Bank. 2002. Building Institutions for Markets. World Development Report 2002, Oxford University Press: New York

41 Daniel W. Bromley (2019). South Sudan: Country Policy and Institutional Environment, Ebony Policy Brief, EPB#2019/1

also an institution. As an institution, the Bank has its own 'working rules of collective action' contained in the articles establishing it as an International Bank for Reconstruction and Development (IBRD). These articles guide (restrain, liberate and expand) the Bank's operations, policies and strategies. And on the other hand, the Bank functions like an organization, governed by rules stipulated in the articles (i.e. working rules of collective action formulated by the founders) establishing the Bank.

Literature suggests that the central role of institutions in economic performance and growth is now widely acknowledged, due largely to the recent empirical evidence, which indicates institutions as one of the key determinants of economic development (Acemoglu[42]; Rodrik[43] et al,). According to Douglas North, institutions may be created (e.g. written constitutions) or may simply evolve over time (e.g. common law). The challenge then is on utilizing existing empirical evidence in the proper design of resilient institutions that would produce effective governance for sustainable peace. Thus, this further affirms my emphasis on the significance of an analytical framework for guiding "which institutions" are more likely to accelerate the implementation of the exit strategy from fragility to sustainable peace.

Weak institutions were a recurrent theme among the root causes of crises of governance and leadership that were identified through grass-roots consultations in South Sudan. In the context of fragile states, four main components of John Commons' definition provide four broad categories of institutions underpinning building resilient institutions for effective governance as one of the three key pillars of a coherent state:

- A new constitution that takes into consideration legitimate grievances and aspirations of all the stakeholders/ethnicities/nationalities/"tribes" as expressed through the National Dialogue process. The working rules of collective action would

---

42 Acemoglu, Daron, Simon Johnson and James A. Robinson. 2016. *Why Nations Fail: The Origins of Power, Prosperity, and Poverty*. Crown Publishing Group.

43 Rodrik, Dani, Arvind Subramanian, and Francesco Trebbi. 2002. *Institutions Rule: The Primacy of Institutions over Geography and Integration in Economic Development*. IMF Working Paper Number

be embedded in such a constitution. The constitution is a critical framework for building resilient institutions for effective governance that would in turn ensure justice, equal access to resources and opportunities for wealth creation, and peaceful coexistence in a post-fragility environment. **Here, resilient institutions would be for the three conventional branches of government – legislature, executive, and judiciary**. That is, a partial approach that focuses on building resilient institutions for one branch of government, say executive would not yield the desired results of having effective governance of a coherent state.

- Restraint (e.g. though shall not…type of constraints/commands) entails that all the citizens/nationalities/"tribes" or members of a given organization are aware of the prevailing rule of law (or what I would prefer to call administration of justice), so that nobody takes the law into her/his own hands. It also calls for the observance of prescribed social values, ethics and moral norms. **Here, law enforcement agencies and security sector organizations derive their existence /legitimacy from this tenet and must be established with this tenet inherent in their behavior**. For instant, these institutions must restrain from taking sides in competitive political party politics.

- Liberation in this context means liberty and freedom of whatever one does, though within the 'working rules of collective action' or the rule of law. This tenet provides legal foundation and institutional frameworks for the establishment of social, political and economic organizations/agencies. Here, a robust judiciary, effective civil society, vibrant private sector, strong press, and active research and academic institutions would act as guarantors for liberty and freedom that lay the basis for effective governance. The tragedy in South Sudan is that these institutions have not been able to provide this important service and obligation.

• Expansion is the third tenet, which provides the dynamic aspect of institution in that it allows change (i.e. technical and organizational change) to occur overtime and space in order to obtain growth and development. Agencies and organizations that focus on innovation and social change would derive their strategic visions from the expansion aspect of the 'working rules of collective action.' That is, the working rules of collective action allow expansion to occur in space and over time. **Here, the role of the universities and research centers - critical thinking and innovation – is the driving force of this tenet.**

Comprehensive Institutional Reform for Sustainable Peace

The question of "institutional reform/transformation for what" refers to institutional evolution and/or reform measures to build appropriate institutions for the functions or purpose of which any viable state is expected to do. If this inquiry is viewed in the context of the common understanding of capacity and institutions as defined in the preceding paragraphs, one could argue that institutional reform or transformation requires a deeper understanding of institutions and associated capacities. In this regard, I concur with Klaus Nielsen and Björn Johnson[44] argument that institution is a core concept for understanding the types of institutional change envisaged to occur during the war-to-peace transition.

The call then for a comprehensive institutional reform, is a realization of the fact that institutions created and/or evolved during the conflict, were in most cases for the overall objective of applying 'working rules of collective action in restraint, liberation, and expansion of individual action' in the pursuit of the war effort.

South Sudan should, in the light of R-ARCSS and National Dialogue, seek to reform or build resilient institutions that would

---

44   Nielsen, Klaus and Johnson, Björn (eds.). 1998. *Institutions and Economic Change - New Perspectives on Markets, Firms and Technology.* Edward Elgar, London, UK

ensure sustainable peace all over the country. But, the first step in this process is institutional readiness assessment, which would help in prioritizing the establishment/strengthening institutions stipulated in the various chapters of the R-ARCSS. Thus, institutional reform with the advent of stability, is required to ensure:

- A functioning (i.e. coherent) state at the macro-level, which would in turn provide an overall governance system through an enabling institutional environment for other levels (meso and micro) of governance to operate. This implies the adoption of a new constitution with a clear definition of intergovern-mental relations, basic principles of human rights and civil liberties, property rights and promotion of private initiative or entrepreneur spirit, rule of law, social values and norms. There is urgent need to first clearly establish the separation of powers between the three branches – legislature, executive, and judiciary – of government and secondly put in place effective institutions of these branches. **By way of illustration, insti-tutions of the economic sector, e.g. central bank and ministries of finance, petroleum, agriculture, trade, transport and so forth will have to be given priority in making them efficient and effective in the mobilization, management, and allocation of scarce public resources to meet the fundamental objectives of: a) sustainable peace; b) economic growth; and c) poverty eradication**.

- A robust system at the meso-level (i.e. regional or state level) of corporate and communal governance within a set of principles, obligations, duties, social responsibility and rules consistent with the overall policy thrust and the constitution as some of the prerequisites for sustainable peace to prevail in South Sudan. The constitution is essentially a social contract between the state and respective communities and /or civil society of South Sudan irrespective of their ethnicity, gender, age, religion, region, political inclinations, and/or socio-economic status.

- Stable household governance at the micro-level (i.e. grassroots) within which core and basic values of morality, ethics and norms of civility and patriotism are learnt, internalized, obeyed and respected. Here the role of household in combating corruption is imperative through emphasis on integrity, human dignity and self-respect. This is where social capital formation is critical for sustainable peace and social cohesion as expressed by the people of South Sudan through grassroots consultations of the National Dialogue.

CHAPTER 3

THE STRUCTURE AND PROCESS OF THE NATIONAL DIALOGUE

◆

...the ultimate test of the value of a political system is whether it helps that society establish conditions which improve the standard of living for the majority of its people, plus enabling the maximum of personal freedoms compatible with the freedoms of others in society[45]. "

I thought it would be most appropriate to start this chapter with the above passage from Lee Kuan Yew the founding father of Singapore. The underlined premise in the quoted passage is what the National Dialogue process in South Sudan is seeking. The structure of the National Dialogue in South Sudan consists of a convener and stakeholders/participants in the dialogue. The convener is the Steering Committee consisting of 100 persons, headed by a nine-person Leadership comprised of eminent sons and daughters of South Sudan with technical backstopping from a Secretariat of thirteen persons drawn from the Ebony Center for Strategic Studies; the Sudd Institute; the South Sudan Council of Churches; the Institute of Peace, Development and Security Studies (IPDSS), University of Juba; and the Islamic Council of South Sudan. The Steering Committee, the

---

45   From Lee Kuan Yew: Lessons for leaders from Asia's 'Grand Master', by Graham Allison, Special to CNN Updated 1817 GMT (0217 HKT) March 28, 2015

Leadership, and the Secretariat were expanded in 2019 to accommodate all the political parties[46].

The literature of the National Dialogue shows that the overall role of the convener is to ensure that the process is sufficiently inclusive of all the stakeholders. How has inclusivity been addressed?

Inclusivity: It is, according to Susan Stigant and Elizabeth Murray, one of the six key principles that would help a National Dialogue process "*to contribute meaningfully to political transformation and peace[47].*" But, more importantly it would enable South Sudanese of all walks of life to manage their own narrative in their determined quest for sustained peace, economic growth, and poverty eradication. Here, inclusivity of ideas is as important as physical participation in the dialogue forums and conferences. I believe that conceptual clarity is necessary, though not sufficient, for understanding the nature of the dialogue process. The first substantive action the Leadership of SSND took was to divide the dialogue process into three distinct phases: a) Preparatory phase; b) Conference phase; and c) Implementation (i.e. Post-dialogue) phase.

The SSND process started on 22 May 2017 and was envisaged to end on 12 May 2018. But, it turned out to be a lengthy process that looks like, at the time of writing this book, more than 30 months (May 2017 – July 2020) to complete. I would nevertheless present the initial schedule of activities to enable me to explain how the Leadership of SSND applied the cardinal principle of inclusivity. The envisaged activities of the three phases and proposed timeframe for their completion are given in Table 3.1 below.

---

46   All the political parties accepted to participate, but the SPLM-IO of Dr. Riek Machar Teny pulled out in September 2019

47   National Dialogue: A Tool for Conflict Transformation? A Peace Brief number 194, October 2015 by Susan Stigant and Elizabeth Murray, United States Institute of Peace (USIP)

Table 3.1: Activities of the Steering Committee by Phases of the National Dialogue

Preparatory Phase1 22 May – 31 October 2017	Conference Phase 1 Nov 2017 – 12 May 2018	Implementation Phase June 2018 & Beyond
1. Building confidence among all the stakeholders through effective measures (e.g. ceasefire, release of political detainees, freedom of expression, etc.) that would in turn create enabling environment for a genuine conversation on the design of the SSND (continuous activity)	1. Selection of delegates by the stakeholders from Boma & Payam to the Local Dialogue Forum/Conference (LDF/LDC) (1 – 4 November 2017)	
2. Internalization of the key guiding principles for the National Dialogue (ND)	2. Convening of LDFs/LDCs (8 – 22 November 2017)	
3. Formulation of the agenda of the dialogue forum at three levels (local, regional, and national) of governance;	3. Selection of delegates from LDFs/LDCs to the respective RDFs/RDCs (20 -21 November 2017)	
4. Establishment of criteria for the identification of stake-holders/constituencies of the dialogue at the above stated levels and the Diaspora	4. Summary of the resolutions of the LDFs/LDCs (23 – 24 November 2017)	
5. Agreement on the number of stakeholders/constituencies, size of a dialogue forum at the relevant level, and respective percentage allocation at each dialogue forum	5. Third Plenary Session of SC: Identification of the emerging consensus from the grass-roots consultations on issues of regional and national dimen-sions, which are to be passed on to the RDFs/RDCs and subsequently to the National Dialogue Forum/Conference (NDF/NDC): (27 November – 7 December 2017)	
6. Adoption of procedures for the selection of delegates (repre-sentatives) by each constituency to the relevant dialogue forum	6. Convening of RDFs/RDCs (8 – 22 January 2018)	1. Agreement on the mechanisms for the implementation of the resolutions & recommendations of the NDF/NDC
7. Seminars on the facilitation of National Dialogues	7. Selection of delegates from the respective RDFs/RDCs to the NDF/NDC (23 January 2018)	2. Establishment of Monitoring & Evaluation (M&E) Commission

Preparatory Phase1 22 May – 31 October 2017	Conference Phase 1 Nov 2017 – 12 May 2018	Implementation Phase June 2018 & Beyond
8. Consultation with stakeholders 1 August 2017 – 30 September 2017	8. Summary of the resolutions of the RDFs/RDCs (24 January 2018)	
9. Second Plenary Session of SC: a) Preparation of Reports of sub-committees on consultation with stakeholders (02 – 05 October 2017) b) Presentation of the reports of sub-committees on consultation with stakeholders (09 – 12 October 2017)	9. Fourth Plenary Session of SC: Identification of the emerging consensus from the RDFs/RDCs on issues of national dimension, which are to be passed on to the National Dialogue Forum/ Conference (NDF/NDC): (5 – 18 February 2018)	
10. Report of the Leadership on consultation with stakeholders (political parties & armed opposition groups) outside the country (12 October 2017)	10. Convening of the NDF/NDC (12 March – 14 April 2018)	
11. Resource mobilization (continuous activity)	11. Summary of the resolutions of the NDF/NDC (16 – 20 April 2018)	
12. Approval by the Steering Committee of the work plan (including the agenda of RDF/RDC and LDF/LDC) for Phase II (Conference phase) of the SSND (16 – 21 October 2017)	12. Presentation of the resolutions & recommendations of the NDF/NDC to the President (? – 12 May 2018)	

The Preparatory Phase

The preparatory phase was, as highlighted in Table 3.1 above, aimed, *inter alia*, at sensitizing members of the Steering Committee about their role as the convener of the SSND. This exercise called for members of the Steering Committee to internalize the underlined principles of a national dialogue before embarking on the process. The success of the SSND is a function of this critical phase upon which the other two phases of the National Dialogue process depend. The challenge then was how to ensure, among other things, participation of all the stakeholders at the national level in the design of the National Dialogue and associated processes.

THE NATIONAL DIALOGUE

A general consensus was needed on each and every activity of the above stated points in the proposed activities of the preparatory phase. The Leadership embarked on series of meetings with all the actors – political parties in the Transitional Government of National Unity (TGoNU), opposition parties inside and outside the country, armed opposition groups, and civil society organizations at the national level. These meetings included meeting with the Former Political Detainees (FDs) both in Juba and Nairobi, Kenya; National Democratic Movement (NDM) in Khartoum, Sudan; and a visit to Dr. Riek Machar Teny in South Africa, though he refused to meet the delegation that was led by Hon. Angelo Beda, Co-chair of the SSND.

The second substantive decision by the Leadership of SSND was the division of the Steering Committee into 15 Subcommittees. These Subcommittees were: a) 10 subcommittees based on the former states since restored in 2019; b) two Administrative Areas of Abyei and Pibor; c) refugees and international outreach; d) security to consult the organized forces; and e) National Capital to consult stakeholders in Juba. Each of these subcommittees was envisaged to have representatives of the opposition political parties outside the country and armed opposition groups. But, this was not achieved until May 2019 when all the political parties of South Sudan joined the SSND process[48]. The following were the generic terms of reference for the subcommittees:

1. *Identify, through grassroots consultations, stakeholders for the dialogue forums at the local, regional, and national levels;*
2. *Sensitize the stakeholders about the objectives of the SSND and general principles of a National Dialogue;*
3. *Identify traditional value-systems that underpin both violence and dialogue traditions to resolve conflicts;*
4. *Specify traditional organizational structures for dialogue and conflict management;*
5. *Develop agenda and rules of procedures for facilitating local and regional dialogue forums;*
6. *Facilitate consultations at the level of: a) grassroots; b) refugees; c) organized*

---

48   The parties are: SPLM, SPLM-IO, FDs, South Sudan Opposition Alliance (SSOA), National Agenda, National Alliance, and Umbrella. The SPLM-IO pulled out later due mainly to internal differences.

forces; and d) national capital

7. *Formulate procedures and criteria for the selection of delegates by respective stakeholders to relevant conferences/forums;*

8. *Assist stakeholders to select their representatives to their respective Regional Dialogue Forum/Conference (RDF/RDC);*

9. *Summarize consensus points of various dialogue forums; and*

10. *Facilitate selection of regional delegates to the National Dialogue Forum/Conference (NDF/NDC).*

The Conference Phase

This is the second phase (see Table 3.1) of the ND, which follows the Consultation/Preparatory stage as described in the preceding section. A bottom-up approach characterizes this phase of the SSND. A review of the literature on the National Dialogue, which is a new phenomenon, indicates that the first (inclusivity) and second (transparency and public participation) principles are critical to the success of the Consultation phase[49]. The third document of the Steering Committee, which is called **"The People Have Spoken"** that was released in August 2018, would, in my view, confirm the validity of this point. **The People Have Spoken** is a summary of the emerging consensus from the grassroots consultations on the root causes of the crises in the country. The root causes were grouped under the following four clusters or themes: a) governance; b) security; c) economy; and d) social cohesion.

Selection of delegates to the various levels of dialogue was designed by the Steering Committee on a constituency-based system. The system is drawn from lessons of experience from the first Convention of the Sudan People's Liberation Movement (SPLM) held in Chukudum in 1994. This was envisaged to enable, through their delegates, all the segments of the society to address the crises of governance and leadership in the country. Figure 3.1 below represents the conceptual underpinning of a constituency-based system in the form of three Venn Diagrams.

---

49   See for instance, National Dialogue Handbook: A Guide for Practitioners, published by Berghof Foundation, February 2017.

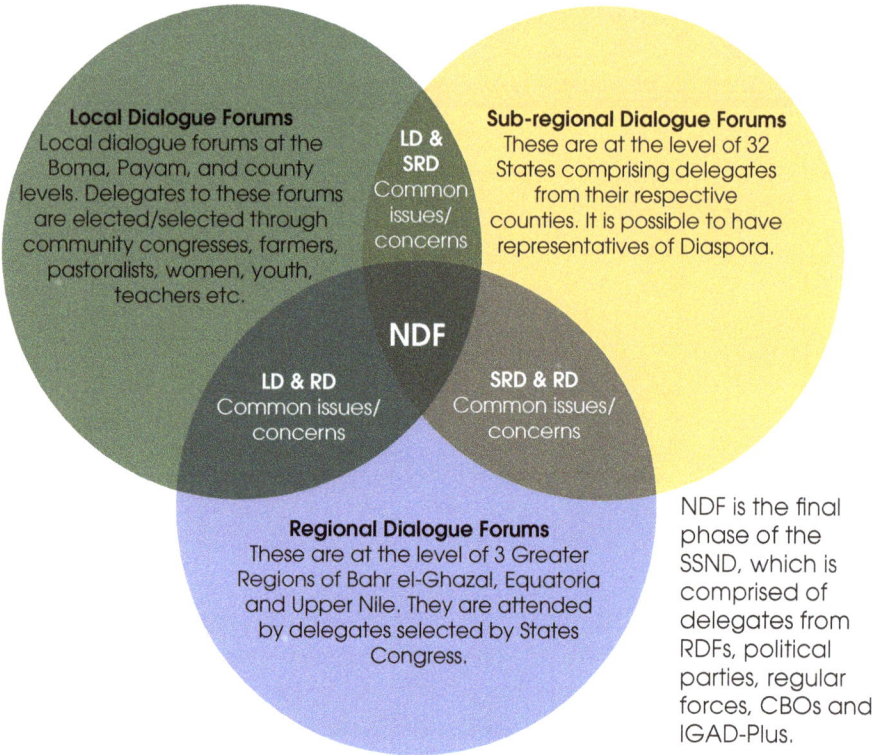

Local Dialogue Forums
Local dialogue forums at the Boma, Payam, and county levels. Delegates to these forums are elected/selected through community congresses, farmers, pastoralists, women, youth, teachers etc.

LD & SRD
Common issues/ concerns

Sub-regional Dialogue Forums
These are at the level of 32 States comprising delegates from their respective counties. It is possible to have representatives of Diaspora.

NDF

LD & RD
Common issues/ concerns

SRD & RD
Common issues/ concerns

Regional Dialogue Forums
These are at the level of 3 Greater Regions of Bahr el-Ghazal, Equatoria and Upper Nile. They are attended by delegates selected by States Congress.

NDF is the final phase of the SSND, which is comprised of delegates from RDFs, political parties, regular forces, CBOs and IGAD-Plus.

Figure 3.1: A Conceptual Framework for Ensuring Inclusivity in the South Sudan National Dialogue (SSND) Process

The three Venn Diagrams represent local (community at the grass-roots level), sub-regions, and regions of South Sudan. There are issues that are exclusively for each of these levels. But, there are common issues between any two of them on the one hand, and between all of them on the other. The common area between the three circles/ diagrams consists of issues, which will constitute the agenda of the National Dialogue Forum/Conference (NDF/NDC). Based on the circles as well as on the activities of the Conference phase stipulated in Table 3.1, it was recommended that the constituency-based system of allocating seats and selecting delegates to the various levels of dialogue forums/conferences be as follows (see Table 3.2):

Table 3.2: Number of Delegates by constituency at each level of dialogue forum

National Dialogue Forum/ Conference (NDF/NDC)		Regional Dialogue Forum/ Conference* (RDF/RDC)		Local Dialogue Forum/ Conference ** (LDF/LDC)	
Stakeholder or Constituency	*Number of Delegates*	*Stakeholder or Constituency*	*Number of Delegates*	*Stakeholder or Constituency*	*Number of Delegates*
1. Regions	1,000	1. Women	250	1. Women	125
2. Political Parties	100	2. Youth	250	2. Youth	125
3. Armed Groups	15	3. Political Parties	150	3. MPs & Counselors	70
4. Civil Society	10	4. Traditional Leaders	50	4. Traditional Leaders	25
5. Diaspora	10	5. Organized Forces	50	5. Organized Forces	25
6. Refugees	10	6. Traders	50	6. Traders	25
7. Business	05	7. Farmers & Pastoralists	50	7. Farmers & Pastoralists	25
8. Youth	05	8. Teachers	50	8. Teachers	25
9. Women	05	9. CBOs	50	9. CBOs	25
10. Faith-based	05	10. Persons with special needs	50	10. Persons with special needs	30
11. Workers	05				
12. Professional Associations	05	**Grand Total**	**1,000**	**Grand Total**	**500**
13. SPLA	05				
14. Police	05				
15. Wildlife	05				
16. Prison	05				
Grand Total	**1,200**				

★ It was initially planned that there would be 12 (i.e. 10 former states now restored plus Abyei Administrative Area and Pibor Administrative area) Regional Dialogue Forums/Conferences (RDFs/RDCs). This phase of sub-regional conferences was eliminated and RDFs/RDCs were now based on the three Greater Regions of Bahr el-Ghazal, Equatoria, and Upper Nile.

★★ It was planned that there would be 100 Local Dialogue Forums/Conferences (LDFs/LDCs)

The number of delegates to each dialogue forum/conference as well as the duration of dialogue forums/conferences was later determined by the availability of resources. Hence, the numbers in Table 3.2 above were indicative and for planning purposes only. Moreover, the dialogue forums are sequenced in that LDFs/LDCs take place first to discuss, *inter alia*, how to end all forms of violence. The LDFs/LDCs select delegates to the RDFs/RDCs, which in turn elect delegates to the National Dialogue Forum/Conference. This process of sequencing is articulated in the SSND Concept Note as depicted by the following Chart:

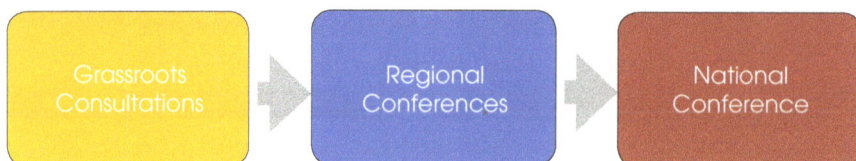

Figure 3.2: A chart showing the flow of the National Dialogue process across different stages

Source: From South Sudan National Dialogue – Concept Note

The next task is to briefly look at what was envisaged to be local and regional dialogue forums/conferences. This is important for it would show how the Leadership ensured the principles of inclusivity, transparency and public participation in the SSND process.

Local Dialogue Forums/Conferences (LDFs/LDCs)

The initial thinking was to have 100 local dialogue conferences with each being attended by 500 delegates from the respective stakeholders (i.e. constituency). This is because grassroots consultations were conceived as part of the national conversation about the challenges and opportunities facing the South Sudanese state. Here, a Local Dialogue Forum (LDF) is essentially a congress of delegates at the County level who are selected by respective Payams (see Table 3.2 above). Stated differently, grassroots consultations were envisaged to be through 100 dialogue forums/conferences of 500 delegates each representing about 100,000 persons (stakeholders). This would translate to 50,000 delegates debating, among other things, what is articulated by the following passage from the Concept Note:

> The first phase shall largely deal with grassroots consultations. The broader aim of these consultations would be to map out grievances that are unique to each community and ones that are encompassing in order to deal with these issues at an appropriate level[50].

---

50   As stipulated in the South Sudan National Dialogue: Concept Note by President Salva Kiir Mayardit, December 2016

It is in the light of the above quotation that a bottom-up approach was likely to give every 250 citizens a delegate (i.e. a representative or voice) in the National Dialogue[51]. In fact, more than 80% of the population of South Sudan is in the rural areas, so every 200 individuals would have one delegate to their respective LDF. There is also another critical factor with respect to the structure of the South Sudanese population. That is, young people below the age of 35 years old constitute 75% of the total population of South Sudan and their views (i.e. revealed needs) must be reflected in the quest for resolving the crises of governance and leadership in the country.

Moreover, women and youth constituencies constitute 50% of the delegates of the LDF. These two categories of our population would therefore have an effective voice in the SSND process. The South Sudan Council of Churches (SSCC), which has the requisite infrastructure and capacity, was to be given the task of facilitating grassroots consultations in areas under the controlled of the armed groups in Greater Upper Nile Region. This was intended to ensure transparency and public participation in the SSND process by offering stakeholders at the grassroots level "an opportunity and guarantee, in the presence of church leaders, of a free environment which is less politically charged, to talk and dialogue freely amongst themselves without mistrust and fear[52]." The subcommittees of the SSND were tasked to coordinate the task of grassroots consultations with the SSCC, which is represented in the Secretariat by three members.

The SPLM-IO did not, however, accept grassroots consultations to take place before the warring parties could sign a revitalized peace agreement. In any case grassroots consultations were carried out in the seventy-nine counties of South Sudan and Abyei Administrative Area (AAA). Only some areas in Akobo County, including Akobo town were not consulted for they were under the controlled of the SPLM-IO.

---

51 Assuming a population of 12.5 million people

52 From SSCC Implementation of Church Action Plan for Sustainable Peace and Reconciliation in South Sudan, 2016 (page 6)

Regional Dialogue Forums/Conferences (RDFs/RDCs)

As stated earlier, 12 Regional Dialogue Forums (RDFs) were envisaged at the planning stage. Each of 12 RDFs was to comprise of 1,000 delegates selected by the LDFs. Besides women and youth who take 50% of the delegates there are eight other stakeholders/constituencies. These are: 1) political parties; 2) traditional leaders; 3) organized forces; 4) traders; 5) farmers and pastoralists; 6) teachers; 7) community-based organizations (CBOs), including faith-based groups; and 8) persons with special needs. RDFs/RDCs provide the linkage (or intersection) between the local and national character of the crises of the South Sudanese state.

Local perspectives on how best to tackle the crises are passed to the national level through regional dialogue forums/conferences. The number of RDFs was subsequently reduced to the three Greater Regions of Bahr el-Ghazal, Equatoria, and Upper Nile. The reduction did not, however, affect the representation of the stakeholders as stipulated in the constituency-based system.

What I have highlighted thus far is the ND process and not the agenda and subsequent outcome of the RDF/RDC. The first RDF/RDC was that of Greater Bahr el-Ghazal to which the reports of the five subcommittees constituted the agenda. The subcommittees were: 1) Abyei; 2) Lakes; 3) Northern Bahr el-Ghazal; 4) Warrap; and 5) Western Bahr el-Ghazal. The agenda was around the four emerging issues/themes from grassroots consultations as documented by the fifteen Subcommittees of the Steering Committee of SSND. Hence, the recommendations of the Bahr el-Ghazal Regional (BGR) conference were as follows[53]:

> After extensive deliberations of the issues, inspired and guided by the objectives and principles of the National Dialogue, and recognizing the complementarity between the National Dialogue and the Revitalized Agreement on the Resolution of Conflict in South Sudan (R-ARCSS), the conference agreed on the following conclusions and recommendations:

---

53 Extracted from the Communiqué of The Bahr El Ghazal Regional Conference Wau, South Sudan, 25th February—2nd March 2019

On Governance
The Conference,

Notes with concern the challenges facing the current decentralized system of governance and recommends the establishment of a federal system;

1. Strongly supports the creation of the current 32 states, and Abyei Administrative Area, as sub-units of the federal system and recommends the creation of more states to meet the legitimate aspiration of the people of the area concerned;

2. Endorses a presidential system of government as opposed to a parliamentary system, recommends appropriate limitation on presidential powers over the states, and also recommends two consecutive five-year term limits for the president;

3. Calls for strict adherence to the normative principles of constitutionalism, including the separation of powers among three arms of government: the executive, legislature, and the judiciary;

4. Recognizes the popular demand for peaceful democratic transfer of power through regular, free and fair elections;

5. Calls upon the government to deliver peace dividends and the expansion of essential services with special focus on the vulnerable groups such as IDP and refugee returnees;

6. Recognizes the importance of land to the people of South Sudan and recommends that the government should own and manage the land.

On the Economy
The Conference,

1. Emphasizes the need for the diversification of the economy through the development of non-oil sectors and strengthening the National Revenue Authority to improve tax collection and revenue management;

2. Strongly urges the government to invest in agriculture as the engine and backbone of the economy and an essential source of livelihood for most of the people of South Sudan;

3. Recognizes modern infrastructure as an essential driver of economic development and social integration, and therefore calls upon the government to give priority to the construction of roads and bridges, river transport, electricity and telecommunication services;

4. Appeals to the government to strengthen social safety net programs through the establishment of cooperatives with the aim of alleviating the cost of living;

5. Calls upon the government to exert more efforts to restore macro-economic stability in the country to accelerate economic growth, sustainable livelihoods, employment opportunities and to accelerate equitable socio-economic programs throughout the country;

6. Recommends the empowerment of women and youth through the establishment of microfinance institutions to expand access to credit and promote inclusive growth;

7. Notes with serious concern the pervasive corruption in South Sudan and calls for strengthening legal, institutional, and regulatory frameworks to ensure accountability and combat impunity;

8. Recommends inclusive and fair allocation and distribution of national resources. It therefore recommends oil and mineral producing states to take 20% of revenue and the national government to take 80%, which shall be shared 70% for the national government and 30% for non-mineral producing states to foster a sense of belonging and equitable development

On Security
The Conference,

1. Calls for an immediate end to all forms of hostilities in the country and urges all armed groups to end violence and seek peaceful means to address their grievances;

2. Expresses serious concern about the impact of small arms and light weapons in the hands of civilians and strongly recommends comprehensive and simultaneous civilian disarmament across the country;

3. Strongly disapproves of violent means for seeking power and mobilization of ethnic communities for the same purpose;

4. Calls for the depoliticization, professionalization and unification of national army through comprehensive security sector reform;

On Social Cohesion
The Conference,

1. Calls for the appreciation, preservation and promotion of the diverse South Sudanese cultures to foster national unity and harmony;

2. Stresses the need to demilitarize and depoliticize communal relations in order to enhance social cohesion and peaceful coexistence;
3. Recommends that the government invest in civic education, through public institutions, as strategy for promoting unity, harmony and national solidarity;
4. Calls for speedy and voluntary return of refugees, internally displaced persons, and South Sudanese on the Protection of Civilian Sites (PoCs) to their homes.

The Greater Upper Nile Regional (GUNR) conference made its recommendations two months later, in May 2019. The agenda of GUNR conference was similar to that of GBR, focusing on the four themes of: governance; economy; security; and social cohesion. Moreover, the GUNR conference was informed by the reports of the four Subcommittees: 1) Jonglei; 2) Pibor Administrative Area (PAA); 3) Unity; and 4) Upper Nile. There are similarities in the recommendations of GUNR with that of GBR, though there are sharp differences on the issue of land ownership. Here are the recommendations of GUNR dialogue conference:

On Governance
The Conference,
1. Notes with concern the challenges facing the current decentralized system of governance and recommends the establishment of a federal system with devolved powers to the states;
2. Strongly supports the establishment of the 32 states and Abyei Administrative Area, as sub-units of the federal system and recommends the creation of more states, as needed, to meet the legitimate aspirations of the people;
3. Endorses a presidential system of government as opposed to a parliamentary system, recommends appropriate limitations on presidential powers over the states, and also recommends two consecutive five-year term limits for the president;
4. Recommends that the 2010 elections be recognized as the first term for the incumbent and the next elections be the second term.
5. Calls for strict adherence to the normative principles of constitutionalism, including the separation of powers among the three arms

of government: the executive, legislature, and the judiciary and further recommends credible independence of the legislature and the judiciary from executive interference;

6. Recommends that any member of parliament appointed to an executive position must resign from parliament and be replaced by the constituency through by-elections;

7. Recommends that the president appoints only those judges recommended by the Judicial Service Commission;

8. Strongly recommends that power can only be transferred from one person to another through legitimate, timely, free and fair democratic elections;

9. Recognizes the importance of land to the people of South Sudan and declares that rural land be owned and managed by indigenous communities and urban gazetted land be owned and managed by the government. Notes further that any government in need of rural land for development and for purposes of other public interests should be granted such land with consent of the indigenous communities;

10. Strongly recommends that state boundaries must be managed and demarcated by the national government as they stood on 1st January 1956;

11. Strongly condemns the abduction and trafficking of children and calls for an immediate end to these practices;

12. Endorses the results of the Abyei Referendum and recommends that the government endorses the same and ensures speedy and final settlement of the status of Abyei;

On the Economy
The Conference,

1. Calls for the diversification of the economy by making agriculture the engine of growth and using oil revenues to fuel this engine through investment in roads, telecommunication and electricity;

2. Strongly urges the government and oil companies to immediately address social and health problems created by environmental degradation of oil production in Greater Upper Nile;

3. Recognizes that there are two types of land - rural and urban land, the rural land is owned by the community, while the gazetted urban land is owned by the Government, leased and distributed to individuals

and allocated to institutions;

4. Calls for the urgent resolution of land disputes between a number of ethnic groups through recognition of boundaries as they stood on January 1, 1956;

5. Appeals to the government to strengthen social safety-net programs through the establishment of cooperatives with the aim of alleviating the cost of living;

6. Calls upon the government to exert more efforts in stabilizing peace and in restoring macroeconomic stability within the overall framework for sustainable peace, economic growth, and poverty eradication;

7. Recommends the empowerment of women and youth through the establishment of microfinance institutions to expand access to credit and promote inclusive growth;

8. Notes with serious concern the pervasive corruption in South Sudan and calls for strengthening legal, institutional, and regulatory frameworks to ensure accountability and combat impunity;

9. Recommends equitable and fair allocation and distribution of national resources and further recommends that oil and mineral producing states take 15% of revenue and the national government takes 85%;

On Security
The Conference,

1. Calls for an immediate end to all forms of hostilities in the country and urges all armed groups to end violence and seek peaceful means to address their grievances;

2. Expresses serious concern about the impact of small arms and light weapons in the hands of civilians and strongly recommends comprehensive and simultaneous civilian disarmament across the country;

3. Strongly Condemns cattle raiding and related killings and recommends that the government formulate and implement policies against this practice.

4. Strongly disapproves of violent means for seeking power and mobilization of ethnic communities for the same purpose;

5. Calls for professionalization and unification of the national army through comprehensive security sector reforms in which all the nationalities/ethnicities are represented proportionately;

On Social Cohesion

The Conference,

1. Calls upon the government to formulate and implement policies against hate speech and propaganda that spread social discord;
2. Recommends that the government ban songs and media outlets that spread hate, fear, violence, and war propaganda;
3. Calls upon the people of South Sudan to embrace and respect diversity of cultures and preserve and promote our cultural heritage;
4. Strongly recommends that the government formulate policies against tribalism, nepotism and favoritism in employment;
5. Recommends that tribal markings and facial scarification as well as the removal of teeth be ended forthwith;
6. Recommends the establishment of national boarding schools that bring students together from diverse ethnic backgrounds so as to foster national unity and identity;
7. Recommends annual regional and national conferences of chiefs to promote dialogue and understanding;
8. Recommends the establishment of national and regional museums;
9. Calls for the formation of a joint committee of the parties to the R-ACRSS to engage citizens at UNMISS PoC sites to return home.
10. Calls for a speedy and voluntary return of refugees, internally displaced persons, and South Sudanese on the (PoCs) to their homes in safety and with dignity.

The third and last regional dialogue conference was that of Greater Equatoria Region (GER). The agenda was similar to that of the other two regions. Here is the summary of the GER:

The delegates representing 24 counties of the 3 former states of Equatoria Region met in Juba from the 26th to 31st of August 2019 under the Co-Chairmanship of H.E. Abel Alier and Hon. Angelo Beda.

The Conference deliberated on the agenda of the Greater Equatoria Regional Conference prepared by the Steering Committee. The agenda contained key issues that emerged from the Grassroots Consultations as reflected in various documents of the Steering Committee. These issues were categorized into four substantive clusters: governance, economy, security and social cohesion.

To facilitate in-depth discussion of these issues and to ensure greater participation, the delegates broke up into groups on the basis of the clusters and specific issues.

After extensive deliberations of the issues, inspired and guided by the objectives and principles of the National Dialogue, and recognizing the complementarity between the National Dialogue and the Revitalized Agreement on the Resolution of Conflict in South Sudan (R-ARCSS), the Conference agreed on the following recommendations:

On Governance
The Conference,

1. Notes with grave concern the challenges facing the current decentralized system of governance and endorses the establishment of a federal system with more powers devolved to the states;
2. Proposes 39 states as sub-units of the federal system to be shared equally among the three regions of Bahr el Ghazal, Equatoria and Upper Nile, each with 13 states;
3. Endorses a presidential system of government and limits federal powers over the states;
4. Recommends four-year term of office for president, and if re-elected can only serve for another four years;
5. Recommends that the post of president should rotate among the three regions of Bahr el Ghazal, Equatoria and Upper Nile;
6. Recommends rotation should start immediately after the end of the transitional period stipulated in the Revitalized Agreement on the Resolution of Conflict in South Sudan;
7. Strongly recommends that state government should have the three arms of government: executive, legislature, and judiciary, with full competences;
8. Calls for strict adherence to the normative principles of constitutionalism, including the separation of powers among the three arms of government: the executive, legislature, and the judiciary, and further recommends the independence of the legislature and the judiciary from executive interference;
9. Calls for the establishment of an independent constitutional court;
10. Recommends that any member of parliament appointed to an executive position must resign from parliament and be replaced

through by-elections;

11. Strongly recommends that access to, and transfer of power should only be through legitimate, timely, free and fair democratic elections;

12. Recommends that land shall belong to the community and be protected by the government and it shall be managed and administered by the local government in collaboration with the indigenous communities;

13. Recommends formation of a border Commission with a strong and clear mandate to protect our national borders and international boundaries;

14. Strongly recommends that state boundaries must be managed and demarcated by the national government as they stood on the 1st January 1956;

15. Strongly recommends the enforcement of affirmative action to enable full participation of women, youth and people with special needs in governance;

On the Economy
The Conference,

1. Calls upon the government to make Peace a priority in order to restore macroeconomic stability in the country, accelerate economic growth, sustainable livelihoods, and employment opportunities, and formulate inclusive and equitable socio-economic programs throughout the country;

2. Recommends inclusive and fair allocation and distribution of national resources and further recommends that the national budget be divided 55% for the federal government and 45% for the states;

3. Recommends compensation for damages caused to the land by allocating 10% of the net revenue to the natural resources producing states;

4. Strongly urges the government to invest in agriculture as the engine of the economy;

5. Calls on government to urgently develop policy for industrialization;

6. Emphasizes the need for the diversification of the economy through the development of both oil and non-oil sectors and strengthening the National Revenue Authority to improve tax collection and revenue management;

7. Recognizes modern infrastructure as an essential driver of economic development and social integration, and therefore calls upon the government to give priority to the construction of roads and bridges, river transport, airports, dams, power plants and the improvement of information technology and telecommunication services;
8. Strongly condemns the rampant corruption in the country and calls for establishment of anti-corruption court;
9. Recommends complete overhaul of public financial management systems and institutions with a view to restoring public trust, credibility and integrity in the economic system;
10. Recommends that as a matter of strategic national interest, South Sudan should build a modern international airport that can handle heavy planes;
11. Recommends development of sound economic and trade policies that promote competitiveness of South Sudanese entrepreneurs through capacity building and access to financing;
12. Appeals to the government to strengthen cooperatives and microfinance institutions and ease access to credit facilities to alleviate poverty;
13. Recommends establishment of social welfare;
14. Recommends economic empowerment of women, youth and people with special needs so as to promote inclusive growth;
15. Calls for the construction of domestic oil refineries in South Sudan;
16. Calls for the adoption of mixed economy in South Sudan;
17. Recommends the establishment of Petro-chemical and agro-industrial schemes;
18. Calls for the revival of the six national parks and 8 game reserves in South Sudan;
19. Recommends the promotion of tourism and the hotel industries;

On Security
The Conference,
1. Calls for an immediate end to all forms of violence and hostilities in the country, urges the government and all the armed groups to seek peaceful means to address their grievances;
2. Appeals to the government to engage directly with the hold-out groups;

3. Calls for full and immediate implementation of the R-ARCSS, especially chapter II on security arrangements;
4. Calls for the establishment of a unified, regionally balanced, and ethnically representative, professional national army and organized forces;
5. Calls for immediate return of all pastoralists currently in Equatoria to their places of origin and further calls for the disarmament of all pastoralists;
6. Expresses serious concern about the impact of small arms and light weapons in the hands of civilians and strongly recommends comprehensive and simultaneous civilian disarmament across the country;
7. Strongly disapproves of accession to and retention of power through violence;
8. Condemns rewarding of rebels with high-ranks and political positions;
9. Recommends that promotion in the army should be based on merits;
10. Calls for the de-politicization, professionalization and unification of the national army and organized forces through comprehensive security sector reforms;
11. Strongly condemns child abduction and trafficking and calls for the criminalization of such inhumane practice;
12. Strongly condemns the practice of cattle raiding and calls for enactment of laws that criminalize the practice;
13. Strongly condemns gender-based violence and calls for immediate enactment of family law;

On Social Cohesion
The Conference,
1. Calls for the dissolution of all tribal political organizations, associations and council of elders, which negatively influence national decision-making processes;
2. Strongly condemns changing of indigenous names of places and calls for reverting to original names;
3. Recommends to the national parliament to enact laws against all forms of discrimination;
4. Urges the government to support and encourage inter-communal dialogue;
5. Calls for the appreciation, preservation and promotion of the diverse

South Sudanese cultures to foster national unity and harmony;

6. Calls for the preservation and protection of all national and local historical sites across the country;

7. Strongly recommends the relocation of national capital to Ramciel, which is more at the center of the country;

8. Stresses the need to create conducive environments to enhance communal relations, social cohesion and peaceful co-existence;

9. Supports multi-party democracy and calls for widening of the political space and funding of political parties;

10. Recommends that the government invests in education, especially civic education, through public institutions, as a strategy for promoting unity, harmony and national solidarity.

11. Strongly recommends the restoration of powers of traditional authority;

12. Calls for the introduction of annual cultural festivals all over South Sudan to foster national identity and national unity;

13. Demands an immediate end to arbitrary arrest and forced disappearance of citizens by National Security Service and other organized forces, and further demands for immediate release of those who were innocently arrested;

14. Calls for the review of the National Security Service Act;

15. Calls for the government to create conducive environment and facilitate the voluntary return of refugees, internally displaced persons, and South Sudanese on the Protection of Civilian Sites (PoCs) to their homes;

16. Demands an immediate enactment of a national law that protects people with special needs and ensures they are given employment and other enabling opportunities;

17. Recommends establishment of national boarding schools from upper primary to secondary to promote nationalism and national unity.

The Conference strongly calls for full implementation of the recommendations and resolutions of the National Dialogue.

The recommendations of the three regional dialogue conferences have provided a comprehensive menu for the agenda of the National Dialogue Conference. There is, for instance, a federal system being recommended to the NDF/NDC to consider. It would, however, require a comparative analysis of federal systems in the world, which will be deliberated upon by the delegates at the ND conference. Another recommendation of the three regional conferences is on presidential system, which will also be one of the agenda items of the ND conference. These examples and more do support the premise of this book that the National Dialogue in South Sudan provides a framework for sustainable peace, economic growth, and poverty eradication. This is because the ND process has created an enabling political and civic space for deliberating on these three issues.

PART II

THE ECONOMY

LEVERAGING PEACE: THE ECONOMY

◆

We have involved ourselves in a colossal muddle, having blundered in the control of a delicate machine, the working of which we do not understand. The result is that our possibilities of wealth may run to waste for a time—perhaps for a long time[54].

John Maynard Keynes' description of "The Great Slump of 1930," would seem as if he was discussing how the South Sudanese ruling elites have been managing their economy. The economy of South Sudan is, in my view, a highly delicate machine in which our policymakers have involved themselves without clear knowledge of how it operates. This knowledge is necessary, though not sufficient for formulating a program for a *"payback time by the SPLM to the Sudanese people who fought and sacrificed"* during the war of liberation. Moreover, our people at the grassroots level have identified the lack of economic growth (i.e. poor economic performance) as one of the root causes of our twin crises of governance and leadership. In fact, they are demanding improved economic performance that would generate economic growth that could in turn lead to sustainable peace and poverty eradication in South Sudan.

The National Dialogue process has provided sufficient political and

---

civic space for all the stakeholders to articulate their views/dreams about the economy. South Sudanese intellectuals of various disciplines, professions, and political orientations have a responsibility in the translation of these dreams into tangible actions, which in turn would contribute to sustainable livelihoods of ordinary people.

Dr. Peter Adwok Nyaba has recently asked the following question: *"What can the South Sudanese intellectuals do in the face of the situation the country is facing; the sterile debate on the number of states and borders, while we are wasting away, dying as we are going to bury soon Moulana Majok Mading who collapsed and died yesterday in Nairobi having being flown in from Juba[55]?"*

South Sudanese intellectuals must condemn and oppose the use of violence in resolving the crises of governance and leadership facing the country. They must be guided in their discourse by what Dr. Francis Mading Deng calls "**the voice of reason and moderation**." I have reproduced, as Box 4.1, the excerpts of my rejoinder on the responsibility of intellectuals, from the DPF discourse as my way of looking at the economy.

Box 4.1: My Rejoinder

The above question by Peter Adwok Nyaba came at the time I was working on this chapter. My initial and brief response to Peter was:

1 The body of Moulana has been laid to rest yesterday Tuesday 31 December 2019 at his village Pan-Piol, Pakeer County, Jonglei State. The people of Greater Bor have ended a difficult year of 2019 with his burial. And we begin today the new decade of 2030s, which also marks the beginning of the 2nd decade of our independence, so the DPF community is in a way paying tribute to Molana Majok by reflecting on: **The Responsibility of Intellectuals: Using Privilege to Challenge the State**, by Noam Chomsky. Two categories of intellectuals are discussed in this article: a) **value-ori-**

---

55   A question he asked through a thread on the Responsibility of Intellectuals by Noam Chomsky, posted on 26 December 2019, on the digital Development Policy Forum (DPF), which is moderated by the Ebony Center for Strategic Studies

ented intellectuals; and b) **technocratic and policy-oriented intellectuals**. Dr. Francis Mading Deng expressed his sorrow and condolences to my family, through an email message to me, by saying the following about Moulana Majok, which I thought is a critical point of departure to examine this topic:

Dear Lual,

I am sorry this message comes rather belatedly, but I wanted to share with you how saddened I was by the news of the passing away of Molana Majok Mading. I met him several times in Juba and was always impressed by his profound, though understated, intelligence and wisdom. He was certainly a much needed voice of reason and moderation, qualities that are tragically compromised by the divisiveness of the crisis afflicting our country. He will be severely missed, but will also live on in the memory of many. Please convey my condolences to the family.

Francis.

2   So, let us keep at the background of debate here, the "voice of reason and moderation," which Dr. Francis Mading Deng has pointed out as among the cardinal principles of intellectualism. These qualities are underpinned by intelligence & wisdom according to Dr. Francis. And Noam Chomsky considers *"Intellectuals as defenders of justice, confronting power with courage and integrity."* Both the title and the definition of the role of intellectuals are, in my view, describing the *"value-oriented intellectuals who pose a challenge to democratic government which is, potentially at least, as serious as those posed in the past by aristocratic cliques, fascist movements, and communist parties."* I would say challenging the state or *"confronting power with courage and integrity"* is one of the legitimate responsibilities of the intellectuals and I would venture to characterize you, Comrade Peter Adwok as one of our leading thinkers in this area or could I call you the dean of our **value-oriented school of thought**. I believe in the division of labor and I therefore see added value to our discourse in having varied schools of thought or varied orientations of South Sudanese intellectuals all in the service of the country and people of South Sudan. The debate on the ideology, which has been initiated by our young scholar Kuir ë Garang falls within this value-oriented intel-

lectuals who see our 52+ political parties (including the SPLM)
to be suffering from "**poverty of ideology!**" I am also reading
the excellent rejoinders of: Dr. Garang Majok Dut, Dr. SAL, Atok
Baguoot, Molana Dr. Biong Deng Kuol, who bring extremely
valuable insights to our determined quest for a political ideology in
South Sudan that would in turn enable us to embark on the second
war of liberation, which is the eradication of poverty in its all forms
and shapes. You and I tried this debate 5 years ago, but we got a
very low response within the DPF. It's never too late to re-start it
again, especially in the light of the challenges the country is facing.
Hence, the debate about the number of states and boundaries is, in
my view, NOT sterile; it provides an important point of departure
for an intellectual journey in search of the most appropriate instruments (weapons, if you wish) for the second war of liberation.

3   The SPLM has, according to Kuir ë Garang, quickly abandoned its
    political ideology after the demise of one of its founders – Dr. JG -
    because Garang had imposed his personal ideology on the SPLM.
    You, Dr. Garang Majok Dut, I, and many others have challenged
    this thesis. I would now farther support my challenge based on
    Chomsky's important article. I would say the new leadership of
    the SPLM deviated from its ideology when Adam Smith's "masters
    of mankind" took over the reign of power in Juba with their "vile
    maxim" articulated by Adam Smith:

*All for ourselves and nothing for other people, seems, in every age of the world,
to have been the vile maxim of the masters of mankind. As soon, therefore, as
they could find a method of consuming the whole value of their rents themselves,
they had no disposition to share them with any other persons[56].*

4   In our situation, the **"masters of mankind"** would be the liber-
    ators (to be fair, a tiny minority of the liberators, but powerful)
    who have captured the South Sudanese state for their own personal
    interest. All the sagas: reports of our own Auditor General, the Sentry

---

56   See Adam Smith: *An Inquiry into the Nature and Causes of the Wealth of Nations* (1776), Book III,
     chapter IV [WN III.iv.10. p 418]

Reports, and so forth, constitute a powerful evidence of this "state capture!" I don't know if this is the third category of intellectuals SAL has hinted in his rejoinder and which he said he is holding the name. But, this statement of mine about some of our liberators is not consistent with Dr. Francis Deng's "voice of reason and moderation" as it could add fuel to fire of what he correctly describes as **"the divisiveness of the crisis afflicting our country."**

5 The second category is the **"technocratic and policy-oriented intellectuals."** They are, according to Noam Chomsky, *"responsible and serious thinkers who devote themselves to the constructive work of shaping policy within established institutions and to ensuring that indoctrination of the young proceeds on course."* I would think that most of us who remained behind after the eruption of conflict in December 2013 fall within this category. I would also add that the Technical Committee of Intellectuals (TCI), which was established in January 2000 by the SPLM leadership following a successful Economic Governance Conference, held in Yambio in November 1999 was the realization of the role of intellectuals in the liberation struggle. The conference was organized by the then newly formed New Sudan Economic Society headed by late Prof. George Tombe. The TCI subsequently provided technical backstopping to the SPLM leadership in the production of key documents, policy briefs, JAM, and notes/position strategies for negotiating the six protocols of the CPA.

6 To answer your intriguing question of: *"What can the South Sudanese intellectuals do in face of the situation the country is facing?"* I would say, it depends on which category of our intellectuals are we asking! I would nevertheless encourage that all should have one common denominator, which is given by Dr. Francis Deng as the **"voice of reason and moderation,"** for the country is too divided for any recklessness from any category of the South Sudanese intellectuals. In this regard, it is the responsibility of intellectuals to persuade President SKM and Dr. RMT to listen to the voices from the grassroots that are calling both of them to step down from the leadership of the country. The intellectuals must provide evidence to support

what the people are demanding, as documented through the ND process, by citing the fact that the two leaders have not been able to form RTGoNU as stipulated in the R-ARCSS. There are so many other empirical evidences that could be provided to enhance this persuasion task by the intellectuals.

I wait for the responses of other DPFers.

Cheers, LD

The first step in the process of fulfilling our responsibility as intellectuals is to adopt a culture of inquiry into the nature of things. Take the economy for instance, where we should be asking: *what is the purpose of an economy; what determines its growth; and how could the economy of South Sudan be revitalized after the devastating violent conflict?*

I strongly believe that one of the responsibilities of the South Sudanese intellectuals is to explain how the economy operates. There should be no disagreement on the purpose of the economy, but definitely on how it performs its functions. How the economy performs its functions is a function of the political ideology of the ruling elites, which is essentially a product of leadership. And there is no such thing called "personal ideology" being imposed on the party by its leader, which is a mistaken notion.

I have stated at the beginning of Chapter Two, how Dr. John Garang had wanted to formulate a program in which the economy was to operate with the primary objective of paying back the people of Sudan for their services during the war of liberation. The payment was to be in-kind and not in-cash in *"areas of physical infrastructure, good governance, financial infrastructure and viable markets, development and provision of social services and basic necessities: health, education, water, food security, employment opportunities…"* These areas underpin the process of broad capital accumulation in an economy and of which Chairman Garang was well informed about it. He was not just a leader of a political organization; he was an intellectual with strong professional conviction to serve his people, which he did superbly. This point on the role of ideology (i.e. leadership) in the development process would become clearer when we discuss the determinants of economic growth based on empirical evidence.

The Purpose of The Economy

It is imperative that we understand the purpose of economy; any economy – developed or developing; small or large. The overall purpose of the economy is the production and distribution (i.e. supply) of goods and services for sustained incremental improvement in the well-being of the people through a well-functioning price mechanism. It could simply be defined as a process of individual and collective wealth creation within the working rules of a coherent state. Sustained incremental improvement in the well-being of the people is what is popularly known as economic growth or economic development. Simon Kuznets points out that: *"A country's economic growth may be defined as a long-term rise in capacity to supply increasingly diverse economic goods to its population[57]."*

Intellectuals (or is it policymakers and the ruling elite) of South Sudan would seem to have, in my view, ignored three requisites for the economy to pursue the cardinal purpose of supplying increasingly diverse economic goods and services to the population. Adam Smith reminded us centuries ago about these preconditions as follows:

> Little else is requisite to carry a state to the highest degree of opulence from the lowest barbarism but peace, easy taxes, and tolerable administration of justice: all the rest being brought about by the natural course of things[58].

---

57 Kuznets, Simon. 1971. "Modern Economic Growth: Findings and Reflections," (Nobel Memorial Lecture, in Kuznets, Simon, *Population, Capital, and Growth: Selected Essays*, London: Heinemann, 165-184

58 Adam Smith on the need for "peace, easy taxes, and a tolerable administration of justice" (1755), from https://oll.libertyfund.org/quotes/436

Peace

Economic growth and peace are, in the case of South Sudan, analogous to the age-old puzzle of "**chicken - and – egg**," as to which comes first in our debate – **peace** or the **economic growth**? I would state unambiguously that it is peace that comes first. In fact, there was relative peace after our independence on July 9, 2011; a peace, which was turned on its head through poor economic management underpinned by our own political recklessness (greed and selfishness) and inexperience (ignorance and arrogance). A point, which Adam Smith had warned against as follows: "*All governments which thwart this natural course, which force things into another channel, or which endeavour to arrest the progress of society at a particular point, are unnatural, and to support themselves are obliged to be oppressive and tyrannical[59]*."

I consider the natural course of things to be the initial conditions on 9 July 2011. The World Bank describes these initial conditions at independence in the following powerful words:

> On July 9, 2011, the Republic of South Sudan celebrated its independence. The country began its life with significant natural resources and a binding narrative of triumph and freedom, but with a legacy of over 50 years of conflict and an extremely low level of physical, human and institutional development.[60]

That "*binding narrative of triumph and freedom*" and "*significant natural resources*" were never utilized by the political elites to address the legacy of marginalization and underdevelopment. The "binding narrative of triumph and freedom" should have provided the necessary and sufficient conditions for sustainable peace, which would have in turn enabled policymakers to embark on building a coherent South Sudanese state. A coherent South Sudanese state is needed to pave the way for the three requisites envisaged by Adam Smith several centuries ago.

---

59 Ibid

60 Interim Strategy Note (FY 2013 – 2014) for the Republic of South Sudan. Report No: 74767-SS

THE NATIONAL DIALOGUE

Daniel Bromley has been warning us over the years, as I have quoted him earlier in this book that:

South Sudan became an independent nation on July 9, 2011. Eight years later it is still not a coherent state. Coherent states require two essential attributes— one of which is structural in nature, the second of which concerns processes. When these two necessary conditions are absent, the economy cannot perform its necessary functions, and civil conflict is inevitable[61].

Our economy has not been able to "perform its necessary functions" of producing and supplying goods and services to the people of South Sudan due to the violent conflict that has ensued since December 2013. This means that although peace is a requisite for taking the South Sudanese people to prosperity, this peace would not be sustainable if the economy were not growing. This economy would not grow until on the one hand we sufficiently understand its necessary functions, and on the other know what makes it grow.

It is in the light of the delicate **peace–growth nexus**, which makes me strongly believe that there is a synergy between the National Dialogue and the R-ARCSS. This synergy is anchored on sustainable peace and comprehensive reform of the institutions of economic governance. Part One of this book has focused on National Dialogue as a critical framework for sustainable peace, which is also the central focus of R-ARCSS.

The people of South Sudan have made similar calls, through the grass-roots consultations initiated by the National Dialogue, for comprehensive reforms in the areas of governance, economy, security, and social cohesion. **Peace is a fundamental requisite for undertaking these comprehensive reforms.**

---

61 Daniel W. Bromley (2019). *South Sudan: Country Policy and Institutional Environment*, Ebony Policy Brief, EPB#2019/1

Easy Taxes

Significant natural resources (e.g. oil, timber, gold, gum–Arabic, etc.) could have in a way substituted the call for "easy taxes" as one of the three requisites *"to carry a state to the highest degree of opulence."* I have argued elsewhere that South Sudan was born with a *"golden spoon"* in her mouth. This is because oil constituted, at independence, more than 75% of the gross domestic product (GDP); more than 95% of government total revenues; and about 99% of exports. Moreover, the Government of the Republic of South Sudan (GRSS) received during the first six months (9 July – 31 December 2011) of independence a total amount of $3.3 billion from oil revenues[62]. It could therefore be stated that the country received "easy taxes" in the form of very impressive average monthly oil revenues of $556.3 million. In fact, September 2011 witnessed the highest level (i.e. $675 million) of GRSS' monthly oil revenues during this period.

The "easy taxes" in the form of steady flow of oil revenues was interrupted through our own political recklessness, when, as described by John Maynard Keynes, *"we involved ourselves in a colossal muddle, having blundered in the control of a delicate machine, the working of which we do not understand."* Corruption is, in my view, the key driver of this "colossal muddle," which has been compounded by three events of our own making. I will discuss the meaning, types, sources, and consequences of corruption after highlighting these events.

The first was in January 2012 when the GRSS voluntarily and suddenly decided to completely shutdown oil production in a dispute with Sudan over transit fees. This decision was taken at the time when daily oil production was approaching 450,000 barrel per day (bpd) and the oil prices in the international commodity market were over $100/barrel of crude oil. That was the beginning of the end of the binding narrative of triumph and freedom. The new independent country entered series of *"man-made"* episodes when the ruling elite of the SPLM started to quarrel over power and rents instead of over the political ideology of the party. That is, the binding narrative of triumph

---

62 MPM Marketing Reports, Volume 1A, Ministry of Petroleum and Mining (MPM), Republic of South Sudan

and freedom was anchored on the SPLM's vision of New Sudan and when the party deviated from it, chaos and indiscipline set in!

The second event is the decision of the GRSS that might have compounded the current economic crisis. That is, the September 2012 Oil Agreement between Sudan and South Sudan and which gave Sudan $24.1/barrel of Dar blend crude exported through its territory. The figure of $24.1/barrel might have been reasonable at the time oil prices were above $100/barrel, but it quickly looked stupid when prices dropped to below $25.0/barrel. Oil production resumed in April 2013 with GRSS receiving average monthly revenues of $111.3 million (i.e. during the period of April 2013 – May 2014). The average monthly oil revenues dropped to $82.0 million during the period June 2014 – May 2015, which is 14.7% of what GRSS was getting during the first six months of independence. This figure dropped to about $24.0 million during the period June 2015 – May 2016.

The third of the "man-made" episodes is the eruption of violent conflict in December 2013. The economy has been one of the major victims of this third "man-made" episode – high fiscal deficits as a consequence of fighting the war through inflationary financing (popularly known as deficit financing), which is characterized by hyperinflation[63] (i.e. consumer price index increased by 77.7% from June 2016 to July 2016). These endogenous factors were compounded by an exogenous element in the form of a drastic decline in crude oil prices in the international commodity market. Moreover, inappropriate macroeconomic policy responses have contributed to deepening the crisis. This is more so due to the fact that institutions of economic governance were already weak before the on-set of the crisis.

A good example of this weakness is the adoption **in December 2015** of a **"managed-float" exchange rate regime**, which ignored experts' advice not to apply such a policy in December on the one hand, and without minimum financial and commodity buffers on

---

63 "In countries with hyperinflation, which is usually defined as an inflation rate higher than 50% per month, the money supply increases much faster than real GDP, causing rapid increases in prices, which causes people to spend the money that they receive as quickly as possible, before it diminishes in value. Hence, a very high inflation rate will also maximize the velocity of money, which will increase the inflation rate even further." From http://thismatter.com/money/banking/money-growth-money-velocity-inflation.htm

the other. Within six months of the adoption of a new exchange rate policy by the monetary authorities, the economy of South Sudan entered, without their knowledge, the third phase of a **"dollarization process!"** That is, our economy is now at the stage in which economic agents think in terms of United States of America dollar (USD) and prices in South Sudanese pound (SSP) are indexed to the daily SSP/USD exchange rate.

It is worth mentioning here that oil revenues are denominated in the United States of America dollar. Stated differently, South Sudan in this sense was highly dollarized, though unofficial, at independence. It is, however, possible that policymakers in general, and monetary authorities in particular might not have been aware of this phenomenon. This is evidenced by the liberal way USD was allocated to commercial banks and forex bureaus. For instance, the Bank of South Sudan (BoSS) used, during the first six months of independence, to sell weekly about USD75.0 million to commercial banks (e.g. a commercial bank was allocated up to USD5.0 million) and forex bureaus – a forex was able to buy directly from the central bank of South Sudan up to USD2.5 million. There was no sense of building foreign exchange reserves for a rainy day!

CHAPTER FIVE

PATHWAYS TO ECONOMIC GROWTH

◆

The annual labour of every nation is the fund which originally supplies it with all the necessaries and conveniences of life which it annually consumes ... bears a greater or smaller proportion to the number of those who are to consume it.... [B]ut this proportion must in every nation be regulated by two different circumstances: first, by the skill, dexterity, and judgment with which its labour is generally applied; and secondly, by the proportion between the number of those who are employed in useful labour, and that of those who are not so employed[64].

On growth, a backward journey through the history of economic thought would reveal that what makes the economy grow has always been the dominant subject of inquiry by economists seeking to understand and explain how the delicate machine operates. This sustained search started, in my view, with the seminal book of Adam Smith: *An Inquiry into the Nature and Causes of the Wealth of Nations* first published in 1776. The above passage from the introduction of the Wealth of Nations supports this view.

My interpretation of the above passage leads me to state two things. First, there is what I would call the "*visible hand*" of Adam Smith in the form of regulations, which explicitly gives a proactive role to the state in regulating the economy. Second, that labor was, according to Adam Smith, the prime driver of economic growth during his time.

---

64   *An Inquiry into the Nature and Causes of the Wealth of Nations* first published in 1776, p. 3

Moreover, Adam Smith viewed the growth process to be endogenous[65].

A careful look at the concept or phrase of the "annual labour" as the "fund" would reveal that Adam Smith was essentially treating labor as a combination of human capital and technology (which is created by this labor through innovation and know-how) that in turn produces what Acemoglu calls "*parameters and policies that have first-order influence on physical and human capital and technology*"[66]. Moreover, I would think that what Adam Smith was referring to, as "*the skill, dexterity, and judgment with which its labour is generally applied,*" is in fact what Simon Kuznets is restating as follows:

> If technology is to be employed efficiently and widely, and, indeed, if its own progress is to be stimulated by such use, institutional and ideological adjustments must be made to effect the proper use of innovations generated by the advancing stock of human knowledge.[67]

It is, therefore, obvious that technological progress is a function of human knowledge – the skill, shrewdness, and judgment in which labor is used in the production of goods and services. In this regard, I would consider the Wealth of Nations as the first economic growth theory in which labor was the prime driver of growth. This point would become clearer if we turn to Daron Acemoglu who defines technology as: "*advances in techniques of production, advances in knowledge, and the general efficiency of the organization of production.*" All these advances are clearly a function of human capital, which is labor in its traditional sense of usage.

Let us now turn to a brief highlight of the determinants of economic growth through a quick review of literature.

The relevance of the literature is for our policymakers as well as the general public to understand how and why growth behind the economic performance differs between countries and over time. That

---

65 Lowe, A. 1954. 'The Classical Theory of Economic Growth', Social Research, 21, pp. 127-58. Reprinted in A. Lowe, *Essays in Political Economics: Public Control in a Democratic Society*, edited by A. Oakley, Brighton 1987: Wheatsheaf Books

66 Acemoglu, Daron. 2009. Introduction to modern economic growth. Princeton NJ: Princeton University Press

67 Kuznets, Simon. 1971. "Modern Economic Growth: Findings and Reflections", (Nobel Memorial Lecture, in Kuznets, Simon, Population, Capital, and Growth: Selected Essays, London: Heinemann, 165-184

is, whatever I recommend in Part Three of the book on the revitalization of the economy of South Sudan is informed by growth theory on the one hand, and by empirical evidence on the other. I would also state here that our country has, since independence, not been making use of her daughters and sons with scarce skills in economic management. These skills are integral part of the human capital of South Sudan, which must be made use of in the production and supply of increasingly diverse goods and services.

I would, nevertheless, continue to recommend to our policymakers what I think should be done to kick-start economic growth in our country, based on my professional conviction and commitment to the service of our people. The starting point of my recommendation is to have a consensus on the causes of economic growth. However, Paschalis Arvanitidis *et al* inform us that there is no unified growth theory:

> Finally, it is worth emphasising that due to the lack of a unifying theory on economic growth, a substantial volume of empirical research has multi-theoretical bases. This means that studies draw on several theoretical frameworks and examine factors highlighted by many paradigms. As a result findings are often contradictory and far from being conclusive.[68]

I am, however, comforted by Daron Acemoglu in that:

> While there is disagreement among macroeconomists about how to approach short-run macroeconomic phenomena and what the boundaries of macroeconomics should be, there is broad agreement about the workhorse models of dynamic macroeconomic analysis. These include the Solow growth model, the neoclassical growth model, the overlapping-generations model and models of technological change and technology adoption. Since these are all models of economic growth, a thorough treatment of modern economic growth can also provide (and perhaps should provide) an introduction to this core material of modern macroeconomics[69].

68 *On the Dynamics of Economic Growth: An Expert Survey* (2008) by Paschalis Arvanitidis ,George Petrakos and Sotiris Pavleas

69 Acemoglu, Daron. 2009. *Introduction to modern economic growth*. Princeton NJ: Princeton University Press

What our policymakers need to know from the above two contra-dictory passages is why the economy of South Sudan has not been growing despite favorable initial conditions for growth? The work of Daron Acemoglu should help in answering this question. This is because his work is extensive in that he utilizes theory and empirics to differentiate between proximate and fundamental causes of economic growth. This is a major contribution, in my view, in understanding economic growth in a fragile and post-conflict setting, such as that of South Sudan.

Let us look briefly at these two general categories of the causes of economic growth. They are imperative in the design of the most appropriate macroeconomic policy frameworks that would guide economic management in the short-, medium-, and long-term.

Proximate Determinants of Economic Growth

Acemoglu and others have identified physical capital, human capital, and technology as the proximate causes of economic growth. I add to this list, saving and investment, which were the focus of earlier theoretical frameworks, such as: a) Harrod-Domar model[70] of economic growth; b) Lewis model of economic growth (i.e. of a dual economy with unlimited supply of labor); c) Neoclassical growth model (especially Solow-Swan model); and d) New growth theory.

There is a general agreement among these four main theoretical frameworks, underpinning this brief review of the growth literature, that physical capital accumulation is one of the proximate determinants of economic growth. I have not included Walt Rostow's stages of economic growth among these frameworks for the focus here is not on stages of growth per se, but rather on determinants of growth[71]. The third stage of Rostow's model (i.e. takeoff) is, however, relevant to this discussion, especially when read together with Lewis and Harrod-Domar growth models.

---

70 The model had been developed independently by Roy F. Harrod in 1939 and Evsey Domar in 1946

71 Walt W. Rostow in his book: *Stages of Economic Growth: A Non-communist Manifesto,* published in 1960, identified five stages of economic growth: 1) Traditional society; 2) Pre-conditions for takeoff; 3) Takeoff; 4) Drive to maturity; and 5) Age of mass consumption

The Harrod–Domar model is sufficient for the purposes of under-standing the causes of economic growth. It is a simple model, especially for explaining the critical role of saving and investment in the process of capital accumulation in a developing country, such as South Sudan. The model simply states that the rate of growth of GDP is equal to savings ratio divided by capital–output ratio. In this sense, we could say that it is mainly concerned with a study of the conditions, which influence the smooth and uninterrupted growth of national income in a given country.

The central premise of this model is the process of capital accumu-lation in which saving is its prime driver. It is based on the following four assumptions, expressed in simple equations:

1. $S=sY$, where S is total savings in the economy, s is saving rate (or propensity to save), Y is total output or income or gross domestic product (GDP). That is, saving is a function of income;
2. $I=\Delta K$ where I is investment, K is capital stock, and Δ change in capital stock;
3. $I=S$ i.e. saving and investment are equal in ex–ante as well as ex–post sense. That is, what is saved is used immediately in construction, say of roads, houses, new cars, computers, in cultivating a new acreage of agricultural land, in increasing the number of your cattle, and so forth; and
4. $g = \Delta Y/Y = s/\sigma$, where g is rate of growth of income, ΔY is change in total output, and σ is capital–output ratio ($\sigma=K/Y$) or productivity of investment.

It is obvious from the third assumption that the model takes into account both the demand side (i.e. investment) and the supply side (i.e. savings) of capital accumulation. Banks and other financial institutions are intermediaries in this process of capital accumulation, for they attract savings from those with extra cash by paying interest rate. The banks, in turn, lend savings to those with less cash at an affordable price (i.e. interest rate) to buy, say, a new car, a house, furniture, computer, a cow, new machinery for road construction, and so forth. This example is for households, and firms and when it is aggregated within an economy, it means total private capital accumulation or wealth creation.

The public sector, through taxation, resource endowment (e.g. oil revenue in our case) and/or borrowing from domestic and foreign sources, undertakes capital accumulation in the form of roads, schools, health facilities, and electric power generation, just to mention few examples. Hence, the total capital accumulation in an economy is the total sum of private and public sectors' wealth creation.

The ideas of foreign aid and external borrowing originated from this model in that developing countries would normally face low investment due to low domestic savings. By way of closing the savings gap, an economy of a developing country, like South Sudan could get development assistance (foreign aid) and/or borrowing from developed countries and international financial institutions (IFIs), such as the World Bank, International Monetary Fund (IMF), African Development Bank (AfDB), and so forth. Moreover, foreign direct investment (FDI) could also contribute toward the closing of savings gap if it is attracted through business-enhancing structural policies.

For ease of exposition we illustrate the Harrod-Domar model of economic growth using visuals. The visuals are in the form of vicious circles in Figure 5.1 below in which increased savings (circle A) would in turn lead to increased investment (circle B), e.g. infra-structure, equipment and machinery, and other capital goods. Increased investment leads to higher stock of capital (circle C), which would in turn be used in the production of what Kuznets calls "*increasingly diverse economic goods.*" And I would add diverse services for the service sector of an economy gains prominence as the economy moves through Rostow's stages of economic growth and approaches the "age of mass consumption."

Increased GDP (circle D) - increases in diverse economic goods and services - would lead to higher levels of income (circle E), bearing in minds that saving in this model is a function of income. And we are back to the point (i.e. circle A) where we started this virtual cycle – increased savings as a consequence of higher national income would lead to increased investment to higher capital stock and the cycle continues.

The policymakers in South Sudan must understand this simple process for it could guide them in their determined quest to kick-start the economy with the attainment of relative peace in the country.

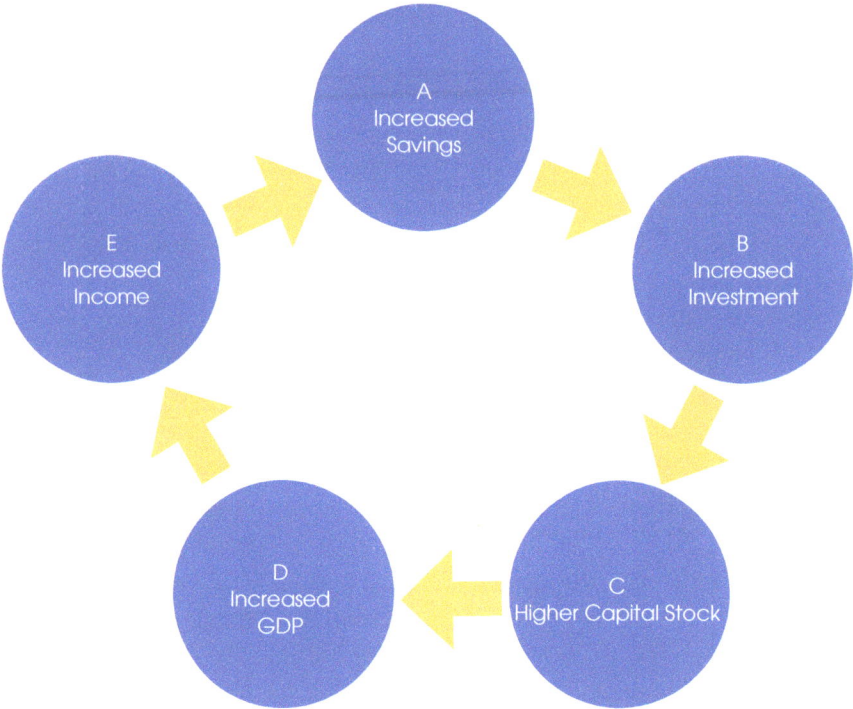

Figure 5.1: Graphical Illustration of the Harrod-Domar Growth Model

The graphic illustration in Figure 5.1 above of the Harrod-Domar growth model is based on a large volume of empirical literature. For instance, Nkurunziza and Gates[72] citing the work of Bosworth and Collins, state, "*that capital accumulation was the key to the successful growth experience of East Asian economies.*" They conclude "*African countries will need to substantially scale up their rates of capital accumulation in order to deliver high and sustainable rates of economic growth.*" This is because capital accumulation is affected in those African countries, according to the growth literature, by low returns to economic activity and high cost of finance.

South Sudan, if it manages the revenues from the sales of its crude oil very well, could easily scale up her capital accumulation. For instance,

---

72 Nkurunziza, J. D. and R. H. Gates. 2003. "Political Institutions and Economic Growth in Africa". The Center for the Study of African Economies Working Paper No. 185.

if the pledged 30,000 barrels of crude oil per day for road construction is strictly adhered to, it could be such a good example of scaling up capital accumulation. This is not withstanding, Dani Rodrik's[73] explanation, using Growth Diagnostic Framework (GDF), of low returns to private investment and "*therefore inadequate demand for investment is due to: government failures; market failures; and problems in other markets.*"

I would be remiss if I do not mention the Lewis model at this point before proceeding to the fundamental causes of economic growth. W. Arthur Lewis is considered as one of the pioneers of development economics[74]. He was awarded the Nobel Prize in 1979 on his path-breaking work on capital accumulation in the dual economy characterized by two sectors – traditional sector dominated by subsistence agriculture and a modern capitalist sector led by industry. There are six assumptions underpinning the Lewis growth model, which are:

1. The model assumes that a developing economy has a surplus of unproductive labor in the agricultural sector;
2. These workers are attracted to the growing manufacturing sector where higher wages are offered;
3. It also assumes that the wages in the manufacturing sector are more or less fixed;
4. Entrepreneurs in the manufacturing sector make profit because they charge a price above the fixed wage rate;
5. The model assumes that these profits will be reinvested in the business in the form of fixed capital; and
6. An advanced manufacturing sector means an economy has moved from a traditional sector to an industrialized one.

I present in table 5.1 below the comparative features of the Lewis dual economy growth model in a tabular format.

---

73   Rodrik, D. 2013. "The Why and How of Growth Diagnostics". At https://www.sss.ias.edu/files/pdfs/Rodrik/Presentations/Growth-diagnostics.pdf

74   Lewis, W. Arthur (1954). "Economic Development with Unlimited Supplies of Labor." The Manchester School. 22: 139–91

Table 5.1: Characteristics of Lewis Dual Economy Growth Model	
Traditional Sector (subsistence agriculture)	Capitalist Sector (industrial sector)
1. Labor-intensive production process	1. Capital-intensive manufacturing process relying on the use of reproducible capital
2. Low average wages	2. Higher average wages
3. Low marginal and average productivity	3. Higher marginal and average productivity
4. Low dependency on capital	4. High demand for labor

I should point out here that the dual economy growth model has other characteristics, such as formal versus informal sector; traded versus non-traded goods; cash versus non-cash economy[75]. These characteristics of dualism are exhibited by the South Sudanese economy and hence the relevance of the Lewis dual economy growth model to this discussion here. For instance, the surplus labor in the traditional sector - rural sector of South Sudan in which more than 80% of the population derive their livelihood from - is being diverted toward the production of violence by both the government and armed opposition groups. And with the return of relative peace, this surplus of unproductive labor in the agricultural sector would be made productive through establishment of agro-industries in the rural areas of South Sudan.

Fundamental Causes of Economic Growth

I now turn to the fundamental causes of economic growth as spearheaded by the new economic growth theory. There are four fundamental causes of economic growth. These are:

---

75   Rodrik, D. 2016. "An African Growth Miracle?" Journal of African Economies, 2016, 1–18, Published by Oxford University Press on behalf of the Centre for the Study of African Economies

1. Leadership;
2. Culture;
3. Geography; and
4. Institutions.

The new growth theory starts from the neoclassical model by endogenizing technological progress[76]. According to Snowdon and Vane "*The central premise of endogenous growth theory is that broad capital accumulation (physical and human) does not experience diminishing returns[77].*" This is because "*the growth process is driven by the accumulation of broad capital together with the production of new knowledge created through research and development.*" Daron Acemoglu further articulates this point as follows:

> In all of our models, especially in those that endogenize physical capital, human capital and technology accumulation, individuals will respond to (profit) incentives. Economic institutions shape these incentives. Therefore, we will see that the way that humans themselves decide to organize their societies determines whether or not incentives to improve productivity and increase output will be forthcoming. Some ways of organizing societies encourage people to innovate, to take risks, to save for the future, to find better ways of doing things, to learn and educate themselves, to solve problems of collective action and to provide public goods.[78]

I like the concept of **broad capital accumulation**, which is now recognized to consist of two components – physical and human. I would, nevertheless, add a third component, which is social capital as conceptualized and defined by Robert Putnam as: "*connections among individuals – social networks and the norms of reciprocity and trustworthiness*

76   Romer, Paul M. 1990. "Endogenous Technological Change." The Journal of Political Economy, Vol. 98, No. 5, Part 2: The Problem of Development: A Conference of the Institute for the Study of Free Enterprise Systems. (Oct. 1990), pp. S71- S102

77   Brian Snowdon and Howard R. Vane. 2005. Modern Macroeconomics: Its origins, Development and Current state. Edward Elgar: Cheltenham, UK and Northampton, MA, USA

78   Acemoglu, Daron. 2009. Introduction to modern economic growth. Princeton NJ: Princeton University Press

that arise from them[79]*."* I have devoted Chapter Ten of this book to broad capital accumulation. It is (i.e. broad capital formation) one of the strategies for revitalizing the economy of South Sudan.

Acemoglu gives the summary of the four fundamental causes of growth in the following passage:

> At the risk of oversimplifying complex phenomena, we can think of the following list of potential fundamental causes: (i) luck (or multiple equilibria) that lead to divergent paths among societies with identical opportunities, preferences and market structures; (ii) geographic differences that affect the environment in which individuals live and that influence the productivity of agriculture, the availability of natural resources, certain constraints on individual behavior, or even individual attitudes; (iii) institutional differences that affect the laws and regulations under which individuals and firms function and thus shape the incentives they have for accumulation, investment and trade; and (iv) cultural differences that determine individuals' values, preferences and beliefs[80].

I will give more focus on leadership after a brief highlights of the other three fundamental causes of economic growth. I believe it is visionary leadership that provides enabling environment for the most appropriate intersection (s) to occur between the proximate and fundamental determinants of economic growth. In this sense, the leadership becomes the primary driver of economic growth.

I want to start with culture as the second fundamental cause of growth, which Acemoglu articulates as follows:

> By culture, we refer to beliefs, values and preferences that influence individual economic behavior. Differences in religious beliefs across societies are among the clearest examples of cultural differences that may affect economic behavior. Differences in preferences, for example, regarding how important wealth is relative to other status-generating activities and how patient individuals should be, might be as important as

---

79   Robert D. Putnam (7 August 2001). *Bowling Alone: The Collapse and Revival of American Community*. Simon and Schuster. p. 19. ISBN 978-0-7432-0304-3.

80   Acemoglu, Daron. 2009. Introduction to modern economic growth. Princeton NJ: Princeton University Press

or even more important than luck, geography and institutions in affecting economic performance. Broadly speaking, culture can affect economic outcomes through two major channels. First, it can affect the willingness of individuals to tradeoff different activities or consumption today versus consumption tomorrow. Via this channel, culture will influence societies' occupational choices, market structure, saving rates and their willingness to accumulate physical and human capital. Second, culture may also affect the degree of cooperation among individuals, and cooperation and trust are often important foundations for productive activities in societies[81].

The above passage is underpinned, in my view, by the work of Max Weber; Banfield; Kuznets; and Putnam[82]. In describing the contribution of Max Weber, Acemoglu summarizes it as follows:

Weber argued that English piety, in particular, Protestantism, was an important driver of capitalists development. Protestantism led to a set of beliefs that emphasized hard work, thrift, saving. It also interpreted economic success as consistent with, even as signaling, being chosen by God. Weber contrasted these characteristics of Protestantism with those of other religions, such as Catholicism and other religions, which he argued did not promote capitalism[83].

In the African context, Chinua Achebe's *Things Fall Apart*, Julius Nyerere's *Freedom and Socialism*, and Francis Deng's [84] *Tradition and Modernization*, are in my view the most relevant creative and scholarly works on culture as a fundamental cause of economic growth. My take away from the work of these three African scholars is trust, which

---

81   Acemoglu, Daron. 2009. Introduction to modern economic growth. Princeton NJ: Princeton University Press

82   Max Weber. 1930. The Protestant Ethic and the Spirit of Capitalism. First published 1930 by Allen and Unwin; Robert Putnam. 1993. Making Democracy Work: Civic Traditions in Modern Italy. Princeton: Princeton University Press; Edward C. Banfield. 1958. The Moral Basis of a Backward Society

83   Acemoglu, Daron. 2009. Introduction to modern economic growth. Princeton NJ: Princeton University Press

84   Chinua Achebe. 1958. Things Fall Apart; Nyerere, Julius. 1968. Freedom and socialism: A selection from writings and speeches 1965-1976. Dar es Salaam: Oxford UP; and Francis Mading Deng. 1971. Tradition and Modernization: A Challenge for Law Among the Dinka of the Sudan, published by Yale University Press

defines and shapes the norms of behavior in a society or community. Trust was always, in our African traditional societies/communities, the foundation of social capital formation.

The trust that, introduction of new ways of life; of new technology; and of alien methods of doing things; would not undermine the dignity of the people or make things fall apart, is one of the fundamental pillars of inclusive development. The body of knowledge embedded in these books should, among other relevant scholarly work, guide our thinking as we enter the second decade of the independence of South Sudan. The power of ideas has highly been underrated, unfortunately, by our policymakers during the first decade of our independence. This was due mainly to the mindsets acquired during the liberation struggle.

Things fell apart in our own case, when we deviated from the prescribed norms of behavior to a culture of "I know it," even if I do not know! This new culture of "**pretense**" is a real challenge, to paraphrase Dr. Francis Mading Deng, for the legal foundation of the development of South Sudan. It undermines Nyerere's foundation of African socialism in which individuals took care of the community, and the community in turn took care of them. And more importantly, it retards what Francis Deng calls "**transitional integration**" of modernity into traditionalism in the process of development and social change. Nyerere expressed, in his *Ujamaa*, the following:

> Our first step, therefore, must be to re-educate ourselves; to regain our former attitude of mind. In our traditional African society we were individuals within a community. We took care of the community, and the community took care of us. We neither needed nor wished to exploit our fellow men[85].

My understanding of transitional integration is that it is a process aimed at dignity-enhancing modernity around which the society (in our case, the traditional society) is to be organized and encouraged *"to innovate, to take risks, to save for the future, to find better ways of doing things, to learn and educate themselves, to solve problems of collective action*

---

85   Julius K. Nyerere. 1962. Ujamaa: The basis of African Socialism, Dar es Salam, April 1962

and to provide public goods.[86]"The challenge before us, we the framers of development policy, is how to operationalize in the current context of South Sudan what was conceptualized half-a-century ago by Francis Mading Deng.

Geography is the third fundamental cause of growth. Let us again turn to Acemoglu for his insights on this:

> By geography, we refer to all factors that are imposed on individuals as part of the physical, geographic and ecological environment in which they live. Geography can affect economic growth through a variety of proximate causes. Geographic factors that can influence the growth process include soil quality, which can affect agricultural productivity; natural resources, which directly contribute to the wealth of a nation and may facilitate industrialization by providing certain key resources, such as coal and iron ore during critical times; climate, which may affect productivity and attitudes directly; topography, which can affect the costs of transportation and communication; and disease environment, which can affect individual health, productivity and incentives to accumulate physical and human capital[87].

Alfred Marshall was the first to have identified geography in his seminal book, *Principles of Economics* (1890), as an important element in economic growth[88]. Others have supported this view through empirical work.[89] Robert Barro gives a powerful case in support of geography as one of the fundamental causes of economic growth:

> Location and climate have large effects on income levels and income growth through their effects on transport costs, disease burdens, and agricultural productivity, among other channels. Geography also seems to affect economic policy choices. Many geographic regions that have

---

86   Acemoglu, Daron. 2009. *Introduction to modern economic growth*. Princeton NJ: Princeton University Press

87   Ibid

88   See Marshall, Alfred.1890. *Principles of Economics*. Prometheus Books

89   Gunnar Myrdal. 1968. Asian Drama: An Inquiry into the Poverty of Nations; Jared Diamond. 1997. Guns, Germs, and Steel: The Fates of Human Societies; John Luke Gallup, Jeffrey D. Sachs, and Andrew D. Mellinger. 1999. Geography and Economic Development

not been conducive to modern economic growth have high population densities and are experiencing rapid increases in population. At particular disadvantage are regions located far from coasts and ocean-navigable rivers, for which the transport costs of international trade are high, and tropical regions, which bear a heavy burden of disease. Moreover, a large portion of population growth over the next thirty years is expected to occur in these geographically disadvantaged regions[90].

Institutions constitute the fourth fundamental determinant of economic growth. I have discussed extensively the definitions of institution in Part One of this book. I would, therefore, not say anything more about them here until part dealing with revitalizing the economy of South Sudan.

Understanding the Intersections Among the Causes of Economic Growth

The reader should by now know that there are five proximate determinants (i.e. saving, investment, physical capital, human capita, and technology) and four fundamental causes (leadership, culture, geography, and institutions) of economic growth. I propose in Table 5.2 below a framework in the form of a policy matrix for a deeper understanding of the intersections between the proximate and fundamental causes of growth. The rows give the proximate determinants of growth, while the columns represent the fundamental causes.

I hope that policy analysts when conducting a comparative analysis of **Garangnomics** and **Kiirnomics** would use this framework. It is important to note here that Garangnomics was never applied due to his tragic death after only 21 days as both the First Vice President (FVP) of the Sudan and President of sub-national Government of Southern Sudan (GoSS). We do, however, have three key pillars of Garangnomics: a) peace through development; b) making agriculture the engine of the South Sudanese economy; and c) taking towns to

---

90   Barro, Robert J. 1991. Economic growth in a cross-section of countries. Quarterly Journal of Economics 106 (2): 407-443

Table 5.2: A framework for Understanding Intersections between Proximate and Fundamental Causes of Economic Growth

Proximate Determinants of Economic Growth	Fundamental Causes of Economic Growth			
	Leadership	**Culture**	**Geography**	**Institutions**
Savings	Visionary leadership ensures: a) Conducive environment for domestic savings; b) Mobilization of development assistance & effective utilization of foreign aid; c) Efficient borrowing from both domestic & external sources	Influences society's savings rates.	Lends natural resources, which directly contribute to growth in nation's wealth	Effective institutions, just like leadership ensure: a) Conducive environment for domestic savings; b) Mobilization of development assistance & effective utilization of foreign aid; c) Efficient borrowing from both domestic & external sources
Investment	Visionary leadership ensures: a) Adherence to the rule of law, which would in turn encourage foreign direct investment (FDI); b) Private property rights; c) Functioning markets underpinned by free movement of goods & services, including capital	Cultural differences that determine individuals' values, preferences and beliefs for undertaking investment activities	Geographical conditions determine the type and priority areas for investment	Inclusive political and economic institutions that ensure effective and efficient allocation of resources to priority areas of public investment, which in turn leads to: a) high returns to economic activity; and b) low cost of financing
Physical Capital	Visionary leadership ensures investment: a) Capital goods; b) Public goods, e.g. roads & bridges, railway, schools; c) Power-generation, tele-communications.	Influences society's willingness to accumulate physical capital.	Geographical conditions determine the nature and magnitude of capital accumulation, which would in turn determine the pace of economic growth	Inclusive political and economic institutions that ensure effective and efficient capital accumulation for sustainable economic growth

Proximate Determinants of Economic Growth	Fundamental Causes of Economic Growth			
	Leadership	Culture	Geography	Institutions
Human Capital	Visionary leadership ensures investment in: a) Education; b) Health; c) R&D	Influences society's willingness to accumulate human capital	Geographical conditions determine the type of educational system that in turn enables the society or country to pursue economic growth strategies consistent with the geography the society finds itself in.	Inclusive political and economic institutions that ensure effective and efficient human capital accumulation for sustainable economic growth
Technology	Visionary leadership ensures: a) Creative destruction of old technology through innovation & adoption of new advanced technologies;	Cultural differences that determine individuals' values, preferences and beliefs for the type of technological change and technology adoption	Geographical conditions determine the type of technological change and technology adoption that in turn enables the society or country to pursue economic growth strategies consistent with the geography the society finds itself in	Inclusive political and economic institutions that ensure effective and efficient systems that encourage advances in techniques of production, advances in knowledge, and the general efficiency of the organization of production

the people in the rural areas of South Sudan. The payback program I have cited in Chapter Two was, in my view, one of the building blocks of the three pillars of Garangnomics.

Leadership as the primary driver of economic growth

I would like to rearrange the nine (or 10 if we add social capital) causes of economic growth in the context of public policy formulation. The goal of any genuine public policy is **sustained economic growth**.

This calls for a programmatic approach in which I categorize the causes of economic growth into four groups. The first group consists of primary drivers and leadership is treated as the primary driver (or first-order condition) instead of being one of the four fundamental causes of economic growth (see Figure 5.2 below).

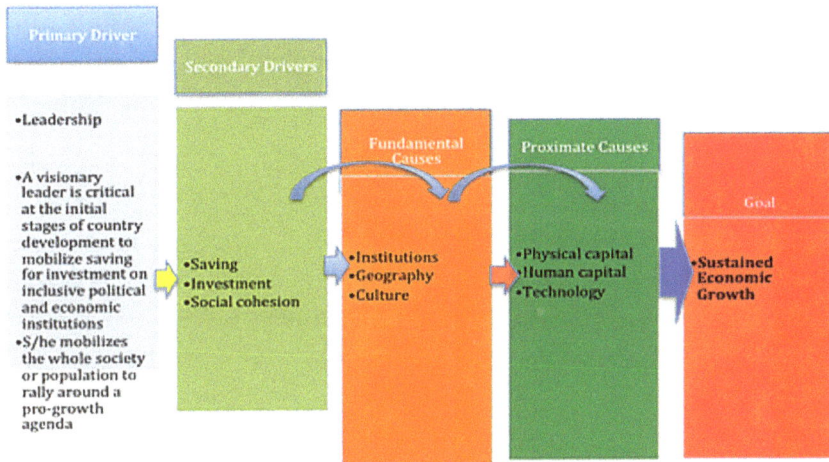

Figure 5.2: Programmatic Illustrations of Economic Growth

I call the second group as secondary drivers (or second-order conditions) of economic growth and it is comprised of saving, investment, and social cohesion (i.e. social capital). The growth literature does not include such a thing called social cohesion, which is, in my view, the basis for social capital formation. The third group of the causes of economic growth consists of three fundamental causes – institutions, geography, and culture. And the fourth group is composed of three conventional determinants of economic growth, which are technology, physical capital, and human capital.

Let us now try to understand the role of leadership in the development process in general, and economic growth in particular. We start with the intriguing question by Daron Acemoglu and James Robinson on *Why Nations Fail?*[91]. Their perspective is underpinned

---

91   Acemoglu, Daron, Simon Johnson and James A. Robinson. 2016. Why Nations Fail: The Origins of Power, Prosperity, and Poverty. Crown Publishing Group

by three paradigms – institutional economics, development economics, and economic history – that they have used in appraising the empirical validity of the four fundamental causes of growth of which leadership is one of them. My answer to their question is simple: **It's leadership, stupid!**

I back up my answer with the work of Benjamin F. Jones and Benjamin A. Olken,[92] who ask the question: **do leaders matter?** They answer their question in the affirmative. They investigated leadership and economic growth since World War II and found that leaders do matter. They conclude:

> We find robust evidence that leaders matter for growth. The results suggest that the effects of individual leaders are strongest in autocratic settings where there are fewer constraints on a leader's power. Leaders also appear to affect policy outcomes, particularly monetary policy. The results suggest that individual leaders can play crucial roles in shaping the growth of nations[93].

Furthermore, Benjamin F. Jones in his *National Leadership and Economic Growth*, brings home the difficult question South Sudanese intellectuals are struggling with to find answers to. I have personally observed since 2005 how some of our leaders have been obstructing growth and Jones gives us the courage by asking: ***"Do leaders act merely to obstruct growth, or do they actively promote it?"*** He then answers it eloquently using African examples, some of which are analogous to the shutdown of oil production in January 2012, followed by bad agreement with Sudan in September 2012. I would breakdown his answer into two parts – positive and negative.

On the positive side of leadership on growth, Jones confirms the influence of a visionary leader on the economy:

> In another view, leaders can be actively good for growth – e.g. by investing in public goods, choosing pro-growth trade policies, or overcoming

---

92 Benjamin F. Jones and Benjamin A. Olken. 2005. "Do Leaders Matter? National Leadership and Growth Since World War II," The Quarterly Journal of Economics, Volume 120, Issue 3, 1 August 2005, Pages 835–864

93 Ibid

national-scale coordination problems. Lee Kuan Yew of Singapore might suggest such a view[94].

David Brady and Michael Spence support the emerging empirical evidence by citing the work of Jones and Olken in their appraisal of the Report of the Growth Commission. They state that:

> In a careful empirical study, Jones and Olken (2005) look across all post–Second World War economies and find 57 cases in which the country's leader suddenly dies or resigns, for example, thus allowing them to use the natural experiment change in leadership for exogenous reasons to solve the endogeneity problem. That is, the unexpected death of a leader gives us a chance to measure the leader's effect on growth. Of course, the change can be positive or negative. They found that the change of national leaders is related to economic growth. The effects were strongest (both positive and negative) in autocratic settings where one or a few leaders have centralized authority[95].

Timothy Besley *et al* motivated by the work of Jones and Olken examined data on about 1,000 political leaders during the period 1875 – 2004. They found that "*heterogeneity among leaders' educational attainment is important with growth being higher by having leaders who are more highly educated*[96]." You do not need to go far to validate this statement, just look at the brief history of the changes in our own leadership.

Look at how the SPLM has splintered, after reuniting in 2004, into a dozen factions; a political disease that has led to the creation of 52 political parties during the first decade of our independence. It is now clear beyond doubt that a visionary leader is critical at the initial stages of a new country, such as South Sudan. This is because a visionary leader is required to lay the foundation for inclusive political and

---

94 Ibid

95 From the Commission on Growth and Development. 2008. *The Growth Report: Strategies for Sustained Growth and Inclusive Development.* Washington, DC: International Bank for Reconstruction and Development and the World Bank

96 Besley, Timothy, and Torsten Persson. 2011. *Pillars of Prosperity: The Political Economics of Development Clusters.* Princeton, NJ: Princeton University Press

economic institutions, which would in turn formulate and execute growth-promoting policies. I have explained in my book: *The Power of Creative Reasoning*, how John Garang effectively utilized a combination of problem-solving approach and Venn Diagram during the Comprehensive Peace Agreement (CPA), which granted self-determination to Southern Sudan that subsequently led to the independence of South Sudan. I conclude this discussion about the role of leadership with a sobering passage from Brady and Spence:

> ...our approach has been to separate the development process into different periods and to analyze leaders' roles at the various stages. The obvious first stage is where the leadership chooses an economic model or strategy, a general overall approach to development and growth, and then builds coalitions, institutions, or both, capable of sustaining a politics that allows the plan time to bring dividends in terms of growth.[97]

On how leaders negatively affect economic growth, he writes:

> In one view, leaders are essentially destructive – highwaymen along the road to economic riches. The tendency to steal, corrupt, and make war are means through which leaders can adversely affect growth and may describe numerous leaders, such as Charles Taylor of Liberia or Mobutu Sese Seko of the former Zaire. In this view, economies would grow well in the absence of such interference[98].

This depressing passage would lead us to examine the invisible hand of corruption and how its risks could be restrained through preventive measures. The next two chapters deal with the curse of conflict and the danger of corruption in the process of economic growth.

---

97 From the Commission on Growth and Development. 2008. *The Growth Report: Strategies for Sustained Growth and Inclusive Development.* Washington, DC: International Bank for Reconstruction and Development and the World Bank

98 Benjamin F. Jones. 2008. *National Leadership and Economic Growth*, Northwestern University, New Palgrave Dictionary of Economics

CHAPTER SIX

THE CURSE OF CONFLICT

◆

The process of capital (physical, human, and social) formation in South Sudan has been undermined by the current civil war that broke out in December 2013. Stated differently, violence has affected investment in public goods, such as roads, electricity, education, public health, water/ sanitation, security[99], and so forth. It has consequently resulted in low private investment on the one hand, and reduced social interaction on the other. Social capital has been eroded and mistrust has risen among communities that used to coexist peacefully.[100]

There are four main sources of financial resources (or total savings) in the economy of South Sudan. These are: GRSS' oil revenues; foreign aid (i.e. development assistance); foreign direct investment (FDI); and domestic savings. Let us see below how the conflict has affected these important sources of savings or investable funds.

Impact of Conflict on GRSS' oil revenues

The impact of conflict on saving (i.e. oil revenues) as one of secondary drivers of economic growth is illustrated by comparing the initial

---

99 It is paradoxical to say that resources have been geared toward the security sector, yet there is high level of insecurity in the country!

100 See Identifying Binding Constraints on Growth in the Context of Fragility: The Case of South Sudan. A collaborative Research Project funded by AERC

conditions at the birth of the Republic of South Sudan on July 9, 2011 with conditions after the onset of conflict. The GRSS received, during the first six months of independence, $3.3 billion from oil revenues, or average monthly income of $556.3 million at that time[101]. The peak was in September 2011 when GRSS received $675 million in that month. This articulates the fact that South Sudan was, during this period, at peace within itself and with her neighbors, especially Sudan. It was, however, a short live prosperity for the leaders of a newly independent country soon took it to violent confrontation with Sudan.

When the brief confrontation with Sudan ended in April 2012, the leaders of South Sudan took it unto themselves on 15 December 2013. This is what I have described elsewhere as political recklessness under-pinned on the one hand by **greed and selfishness**, and on the other by **ignorance and arrogance**. It is a dangerous phenomenon that must be addressed head on by the TCoS for it is a reflection of leadership failure.

Some lessons of experience could be drawn from the Comprehensive Peace Agreement (CPA) of 2005 with respect to the role of intel-lectuals in the articulation of issues underpinning the six protocols. The current leadership of the country has the opportunity to revisit that mechanism (e.g. technical committee of intellectuals), which was used effectively by the SPLM leadership then to formulate various position papers on issues being negotiated. The role of leadership in the CPA could not be over emphasized, for everyone in the current leadership knows it. A visionary leadership would mobilize our intel-lectual resources to take full use of R-ARCSS to address the culture of greed and selfishness in the management of public resources.

One of the consequences of our political recklessness, greed, and selfishness is deficit financing. The research by the Ebony Center, has confirmed, using the Key Informant Interview (KII) technique, that the GRSS was facing a high saving-gap (e.g. fiscal deficit) due to "man-made" crisis. This "man-made" crisis is the violent conflict during the period December 2013 – February 2020. So, even if the R-ARCSS has put an end to the violent conflict, and the phenomenon of recklessness is not tackled, GRSS would not be able to start building up savings. All

---

101 I am reproducing these figures for analysis sake, since I have already given them earlier in the previous chapters of the book

members of the new Collegial Presidency must, in my view, internalize this point if they were to succeed in starting to build up savings.

I have indicated in the preceding chapters of the book that this phenomenon of political recklessness began as far back as January 2012, when oil production was shut down over a dispute with the Sudan. This situation was subsequently compounded by the eruption of internal violent conflict in 2013. First, production stopped completely. Second, global oil prices hit an all-time low in 2015. Since then, the government has struggled to meet its fiscal obligations, let alone allocating resources for production and trade. The limited resources that still flow to the government get spent on salaries and operation (i.e. running cost of public sector operations), which are often in arrears.

By way of explaining the KII findings, oil production before January 2012 was to the tune of 350,000 bopd (i.e. barrel of oil per day) compared to 170,000 bopd at in 2020. The impact of the drastic decline in the daily oil production would be understood if it were stated in terms of budget financing. The first fiscal year (FY) of independent South Sudan was from 1st July 2011 to 30th June 2012. Oil revenues constituted, before the shutdown, 98% of total government revenues; 100% of exports; and 60% of GDP. Hence, the consequences of conflict were drastic and catastrophic to the economy. This is because the GRSS' revenues declined by 98 percent and national income by 80 percent in the FY2012/2013. This means that GRSS' annual expenditure was and continues to be a function of oil revenues accruing to the government.

The saving-gap is explained by a monotonic direct relationship between oil revenues and government spending (see Figure 6.1 below). That is, with shutdown of oil production, GRSS' revenues declined monotonically from $675 million of oil revenues in September 2011 compared to only $25 million in September 2016 when the country was at war with itself. In terms of oil production, it was 350,000 bopd (i.e. barrel of oil per day) in September 2011, compared to 110,000 bopd in September 2016. It is also consistent with the empirical literature that spending in general, and security sector spending in particular is not only influenced by economic conditions. Political decisions and strategic national interest do determine, in most cases, the nature and magnitude of security sector spending.

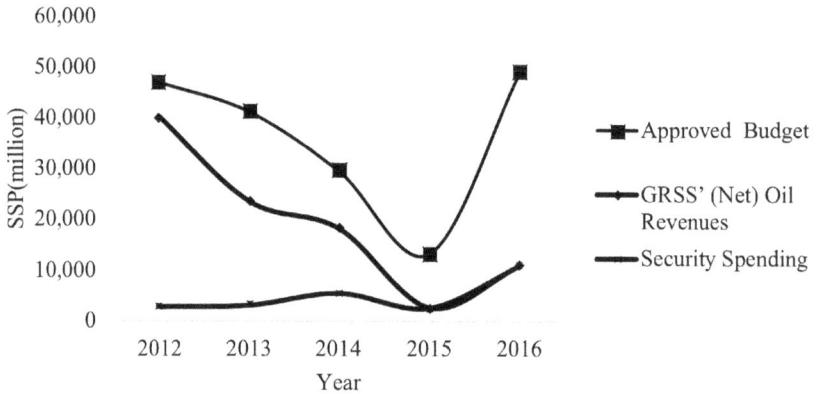

Figure 6.1: Security Sector Spending, net oil revenues, and approved budget in South Sudan, 2012-2016

Security sector spending as a percentage of annual budget[102] (see Figure 6.2 below) is more than one-third (i.e. 35%) during the period July 1, 2011 – June 30, 2017. The highest percentage (43%) was in FY2015/2016, hence our conclusion of 40 percent. In terms of GDP, security sector spending during the period under review constitutes an average of 5.6% of gross domestic product.

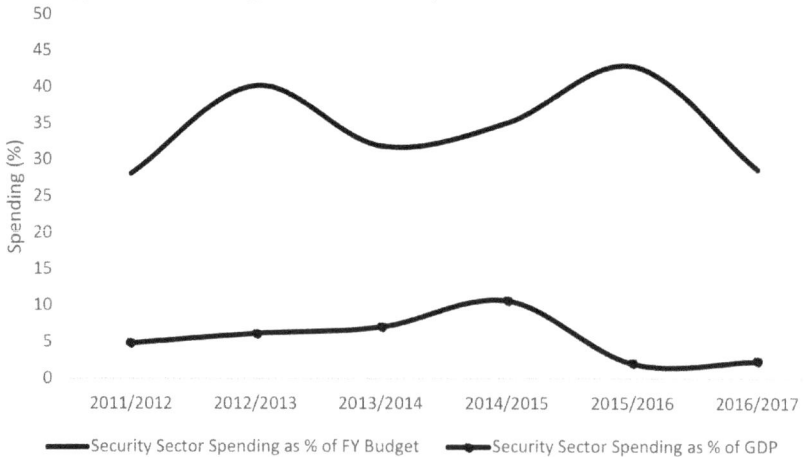

Figure 6.2: Security sector spending as percent of total GRSS budget and GDP, 2012-2016

---

102 The World Bank estimates to be 60%, see Country Engagement Note (CEN) for The Republic of South Sudan, A Report No. 120369-SS, issued by the World Bank, November 2017

The highest (11%) was in FY2014/2015. In absolute nominal terms, the security spending rose from $1.1 billion in the FY2012/2013 to $1.9 billion in FY2013/2014 and dropped to $1.366 billion in FY2014/2015 (see Table 4.3), which made South Sudan the biggest military spender in the IGAD region (see Figure 6.3 below) during that period. The country has nearly doubled its military spending since 2010 as the civil war has been raging in recent years. It is interesting to note that South Sudan imports all its security sector's requirements, even boots and uniforms. South Sudan spends three times of what Ethiopia and Uganda each spends on their military. This is because the two countries have enjoyed decades of relative stability underpinned by sustained investment in physical infrastructure, social cohesion, education, and health sectors.

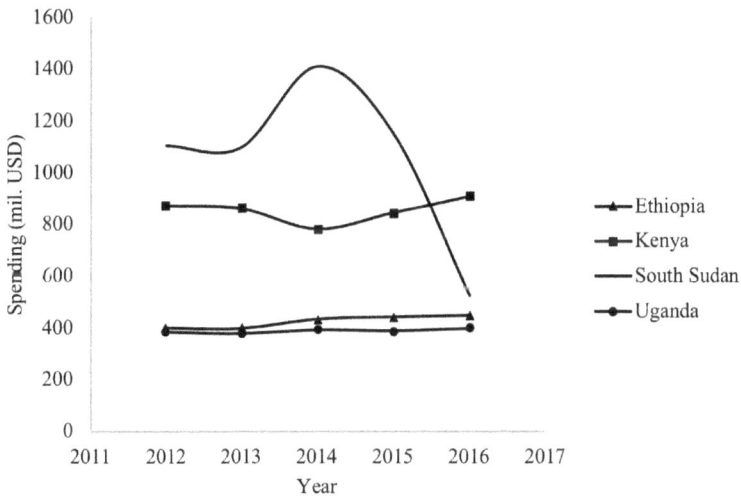

Figure 6.3: Military spending in the IGAD countries, 2012 -2016

Finally, it is observed that the security sector spending has overshadowed budgetary annual allocations for public investment. This in turn negatively affects economic growth. It is understandable that the government would allocate more public resources to the security sector as by way of attempting to have a monopoly of violence. But, in doing so it has depleted funds (savings in the form of oil revenues) for investment in the critical areas of: rule of law, infrastructure, social cohesion, education, health, public administration, and economic governance. Moreover, one of the consequences of keeping constant spending on the security sector, in the light of falling oil revenues, has been a recurrent huge fiscal deficit (i.e. widening saving-gap).

Impact of Conflict on Development Assistance and Foreign Direct Investment

The conflict has, according to our findings through the KII, on the one hand diverted development aid to humanitarian assistance and deterred the in-flow into the country of foreign private investors on the other. Let us first look at Foreign Direct Investment (FDI). The interviewees stated that before the 2013 conflict, there was an investment conference at which about 250 investors made pledges to undertake investment in various sectors of the economy, such as infrastructure. But held broke loose on 15 December 2013 and that hope vanished. The conflict has also raised the cost of doing business in South Sudan and thereby creating unfavorable environment for foreign direct investment. A point well captured by Daron Acemoglu in the following passage:

> An obvious deterrent to the free flow of capital from rich to poor countries arises from the greater risk involved in investing in countries characterized by macroeconomic instability, trade barriers, inadequate infrastructure, poor education, ethnic diversity, widespread corruption, political instability, disadvantageous geography and frequent policy reversals[103].

The in-flow of development assistance was robust, according to Anna Osborne, during the first two and half years of independence in which South Sudan had received $4.3 billion.[104] This flow of development aid was re-directed to humanitarian assistance after the eruption of violence in Juba in December 2013. I consider this annual volume of development assistance that was coming into the country before

---

103 Daron Acemoglu. 2005. *Introduction to Modern Economic Growth*. Department of Economics, MIT

104 Anna Osborne. 2014. "South Sudan, Donor Response to the Crisis," Global Humanitarian Assistance, January 2014

the onset of violent conflict as an integral part of total savings, which could have been invested in productive sectors of the South Sudanese economy. Hence, stopping the war and implementing the peace agreement would lead to generalized-peace dividends in the form of savings by a majority of economic agents in the economy.

Moreover, and according to the interviewees through the KII, efforts to build and maintain basic infrastructure in selected areas using support from the Chinese EXIM bank and the African Development Bank (AfDB) have been incredibly slow and spotty. They farther stressed that one way through which the conflict has constrained long-term economic growth, is the diversion of resources from areas of long-term development to short-term emergencies and humanitarian assistance. Foreign aid (i.e. development assistance), particularly for capacity building programming, has been redirected to humanitarian assistance and to the IGAD-led peace process.

The US Congress, for example, is only able to fund food aid and thereby crowding out investments in productive economic activities and governance strengthening. The United Kingdom (UK) government, it was reported, uses two-thirds of its funding for humanitarian assistance, with the remainder on human capital formation (i.e. health and education).

The change in donors' priorities has meant no direct support to the secondary drivers of economic growth in South Sudan. This humanitarian support has, however, enabled communities to continue to receive basic services. In addition, focusing primarily on consumption has meant that the conflict has eliminated or nearly eliminated private sector investment, consequently contributing to the poor performance of the economy in the production of diverse goods and services.

Impact of Conflict on Private Domestic Resource Mobilization

A brief look at the economics of violence literature would enable us to understand the impact of conflict on private domestic resource mobilization for productive activities in the economy of South Sudan. The ability (capacity) of the economy to supply more (i.e. growth) goods and services to the population is reinforced by a system of sustained transactions and exchanges between economic agents within the country and/or with the rest of the world through international trade. And when this sustained transactions and exchanges are interrupted by violence, the ability of the economy to perform its core functions is reduced proportionately.

The most appropriate tool of analysis here is the microeconomics theorizing, which seeks to understand the behavior of economic agents in an environment of violence and fragility. In this regard, the two theories – growth and economics of violence – are complementary to each other in explaining the impact of violent conflict on the factors influencing economic growth in South Sudan. This is because micro-economics provides appropriate analysis of the behavior of economic agents within a macroeconomic policy framework.

How do economic agents respond to macroeconomic policy measures, such as deficit financing? Such a question is answered through tools drawn mainly from microeconomics. This approach would in turn enable those interested in the growth and stability of South Sudan to understand and appreciate the opportunities, incentives, preferences, and scarcity constraints, which influence the choices people of South Sudan and their leaders make in a conflict environment. And we by now know the behavior of our policymakers during peacetime – propensity for crisis in a strangely reckless manner.

Let us start with Bram van Besouw, Erick Ansink, and Bas van Bavel, who stress the centrality of understanding violence in the context of development:

> Violence is key to understanding human interaction and societal devel-opment. A society that is unable to contain violence will be disrupted and cannot be expected to sustain high levels of welfare, as is painfully illustrated by the current situation in Afghanistan, Libya or, perhaps most conspicuously, parts of Sub-Saharan Africa. Countries like Congo, Somalia, and Sudan are almost continuously torn up by extortion and coercion under the threat of violence, factional strife, and intermittent periods of open violence. Such conditions may destroy lives and capital goods, and deter interaction, exchange, investment, trade, and the benefits of special-

ization that come with trade, leading to significant welfare losses[105].

In his Nobel Prize Lecture on 8 December 1979, Theodore W. Schultz had this to say:

> Most of the people in the world are poor, so if we knew the economics of being poor, we would know much of the economics that really matters. Most of the world's poor people earn their living from agriculture, so if we knew the economics of agriculture, we would know much of the economics of being poor[106].

Following Schultz's tradition of inquiry, we see that about 80% of the population in South Sudan is affected by violent conflict - many South Sudanese are insecure for they derive their livelihood in a conflict environment. So, if we knew, to paraphrase Schultz, the economics of violence, we would know much of the economics of being insecure. That is, "we would know much of the economics that really matters." Daniel Akech Thiong contextualizes this as follows:

> The security dilemma framework and empirical data are used to show that the effects of politics of fear reactivated the once-dormant conflicts in South Sudan in 2013 and have continued to intensify ongoing conflicts[107].

Furthermore, Bromley articulates this profound economic dimension (i.e. the economics of being insecure) by stressing that what "*really matters*" is that "*Civil conflict arises and persists when young males cannot find superior livelihood prospects. Predatory behavior is an expected response to material want and unwanted leisure.*[108]" Such a situation also creates according to Besouw et al an opportunity for "*a group of individually*

---

105 Besouw, B.V., E. Ansink, and B.V. Bavel .2016. "The economics of violence in natural states". Journal of Economic Behavior & Organization 132 (2016) PP 139 -156

106 Theodore W. Schultz. The Economics of Being Poor. Prize Lecture to the memory of Alfred Nobel, December 8, 1979

107 Thiong, Daniel Akech. 2018. "How The Politics Of Fear Generated Chaos In South Sudan." African Affairs, 1–23. Published by Oxford University Press on behalf of Royal African Society

108 Bromley, D.W.2014. Toward Sustainable Livelihoods in South Sudan: The Necessary Institutions of Governance. Paper presented to the Development Policy Forum (DPF) organized by Ebony Center for Strategic Studies, Juba, South Sudan in February 2014.

optimizing violence specialists" to recruit young males to advance its own agenda and thereby reducing the size of labor force that would have been engaged in productive economic activity. This "*group of individually optimizing violence specialists*," fits D'Agoôt's 'gun class.'

The behavior of the ruling elite was underpinned by the inability to internalize the economics of peace within the newly independent state as well as with her neighbors. Understanding the economics of peace would have enabled the South Sudanese policymakers to embark on the process of building up savings instead of war. However, there was no one listening and/or ready to be given any advice and this would seem to be normal in an environment of political recklessness underpinned by greed and selfishness. It is an environment of "*I know it!*" For instance, Alemayehu Geda and Steve Kayizzi-Mugerwa did offer the following advice to the Sudanese and South Sudanese policymakers:

> Notwithstanding the number of outstanding issues that need the immediate attention of the two governments, the agreement on future economic relations is undoubtedly the most pressing one. Specifically, the immediate task should be to negotiate on the issue of oil, debt, currency and related economic issues. The viability of the two economies is to a large degree conditional on a workable agreement on these issues and having a stable macroeconomic environment in both North and South Sudan. This stable macroeconomic environment relates to the issue of low inflation, stable exchange rate and prudent fiscal and external balance[109].

The above advice was ignored by the leadership of the new nation, evidenced by the shutdown of oil production just six months after independence from Sudan. Alemayehu et al proposed analytical framework for negotiating issues of oil, debt, and currency, which could have yielded a win-win outcome, had the GRSS' experts understood its theoretical underpinning. They didn't and the consequences of that failure are vividly captured by the huge saving-gap South Sudan is witnessing today.

It should, however, be stated here that I do not have data on

---

109 Alemayehu Geda and Steve Kayizzi-Mugerwa. 2012. "Sudan: A Macroeconomic Framework for Negotiation and Cooperation between North and South Sudan." IAES Working Paper Serious No. A02/2012

savings (e.g. saving rate) and on the level of domestic resources by South Sudanese private sector. This shortcoming, notwithstanding, R-ARCSS will definitely enable the economic agents, especially the households, to reverse the findings of the Ebony Center's AERC funded research project, which concludes that:

> Violence affects private investment … through low returns to economic activity, which in turn discourages both saving and investment. This is due to the fact that the GRSS (or TGoNU) is fighting various armed groups in the countryside. Both GRSS/TGoNU and rebels compete over household resources (e.g. labor, land, and livestock), especially in the rural areas, for use in the power struggle among the elites; a struggle that is underpinned by violence. In such an environment, the government's role of protecting household savings, labor, and property (e.g. livestock and farm land) and combating corruption had taken a backseat[110].

---

110 See Identifying Binding Constraints on Growth in the Context of Fragility: The Case of South Sudan. A collaborative Research Project funded by AERC

CHAPTER 7

THE DEAD HAND OF CORRUPTION

◆

The political act of graft (American English), is a well known and now global form of political corruption, being the unscrupulous and illegal use of a politician's authority for personal gain, when funds intended for public projects are intentionally misdirected in order to maximize the benefits to illegally private interests of the corrupted individual(s) and their cronies[111].

The above passage from Wikipedia, is an articulation of the dead hand of corruption or of the plundering of natural resources. I would first provide a common understanding of the meaning of corruption. This would in turn contribute to our appreciation of the risks and consequences of the mismanagement of public resources. That is, this chapter focuses on the sources of risk of corruption and tolerable administration of justice.

There are two definitions of corruption. The first is by Vito Tanzi, who defines corruption as "*the intentional non-compliance with the arm's-length principle aimed at deriving some advantage for oneself or for related individuals from this behavior[112]*." The second definition, which is more relevant to the case of South Sudan, is the one given by the World Bank in that corruption is "*the abuse of public office for private gain.*"

---

111 https://en.wikipedia.org/wiki/Corruption

112 Tanzi, Vito. (1995): "Corruption: Arm's-length Relationships and Markets," u: Fiorentini, G. i Pelzman, S.M (ur.): The Economics of Organised Crime, Cambridge: Cambridge University Press

The two definitions of corruption are sufficient for the purpose of understanding the idea of "easy taxes". We should then look at the types of corruption. There are three general types of corruption: a) corruption for accelerating a process, e.g. bribing an official responsible for, say issuing of a driver's license, to let you jump a long line of people waiting to be issued licenses; b) administrative corruption, such as nepotism, favoritism, clientelism, extortion, abuse of discretion, and so forth in which procedures and rules are not followed; e.g. procurement of goods and services are not subjected to competitive bidding as stipulated in the Public Financial Management (PFM) system and law; and c) "state capture" in which corruption is institutionalized[113], e.g. graft, theft, fraud, and embezzlement are norms of behavior than exceptions.

Following the brief highlights of the meaning and types of corruption, the logical question would be what are the sources of corruption? A study in 2017 by Eugen Dimant and Guglielmo Tosato has identified the following 16 causes/sources of corruption[114]:

1. *Greed for money or desires;*
2. *Higher levels of market and political monopolization;*
3. *Low levels of democracy, weak civil participation and low political transparency;*
4. *Higher levels of bureaucracy and inefficient administrative structures;*
5. *Low press freedom;*
6. *Low economic freedom;*
7. *Large ethnic divisions and high levels of in-group favoritism;*
8. *Gender inequality;*
9. *Resource wealth;*
10. *Poverty;*
11. *Political instability;*
12. *Weak property rights;*

---

113 For more on this, see Charap, J. and Harm, C. (1999): "Institutionalized Corruption and the Kleptocratic State," IMF Working Paper, WP/99/91, Washington: International Monetary Fund

114 Dimant, Eugen; Tosato, Guglielmo (1 January 2017). "Causes and Effects of Corruption: What Has Past Decade's Empirical Research Taught Us? A Survey." Journal of Economic Surveys. 32(2): 335–356.

13. Contagion from corrupt neighboring countries;
14. Low levels of education;
15. Lack of commitment to the society; and
16. Extravagant Family (i.e. unsustainable lifestyle)

The Steering Committee of the National Dialogue has added impunity to the above 16 sources of corruption in the case of South Sudan. These sources are more or less captured by an expanded equation by Robert Klitgaard, which is stated as follows[115]:

Degree of corruption = Monopoly + Discretion –Transparency – Morality

I would reformulate this equation as follows:
$$DC = RW + DD - TA - PM$$

Where DC is degree of corruption; RW is natural resource wealth, such as oil in our case; DD is degree of discretion in the use of public resources, such as oil and non-oil revenues; TA is transparency and accountability in the use of public resources; and PM is political morality of public officials at all levels of government. This formula would be of great value in the exercise of identifying, assessing, and understanding the risks of corruption and its consequences on the economy of South Sudan in which the government has the monopoly of oil revenues as well as the discretion to utilize them.

The last two terms with minus sign on the right-hand side of the above equation should, in my view, inform any strategy to combat corruption in South Sudan. It is a simple expression, but powerful in explaining the degree of corruption. That is, the higher the level of transparency and accountability combined with strong political morality, the lower the degree of corruption in a country and/or society. This is because resource wealth (RW) is grounded on a solid public financial management (PFM) system, which is underpinned by robust procedures of accountability. And discretion in the use of resource wealth (RW) is informed by ethics and moral values of those

---

115 Klitgaard, Robert (1998), Controlling Corruption, University of California Press, Berkeley, CA

charged with the public office in the sole service of the people of South Sudan.

It should be mentioned here that political morality is a function of social norms and values of the community in which the concept of **commonwealth** is well understood and internalized. For instance, the dignity (i.e. dignified living) of the community is treated as a commonwealth in some of our communities and people do lose lives in its defense. Communities that have such inherent beliefs in their value systems are likely to have low level of degrees of corruption in the management of public resources (i.e. commonwealth). The danger is, however, when members of such communities are given the responsibility of managing national public finances, they perceive as belonging to alien body (i.e. colonial government introduced the system of taxation) that must not be respected. That is, it is not immoral or unethical to cheat a "government," which is seen by your own community as alien!

The main objective of my interest in the meaning, types, and sources of corruption, is, therefore, to improve the understanding of policy-makers about the consequences of corruption. A brief review of the literature on corruption shows that there are five consequences. That is, corruption leads to:

1. *High costs on each and every transaction with respect to public goods and services;*
2. *Violations of PFM procedures and regulations;*
3. *Dysfunctional market economy, e.g. distorted property rights;*
4. *Kleptocratic behavior in all aspects of social, political, and economic life of society; and*
5. *Corruption-induced violent conflict leading to low level of service delivery and possibility of state collapse.*

Sources of Risk of Corruption

The five consequences of corruption do call, in my view, for credible preventive measures to be put in place. This requires that we look at the potential sources of the risks of corruption in our Republic. Two main sources of risks are: (1) the budgeting process; and (2) the PFM system.

The Budgeting Process

The budget cycle consists of four phases in which the risks of corruption could be identified, assessed, and understood. I present these phases in Figure 7.1 below:

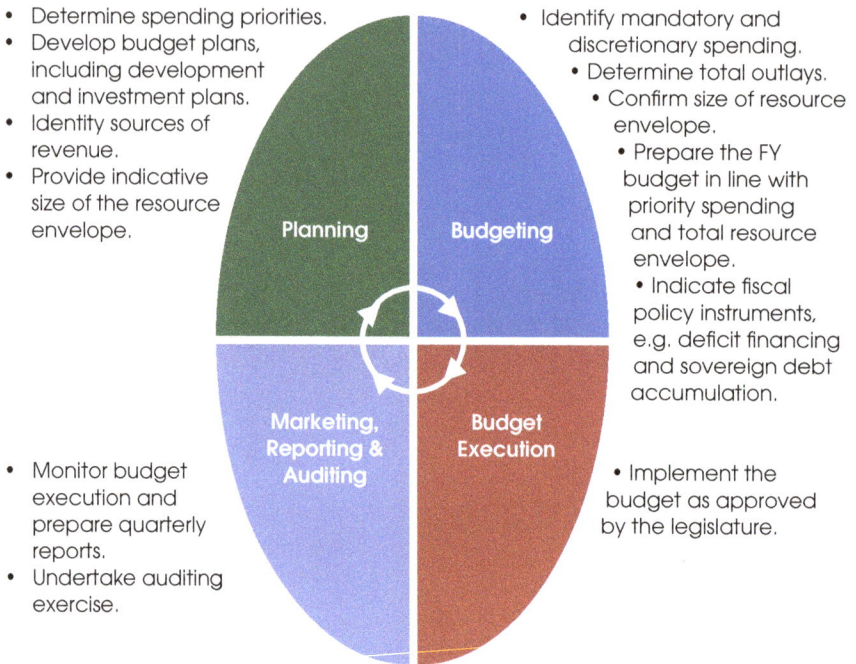

- Determine spending priorities.
- Develop budget plans, including development and investment plans.
- Identify sources of revenue.
- Provide indicative size of the resource envelope.

Planning

- Identify mandatory and discretionary spending.
- Determine total outlays.
- Confirm size of resource envelope.
- Prepare the FY budget in line with priority spending and total resource envelope.
- Indicate fiscal policy instruments, e.g. deficit financing and sovereign debt accumulation.

Budgeting

Marketing, Reporting & Auditing

- Monitor budget execution and prepare quarterly reports.
- Undertake auditing exercise.

Budget Execution

- Implement the budget as approved by the legislature.

Figure 7.1: The Four Phases of the Budget Cycle

I do think that the key framework for identifying the risks of corruption within the budgeting process is the Public Expenditure and Financial Accountability (PEFA). It has seven pillars each in which the risks of corruption could be identified, assessed, and understood. These are:

1. **Budget reliability**: The relevant example here is payment on time of wages and salaries of public sector employees as approved by the legislature and signed into appropriation act

by the president. When wages and salaries are not paid on time, there is a high risk of corruption; especially during periods of non-payment that go for six months and/or more. Another example concerns the payment of suppliers (contractors) of goods and services to the public sector, which creates a major source of corruption in the form of "kick backs" in an environment of unreliability and uncertainty of payment.

2. **Transparency of public finances**: This is critical at the planning phase of the budget cycle where all sources of revenue must be known. Moreover, the size of the resource envelope – total public finances available to be spent should be known by all the spending agencies, by the national legislature, and by the general public. This includes oil revenue, taxes, loans, grants from development partners, and so forth.

3. **Management of assets and liabilities**: This concerns acquisition and disposal of government (i.e. public) properties, such as vehicles, office furniture, land, and so forth. These assets must have identification number kept in a central registry and their acquisition and disposal must be through transparent and accountable system.

4. **Policy-based fiscal strategy and budgeting**: Fiscal policy instruments, e.g. deficit financing, sovereign debt accumulation, oil-collateralized borrowing, and so forth, are major sources of risks of corruption.

5. **Predictability and control in budget execution**: Flow of financial resources during the budget year must be predictable, so as to ensure credibility and integrity of the budgeting process. And when the flow of financial resources is unpredictable, the risk of corruption is increased.

6. **Accounting and reporting**: A system of internal audit units in all the spending agencies of the government is fundamental for ensuring a strong mechanism for accountability and reporting on how public resources have been utilized.

7. **External scrutiny and audit**: The risk of corruption arises when the reports of the Auditor General are not acted upon on time by both the presidency and national legislature.

The PFM system

I have developed a programmatic approach with the overarching objective of ensuring transparency and accountability in the management (TAM) of public resources in the Republic of South Sudan. For ease of understanding, good economic governance is conceptualized as better financial accountability and transparency in the management of public resources. The question of pervasive corruption has been a recurrent concern of the people of South Sudan throughout the grassroots consultations and it, therefore, requires innovative approaches toward proper understanding of its risks. Figure 7.2 below is the schematic illustration for understanding the risks of corruption in South Sudan.

The schematic illustration utilizes the three components of PFM as pillars through which risks of corruption are highlighted:

1. *Aggregate financial management (AFM);*
2. *Operational financial management (OFM); and*
3. *Fiduciary risk management (FRM).*

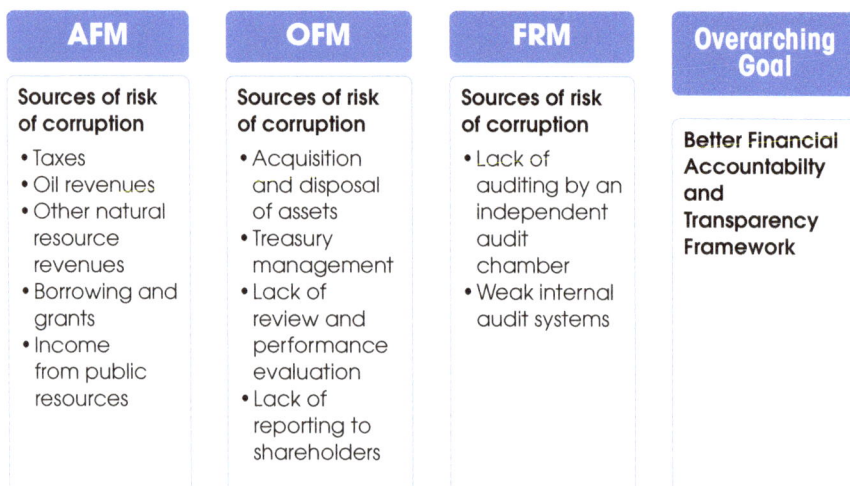

AFM	**OFM**	**FRM**	**Overarching Goal**
Sources of risk of corruption	**Sources of risk of corruption**	**Sources of risk of corruption**	**Better Financial Accountabilty and Transparency Framework**
• Taxes • Oil revenues • Other natural resource revenues • Borrowing and grants • Income from public resources	• Acquisition and disposal of assets • Treasury management • Lack of review and performance evaluation • Lack of reporting to shareholders	• Lack of auditing by an independent audit chamber • Weak internal audit systems	

Figure 7.2: Enhanced PFM Framework for understanding the risks of corruption in South Sudan

Tolerable Administration of Justice

Administration of justice is one of the requisites for the economy to perform its necessary functions of producing and supplying increasingly diverse goods and services to the population of South Sudan. I take "**tolerable administration of justice**" in our case to mean equity and efficiency in the allocation of resources, including opportunities for undertaking any economic activity. Our people have complained that the government has crowded out the domestic (private) sector through maladministration of justice with respect to awarding of contracts to constitutional office holders and foreigners. It would seem to me that we have not yet understood the fundamental function of a free market economy. There is no absolute free market for it has to be well regulated. Henry Hazlitt gives the working meanings of market and private property:

The free market means the freedom of everybody to dispose of his property, to exchange it for other property or for money, or to employ it for further production, on whatever terms he finds acceptable. This freedom is of course a corollary of private property. Private property necessarily implies the right of use for consumption or for further production, and the right of free disposal or exchange[116].

Public property cannot be freely disposed of or exchanged for private and personal use by the government employee (s) in charge of its management. Administration of justice breaks down when government employees abuse their "***public office for private gain***." Land grabbing, especially in Equatoria, and the inability to enforce laws to protect the owners of the land, is one of the examples of maladministration of justice, which has in turn contributed to pervasive corruption in the country.

Moreover, there is a general concern within the business community about "**tolerable administration of justice**." For instance, in a conference organized by the National Dialogue Leadership for the South Sudanese business community, the conferees made the

---

116 Quoted from https://fee.org/articles/the-five-institutions-of-the-market-economy/

following two statements: "*Note with great concern the negative role some senior government officials play in distorting the market; they award themselves government contracts, breaching the principles of conflict of interest and fair competition;*" and therefore "*Call for transparency and fairness in the allocation of contracts and further call for strict adherence to the principle of fair competition*[117]."

The Business Community called, in that conference, upon the government of the Republic of South Sudan to immediately restore peace and tranquility in the country stating, "*there is no business without peace and therefore peace is a necessary condition for the revival of the economy*". They also called for the enforcement of laws and regulations in the economy, to foster fair competition, elaborating that without the rule of law; there can be no business. The leaders also urged the government to formulate and adopt a private sector development strategy and to support and protect national entrepreneurs.

I have discussed in this Part Two of the book, the purpose of the economy and the requisites for it to perform its necessary functions. I will now turn to how to make the economy of South Sudan grow. This is done by looking at the role of the Presidency in revitalizing the economy and then highlight associated policies for economic growth and poverty eradication.

---

117 From a Communiqué issued by the Business Community Conference held in Juba on 21 – 22 November 2019

PART III

REVITALIZING
THE ECONOMY

CHAPTER EIGHT

REVITALIZING THE ECONOMY: THE ROLE OF THE PRESIDENCY

◆

The second stage is in some sense not delimited in time because it concerns how leaders adjust strategies and choices to changing circumstances—economic and political. These adjustments can be responses to shocks or unanticipated external events, but they also occur in response to the endogenous evolution of characteristics of the economy in the course of growth. These latter challenges can and do range from rising income inequality, a rising middle class, competitive pressures from the global economy, rising incomes and wages causing shifting comparative advantage, and institutions not adapted to the evolving characteristics and state of development economy[118].

The choice of the above passage is deliberate, for I want to contextualize the role of leadership in the revitalization of the South Sudanese economy after a decade of conflict and mismanagement. The word "revitalize" would seem to have been overused toward the end of the first decade of the independence of South Sudan. I could not, however, find a better word other than the term "revitalize" to express at the beginning of the new decade, the views of ordinary South Sudanese people on the economy and how its management could be adjusted.

---

118 From the Commission on Growth and Development. 2008. The Growth Report: Strategies for Sustained Growth and Inclusive Development. Washington, DC: International Bank for Reconstruction and Development and the World Bank

The National Dialogue Steering Committee has called its recommendations on the economy in the question form: **How to Rehabilitate and Kick Start South Sudan Economy and Social Rehabilitation?** I would say that the economy was kick started at independence in 2011, though inappropriately, so the word "revitalize" would, therefore, be relevant for the second stage of our attempts to develop our country.

Our leaders now have the opportunity to rise to the occasion by making necessary adjustments to their strategies and choices in response to a combination of external and internal factors, such as oil prices in the international market; the coronavirus (i.e. COVID-19 pandemic); the dwindling purchasing power of the South Sudanese pound; ethnic-induced violence, the demand of ordinary people for better living conditions; and above all the people's demand for a coherent South Sudanese state at peace with itself and with its neighbours.

It is now appropriate to discuss, the task of revitalizing the economy in the light of the four groups of the causes of economic growth that I have discussed in Chapter Five. I would like to state here unambiguously that the economy of South Sudan would not be turned around to perform its core functions without a strong and **visionary leadership**. It is reassuring to note that the question of leadership in South Sudan has been the focus of the framers of the R-ARCSS. This is stipulated in Articles 1.5 and 1.9 of Chapter One of R-ARCSS.

Article 1.5 is on the structure of the executive of RTGoNU, while Article 1.9 is about powers, functions, and responsibilities to be exercised by the President, the First Vice President (FVP), and the four Vice Presidents (VPs) through sustained consultations and agreements. Article 1.9.1 specifically states:

> The RTGoNU is founded on the premise that there shall be collegial collaboration in decision-making and continuous consultations within the Presidency, between the President, the First Vice President, and the Four Vice Presidents, to ensure effective governance during the Transitional Period[119].

---

119 See page 12 of the Revitalized Agreement On The Resolution of the Conflict in the Republic of South Sudan, Addis Ababa, Ethiopia, 12 September 2018

Hence, Article 1.9.1 on the Collegial Presidency provides a critical point of departure for addressing the concerns of the people of South Sudan about the performance of the economy as documented by the National Dialogue Secretariat. I know there are some members of the TGoNU team that participated in the negotiation of R-ARCSS who will arrogantly say that Article 1.9.1 does not mean a collegial presidency! I would, nevertheless, continue with my understanding of Article 1.9.1, especially with reference to "*ensure effective governance during the Transitional Period.*" It is imperative for our leaders to collectively work toward revitalizing the economy in the context of the four groups of the determinants of economic growth I have highlighted in Chapter Five. The groups are:

1. *Group One in which leadership is the primary driver of economic growth;*
2. *Group Two, which consists of secondary drivers (i.e. saving, investment, and social cohesion) of economic growth;*
3. *Group Three, which comprises of fundamental (i.e. geography, culture, and institutions) causes of growth; and*
4. *Group Four, which consists of proximate (technology, physical and human capital) determinants of economic growth.*

The Primary Driver of Economic Growth in South Sudan

The primary driver of economic growth in South Sudan is the Collegial Presidency as stipulated in the R-ARCSS (Article 1.9.1). I would recommend that Article 1.9.1 be literally memorized by members of the Presidency, members of the National Legislature, and the general public to whom the Collegial Presidency is accountable. The framers of R-ARCSS conceptualized, according to my reading, the Collegial Presidency as the ideal answer to this intriguing question.

The R-ARCSS model of the Collegial Presidency divides the Council of Ministers or Cabinet into five clusters[120] (Articles 1.10.1

---

120 Mr. Bona Malwal Madut has recently called them five confederates when he was addressing the Steering Committee of the National Dialogue. He stated the same in his meeting on 4 August 2020 with Dr. Riek Machar Teny, FVP

– 1.10.7): a) Governance cluster with 12 ministries; b) Economic Cluster with 11 ministries; c) Service Cluster with five ministries; d) Infrastructure Cluster with three ministries; and e) Gender and Youth Cluster with four ministries. The President is the head of the Collegial Presidency and the five vice presidents are members, making a total number of six (6) in the collective leadership of South Sudan during the Transitional Period of 36 months.

I would modify R-ARCSS model of Collegial Presidency with the view to making it a genuine **collective leadership** that meets the characteristics of a primary driver of economic growth I have conceptualized in Chapter Five. I am now thinking outside the box of R-ARCSS on the one hand, and the Vatican-mediated peace process on the other. This is especially with respect to the tenure, name, and composition of Collegial Presidency. I recommend that a Collegial Presidency or Council of State be comprised of nine members and chaired by the President. This calls for the reorganization of the Cabinet into eight (8) clusters, with each being supervised by a member of Collegial Presidency (i.e. VP). The composition of the eight clusters is given below.

A. Governance Cluster (four ministries):
1. Presidential Affairs;
2. Cabinet Affairs;
3. Foreign Affairs and International Cooperation; and
4. Information, Communication Technology and Postal Services.

B. Security Cluster (four ministries):
1. Defense and Veterans Affairs;
2. Interior;
3. National Security; and
4. Wildlife Conservation and Tourism.

C. Economic Cluster (five ministries):
1. Finance and Planning;
2. Petroleum;
3. Mining;
4. Agriculture and Food Security; and
5. Trade and Industry.

D. Decentralization Cluster (five ministries):
1. Federal Affairs;
2. Peace Building;
3. Livestock and Fisheries;
4. Land, Housing and Urban Development; and
5. Environment and Forestry.

E. Service Cluster (four ministries):
1. Higher Education, Science and Technology;
2. General Education and Instruction;
3. Health; and
4. Labor.

F. Infrastructure Cluster (four ministries):
1. Energy and Dams;
2. Transport;
3. Roads and Bridges; and
4. Water Resources and Irrigation.

G. Legislative Cluster (five ministries):
1. Justice and Constitutional Affairs;
2. Parliamentary Affairs;
3. East African Community Affairs;
4. Investment; and
5. Public Service and Human Resource Development.

H. Gender and Youth Cluster (four ministries):
1. Gender, Child and Social Welfare;
2. Humanitarian Affairs and Disaster Management;
3. Culture, Museum and National Heritage; and
4. Youth and Sports.

The R-ARCSS calls for comprehensive institutional reforms in general, and in particular institutions of economic governance as stipulated in Chapter IV. These reforms require longer period than 36 months of the Transitional Period. I am, therefore, proposing a Transitional Period of 60 months starting from 9 July 2021 and ends on 8 July 2027.

I would also rename the Collegial Presidency and call it Transitional Council of State (TCoS). It is to be composed of nine members representing the three former colonial provinces of Bahr el-Ghazal, Equatoria, and Upper Nile. These were also the three regions out of five regions in the Civil Authority of New Sudan (CANS) of the SPLM Administration during the war of liberation. I would use Joseph Lagu-Abel Alier formula of 1972 to ensure equal representation in TCoS. This means that each region will be represented by three of which one must be a woman.

The chairmanship (i.e. President) of TCoS shall be by rotation between the three former regions of CANS, with each having the presidency for a period of 24 months. The system of rotation presidency shall be as follows:

1. President Salva Kiir Mayardit shall continue as President of TCoS until 8 July 2023.
2. The First Vice President (FVP) stipulated in R-ARCSS (Article 1.7.2) shall be FVP of TCoS until 8 July 2023 and he or one of the other two VPs from Upper Nile shall become the President of TCoS from 9 July 2023 to 8 July 2025. When FVP who is from Upper Nile becomes the President, one of the three VPs from Equatoria becomes FVP.
3. One of the three Vice Presidents (VPs) from Equatoria shall become the President of TCoS for the remaining two years of the Transitional Period, which is from 9 July 2025 to 8 July 2027.

The R-ARCSS stipulates five Vice Presidents of which three are from Greater Upper Nile, with Greater Bahr el-Ghazal and Greater Equatoria taking one each. I would propose that the three additional VPs be given to the two regions that have not reached their quota: a) one for Greater Bahr el-Ghazal who must be a woman; and b) two for Greater Equatoria of which one must be a woman. Moreover, two of the proposed three additional VPs could be allocated to the non-signatories of the R-ARCSS, specifically the South Sudan Opposition Movements Alliance (SSOMA) and who will not have ministerial portfolios.

I follow the R-ARCSS model of assignment of VPs to the clusters within TCoS and under the overall coordination and supervision of the President. The TCoS shall perform functions and responsibilities stipulated in the R-ARCSS (Articles 1.6 to 1.9). Friends of South Sudan must invest resources to make the TCoS a truly collective leadership of the country by implementing fully all the Articles of R-ARCSS. The TCoS is envisaged to perform the functions of an executive president, which implies that the Cabinet is an implementing body of the decisions of the TCoS. This clarity will enable the TCoS to be the primary driver of economic growth in South Sudan during the six-year Transitional Period.

It is in the light of the above understanding that I recommend the following assignment, which could be changed every 24 months, consistent with the rotation arrangement:

1. *First Vice President, Governance Cluster;*
2. *Vice President for Economic Cluster;*
3. *Vice President for Legislative Cluster;*
4. *Vice President for Decentralization Cluster;*
5. *Vice President for Gender and Youth Cluster;*
6. *Vice President for Infrastructure cluster,*
7. *Vice President for Service Cluster; and*
8. *Vice President for Security Cluster.*

I have provided the basic idea of TCoS as a collective leadership or Collegial Presidency during a Transitional Period of six years, beginning from 9 July 2021. This basic idea is informed by documents generated through critical and complementary processes that were all launched, almost at the same time in 2017.

The first is the National Dialogue process. It was launched in May 2017 and is a bottom-up forum in which all the stakeholders of our country have expressed their views through a consultative conversation, from the grassroots to the national level, about what has gone wrong and how to fix it. The second process is the IGAD led High-Level Revitalization Forum (HLRF) that was launched in August 2017 in which the elites deliberated on what they perceived to have gone wrong and subsequently provided a solution through the R-ARCSS.

I encourage other South Sudanese intellectuals to join me in this journey of ideas in search for implementable framework, which addresses, among other things, the concerns of our people about how to make our economy produce for them; diverse goods and services. The collegial presidency in the form of TCoS is this framework. I have taken a quick review of the collegiality literature and found that four binding principles must be met in order to ensure harmony within the TCoS and, therefore, its effectiveness in revitalizing the economy. That is, the first order of business for the TCoS is to revitalize the economy through evidence-based and well-tested economic policies that promote inclusivity while maintaining growth and enhanced food security.

But, first let us have a common understanding of collegiality. A simple definition of collegiality is given as "*shared power and authority among colleagues.*[121]" Leila Shrifian farther states "*collegial models assume that organizations determine policies and make decisions through a process of discussion leading to consensus. Power is shared among some or all members of the organization who are thought to have a shared understanding about the aims of the institution.*[122]"

The overarching goal of the proposed TCoS is sustainable peace, economic growth, and poverty eradication. Hence, Shrifian's definition is, in my view, consistent with this overarching goal and with what the framers of the R-ARCSS envisaged for the Collegial Presidency, which I have modified to ensure it is sufficiently inclusive and sensitive of gender, of ethnicity, of geography, and of national character. Moreover, most members of the Collegial Presidency stipulated in the R-ARCSS are comrades of the liberation struggle, which led to the independence of South Sudan. They must, therefore, share what the World Bank has appropriately described as "*a binding narrative of triumph and freedom.*[123]" This narrative must be internalized by all the members of the TCoS so as to ensure a viable South Sudanese State at peace with itself and with all its neighbors.

---

121 American Heritage Dictionary of the English Language Online, 2009

122 Leila Shrifan (2011: 1170). Collegial management to improve the effectiveness of managers' organizational behavior in educational institutions, Procedia - Social and Behavioral Sciences 29 (2011): 1169 – 1178

123 Cited from the Interim Strategy Note (FY 2013 – 2014) for the Republic of South Sudan. Report No: 74767-SS, World Bank

It is also important to note here that the leaders of the five political groupings that are sharing power during the Transition Period have agreed to equally *"lay the foundation for a united, peaceful and prosperous society based on justice, equality, respect for human rights and the rule of law.*[124]*"* This understanding of the vision of the RTGoNU constitutes the common purpose of the TCoS that is tasked with the leadership of RTGoNU. But, this shared understanding about the vision, mission, and objectives of RTGoNU requires TCoS to have four binding principles, which underpin the rules of behavior that must be observed within it. These are: a) partnership; b) mutual co-existence; c) self-discipline and self-actualization; and d) equal level of motivation and sense of responsibility.

The first requirement is that the six-year Transitional Period be regarded as a staging period for the creation of a permanent system of governance that is productive, efficient, effective, caring, and above all honest. This calls for a strong partnership among all the political parties in the RTGoNU and who are represented in the TCoS. Lessons of experience from the Sudan Government of National Unity (GoNU) that was co-led by the National Congress Party (NCP) and the Sudan People's Liberation Movement (SPLM) would tend to indicate that one of the key failures of GoNU was a dysfunctional partnership, which eventually resulted in the breakup of Sudan.

Hence, the binding foundation of the partnership of the RTGoNU is the shared understanding to *"lay the foundation for a united, peaceful and prosperous society based on justice, equality, respect for human rights and the rule of law."* This is essentially the meaning of a coherent state that the people of South Sudan so desire.

The key to coherent, agile, and honest governance is a strong partnership that is able to create a governing atmosphere of urgency and expectancy among all the political parties holding essential appointments in the TCoS. The essential aspect here is that all members of the TCoS must be held accountable for outcomes that improve livelihoods of ordinary South Sudanese citizens. They must not be passive occupiers of valued seats of political power. They must, however, perform their tasks as a team and not as competing members repre-

---

124 From the preamble of R-ARCSS, page 1

senting the narrow interest of their respective political parties and/or their own personal interest.

The future of South Sudan as a state and nation lies in the hands of the nine individual sons and daughters in the TCoS, which is tasked to rescue this great country from self-destruction and likely disintegration at the end of the Transitional Period of six years if the R-ARCSS is not implemented wisely and comprehensively. Hence, my proposal to have a Transitional Period of six years is to give sufficient time for the TCoS to lay a strong foundation for a coherent South Sudanese state that is capable of creating a vibrant economy.

The second binding principle is mutual co-existence, which is one of the pillars of a coherent and accountable Collegial Presidency. The President and his eight (or five currently) vice presidents must respect and pursue the principle of mutual co-existence in the implementation of the recommendations of the National Dialogue and R-ARCSS. They are all in this together; whether in success or failure and must, therefore, develop a sense of collective responsibility in everything they do.

The eight Vice Presidents are all aspirants to become President at the end of the Transition Period. They must, therefore, distinguish themselves within the Collegial Presidency (i.e. TCoS) that anyone of them could one day be the President of South Sudan. This calls for self-discipline and self-actualization in the pursuit of the shared goal of laying the foundation for a unified, peaceful and prosperous South Sudanese society. The Vice Presidents must strive to utilize a cadre of well-educated "youngsters" who are eager to play a role in the re-vitalization of South Sudan. The clusters provide a unique platform for demonstrating the skills and characteristics of cooperative management that the country needs in turbulent times. It is essential that a new generation of leaders is able to emerge during the period of transitional governance.

The TCoS should set, over the six-year Transitional Period, as its goal the retirement of approximately one-third of the Cabinet in the first round of rotation of the chairmanship of TCoS. This policy would create between twelve and thirty-three opportunities for fresh new thinking being brought into the government. Those elders replaced in this process should be given a small stipend and retained for one year or two years as "senior advisors." There are people who have been in the Cabinet since 2005 without significant and positive contributions to the development of our people. Such elements have proven to be *"dead-enders"* with no vision for South Sudan[125].

The fourth principle calls for innovation within the TCoS, which would in turn create a sense of responsibility and motivation in serving the people of South Sudan. Moreover, it would be necessary for each office of the TCoS to have a core technical staff of at least eight individuals – each tasked with policy analysis of a given cluster. That is, there will be at least sixty-four technical staff (i.e. policy analysts) within the TCoS.

The best way to create a climate of equal level of motivation and performance is to move these individuals around within the TCoS at least twice during the six-year Transitional Period. The supervision of the eight clusters should be an opportunity for some very promising VPs to aspire for the leadership of the country after the Transitional Period. The poor performing VPs will have to quit the TCoS voluntarily or their political parties are asked to withdraw them during the Transition Period.

It is necessary to determine who, among this initial cadre of presumably trusted elites, is really serious about job performance; and who among them wishes to coast and enjoy the privileges associated with high office. Frequent reassignments create a climate, and an expectation, that excellent performance will be rewarded with new and important opportunities. Few motivated individuals are satisfied to sit and be ignored or ridiculed for bad behavior. South Sudan must create a culture of striving and advancement within the institution of the Presidency.

---

125 Ambassador Stuart Symington, U.S. Special Envoy to South Sudan, articulated this phrase in his meeting on 12 March 2020 with a group of South Sudanese intellectuals. This was in the context of hardliners who opposed the decision of the Presidency to return the country to 10 states instead of 32 states; so, Ambassador Symington thought that such individuals are not hardliners, but dead-enders on the argument that hardliners would have a vision for South Sudan. The consensus at the end of the meeting on the vision thing was: A Viable South Sudanese State at peace within itself and with its neighbors.

CHAPTER NINE

REVITALIZING THE ECONOMY: IMPERATIVE OF POLICY MANAGEMENT

◆

Carry out radical reforms and transformation of public financial management systems to ensure transparency and accountability; Ensure prudent, transparent and accountable management of national wealth and resources to build the nation and promote the welfare of the people; Carry out the functions of government; Restructure, rehabilitate, and ensure radical reform of the civil service; Design and implement security sector reforms and security sector transformation, to include the restructuring and reconstitution of institutions; Rebuild and recover destroyed physical infrastructure and give special attention to prioritizing the rebuilding of livelihoods of those affected by the conflict; and ...Devolve more powers and resources to the State and Local Government levels[126].

The above passage is from Chapter One of the R–ARCSS document (12 September 2018), which calls, inter alia, that the Revitalized Transitional Government of National Unity (RTGoNU) should undertake those stated functions. That is a very tall order, but it is premised on the effectiveness and the **political will** of the envisaged Collegial Presidency.

---

126 These are Articles 1.2.7 – 1.2.15 on page 3 of the Revitalized Agreement On The Resolution of the Conflict in the Republic of South Sudan, Addis Ababa, Ethiopia, 12 September 2018

It is, nevertheless, a tall order in the light of the historical poor perfor-mance of our economic policy management. Hence, the importance of looking at the status of our policy management first before embarking on likely policies for revitalizing the economy.

I use the Country Policy and Institutional Assessment (CPIA) index of the World Bank to give us an idea of the nature and magnitude of the decision-making on the determinants of economic growth. The index clearly shows the nature and magnitude of the mismanagement of our economy. A score of 6 gives the highest quality of policies and institutions of a country, while a score of 1 indicates poor quality (i.e. the lowest level) of policies and institutions. The overall CPIA score for South Sudan ranges between 2.1 in 2012, which is the highest so far to a low of 1.5 in 2018 (see Table 9.1 below).

Moreover, South Sudan in 2018 compares poorly to the World Bank's International Development Agency (IDA) eligible countries with a CPIA score of 3.2; Sub-Saharan Africa (SSA) with a CPIA of 3.1; and fragile states with a CPIA score of 2.8. It is reassuring to note that our people at the grassroots level have identified, without looking at the CPIA, how our government has been poorly managing our economy. Low scores of CPIA index (see Table 9.1 below) for South Sudan are indicators of the inappropriate mixture of lubricants for our economic machine.

Cluster	CPIA Scores by Year							Change in CPIA Scores from 2012 to 2018
	2012	2013	2014	2015	2016	2017	2018	
Economic Management	1.8	1.8	1.8	1.5	1.0	1.0	1.0	-0.8
Structural Policies	2.3	2.2	2.2	2.2	2.0	2.0	2.0	-0.3
Policies for Social Inclusion and Equity	2.3	2.2	2.1	2.1	1.8	1.7	1.5	-0.8
Public Sector Management and Institutions	2.0	2.0	1.9	1.7	1.5	1.4	1.4	-0.6
Overall CPIA	2.1	2.1	2.0	1.9	1.6	1.5	1.5	-0.6

Source: Constructed by the author from Assessing Africa's Policies and Institutions, World Bank (2019)

Table 9.1: The Nature and Magnitude of Decision-making in South Sudan As Measured by CPIA During the period 2012 – 2018

I have said earlier that the lubricants for our economic machine are in the form of public policies and associated responses of the private sector to these policies. This point would be understood if we look at the macroeconomic policy framework (i.e. fiscal and monetary policy measures), which is the key instrument for steering the economy toward the twin objectives of full employment and low level of inflation in the process of producing goods and services for the people of South Sudan and the rest of the world.

I have stated earlier in this book that South Sudan economy has been, since mid-2012, witnessing macroeconomic instability characterized by deficit financing, which in turn triggered high inflation rates and volatility in the exchange rate market. One of the major consequences of macroeconomic instability is the erosion of the purchasing power of the income of all the people of South Sudan. And when people do not buy, the economy stagnates as we have seen in the case of COVID-19 pandemic on the global economic machine. This further illustrates the point that economic growth is a measure of the speed of the economy. It is on how the economic machine moves over a given period of time and in a specific location.

The movement of this machine is the process of producing diverse goods and services, sum of which is called gross domestic product (GDP). The fuel and lubricants of this economic machine are public policies and associated private sector strategies in response to such policies. That is, the market (i.e. private sector) reacts to public policy measures by either producing more goods and services or by producing less of them, depending on the nature – pro-business or anti-business – of these measures.

Policymakers monitor the growth rate of the economy in addition to per capita GDP; with the view to formulating appropriate mixture of policies (lubricants) to keep the machine on a steady path of producing increasingly diverse goods and services for the population. Moreover, policy analysts use, among other measures, per capita GDP (or per capita income) to compare the performance of economies across countries. For instance, the per capita GDP for South Sudan in the year 2012 was relatively strong in comparison to its neighbors (see Figure 9.1 below).

The rosy picture of South Sudan's per capita GDP in 2012 has been

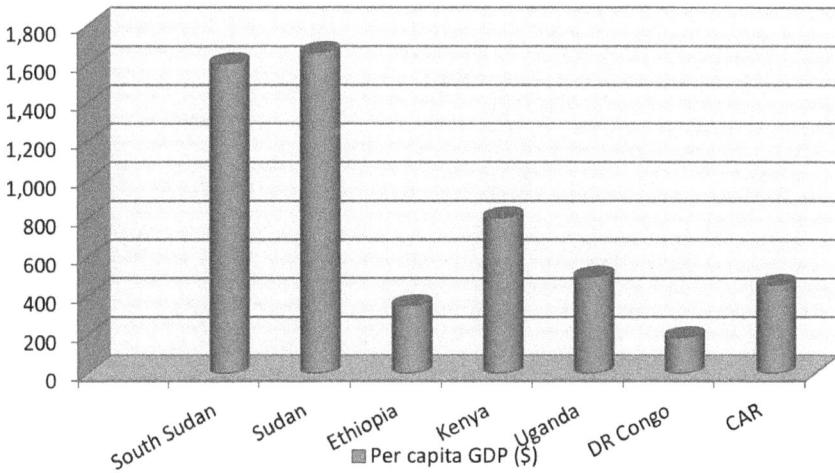

Figure 9.1: Per-capita GDP ($) for South Sudan in 2012 & Neighboring Countries

diminished, through our own recklessness in the management of our resources, as I have explained in the previous chapters of this book. For instance, South Sudan was on top of the list of the ten poorest African countries in 2019 as illustrated by Box 9.1 below. Something unthinkable nine years ago when we celebrated our independence on 9 July 2011 with significant natural resources and a binding narrative of victory and freedom.

Box 9.1: Ten Poorest African Countries in 2019

Africa is one of the richest continents in the world with favorable weather, land-soil, and minerals. However, this is a different story for some of the poorest countries in Africa. With regard to many years of cruel leadership, political instability, insecurity, disasters, countless embezzlement of public funds, and poor decision making, several countries in Africa have been bedeviled by poor economic standards. Here is a detailed list of the top 10 countries that are in poverty in Africa by GDP per capita.

1. South Sudan: GDP per capita: $237.44

South Sudan is the poorest country in Africa and the youngest nation in the world. Born on July 9, 2011, after the agreement that stopped the conflict with Sudan, the longest civil war in Africa. However, violence has still embraced this land-locked state. The conflict started in 2013 when President Salva Kiir accused his former deputy rebel Riek Machar, of organizing a coup. The clashes led to the killing of an estimated 400,000 people and more than 4 million people were displaced.

The country is a potentially wealthy nation, but with oil contributing a lot towards the country's exports, the rising insecurity and falling commodity prices have had a massive blow on the country's economy. In August 2018, Salva Kiir and Riek Machar signed a power-sharing and a ceasefire agreement. Since then, they have worked together in maintaining peace. This could improve the country's economy in the long run.

2. Burundi: GDP per capita: $292.01

Burundi's economy is highly dependent on the agriculture sector which contributes 54% of the country's GDP and 70% of its labor force. Sadly, its economy remains crippled due to the less developed manufacturing sector, inadequate resources, a weak rule of law, and misappropriation of funds. In a bid to overcome future financial issues, Burundi is focusing on self-sufficiency and also seeking external financial aid.

3. Malawi: GDP per capita: $338.48

The third poorest country in Africa is Malawi with a GDP per capita of $338.48. Malawians rely mostly on the agriculture sector which contributes more than 70% of the country's GDP. In addition, the largest population of Malawians live in rural areas, making agriculture the most sustainable economic activity in the country. Due to several unfavorable factors, life in Malawi is considered to be miserable with the life expectancy of its citizens standing at 50 years.

Although the Malawian government is putting more effort in improving the country's export revenue, the country is still plagued with several challenges including inadequate education system, poor health care system, the spread of HIV/AIDS, massive deforestation, poor infrastructure, and high corruption rate.

4. Niger: GDP per capita: $378.06

With a GDP per capita of 378.06, the country has substantial mineral capabilities and a vibrant agriculture sector. The economy is further strengthened by a high volume of domestic production and foreign exports. Despite its high productivity levels, the country hasn't yet achieved standardized economic growth because most of its exports are channeled towards the less-developed countries in Africa. Flexible privatization policies have been implemented by the Nigerien government to stabilize the economy.

5. The Central African Republic: GDP per capita: $418.41

The Central African Republic is one of the African countries that has [sic] been through tough times with years of war. With a GDP per capita of $418.41, the nation's economy has been weakened by the long period of political instability. The country's mineral and timber potentials are a perfect opportunity for raising the national revenue, but on a negative note, corruption incidences have devalued them. President Francois Bozize (2008 – 2012) made great strides in restoring the country's stability, and within his four years rule, he achieved considerable progress. However, in 2013 he was overthrown from power by the Seleka rebel group, putting an end to his achievements.

6. The Democratic Republic of Congo: GDP per capita: $462.78

The country generates the lion share of its revenue from its most active sectors such as agriculture and forestry. Also, its oil sector yields petroleum both for domestic needs and exportation. However, the country is faced with unemployment due to the budget crisis. Though, the country experiences acute economic drawbacks, the incumbent administration is doing its best to implement the use of modern technology to generate electricity from natural gas.

7. Somalia: GDP per capita: $478.34

The question, "Is Somalia the poorest country?" might have popped up in your mind at some point. Well, it ranks as the seventh poorest in Africa, with a GDP per capita of $478.34. A report issued by the United Nations states that Somalia ranks among the poorest countries in Africa and the world.

The crippled economy in Somalia is as a result of the civil war that has been ravaging the country for years. With an economy that is underdeveloped and under the military's control, the country has remained one of the poorest countries in Africa. Its best-untapped resources which could have been harnessed in boosting the economy have been botched by the Somalian army. Economically, the country depends on livestock, foreign remittances, and telecommunications. However, these are still not sufficient to strengthen the country's economic condition.

8. Liberia: GDP per capita: $694.32

With a GDP per capita o $694.32, Liberia depends mostly on mineral resources and agriculture. The nation relies heavily on the exportation of minerals including iron ore and rubber to increase the GDP level. Previously the economic standards of Liberia were sustainable, but as a result of civil war, the economy has been crippled with poor infrastructure, political unrest and lack of capital resources. The Liberian government is putting more effort towards implementing modern technology in enhancing the agricultural sector to revive the economy.

9. Gambia: GDP per capita: $709.01

Which country is the poorest in Africa? Gambia is considered the ninth poorest country in Africa with a GDP per capita of $709.01. It is one of the countries in Africa with insufficient mineral resources. It barely generates significant export revenues, making livestock the main source of economic sustenance. The country has insufficient agricultural land hence difficult to increase the volume of production. The country is depending largely on foreign donations. For the economy to be sustainable, the Gambian government advised its citizens to establish small-scale businesses.

10. Madagascar: GDP per capita: $10,721.61

Madagascar has over the years taken advantage of its sufficient natural capacities such as agriculture and mining to facilitate its exportations. It has, therefore, maintained income stability. It remains to be one of the poorest African nations as a result of recurring political instability, which have discouraged foreign investors. Meanwhile, the country focuses on its tourism sector which is an additional source of revenue generation.

Now you have a complete list of the poorest countries in Africa. As much as the economy might be stagnant at the moment, there is still a bright future for these countries.

Source: http://news-af.feednews.com/news/detail/e3f26c5d82ae93afc28a2b2cead688be?country=ss&language=en&share=1&client=

Figure 9.1 and Box 9.1 are a clear articulation of the nature and magnitude of poor decision-making in South Sudan since January 2012. The first victim of macroeconomic instability is saving; both public and private. This is because economic agents are forced to dis-save in an environment of rising cost of living. For instance, the purchasing power of the money income, especially wages and salaries, was eroded within six months of the adoption, in December 2015, of a new exchange rate regime. The annual inflation rate stood at 700% at end-September 2016. The exchange rate of SSP to USD in July

2020 was SSP340 to one United States of America dollar, which had declined to SSP280/$1.0 after the formation of RTGoNU; but rose due to a number of intervening factors among them the inability to appoint governors of the States and to formulate appropriate policy response to the COVID-19 pandemic.

Let us, by way of illustration, take a monthly salary of a member of the Transitional National Legislative Assembly (TNLA), which is **SSP9,800 (nine thousand–eight hundred)**. This amount was equivalent to **USD 3,322** before the realignment of the exchange rate in December 2015. It was equivalent to **USD10.06** (i.e. dropped by **99.69%**) in July 2020.

The above example of the salary of a member of TNLA (parliament) only tells a story of the status of money income of the elites. Looking at a monthly income of SSP300 for those on minimum wage would capture a true picture of the drastic erosion of the money income of ordinary people. This amount was equivalent to USD101.7/month in December 2015 compared to USD0.909/month (i.e. one dollar per month and not per day, which is the global poverty line) in July 2020. Although the percentage drop in the monthly money income is the same for a member of TNLA and a person on minimum wage, the latter would bear more, the brunt of skyrocketing prices than the former. This is because they both buy their goods and services from the same market. Moreover, the disparity (i.e. gap) is still acute in that what the member of TNLA gets is 10 times that of minimum wage earner.

The situation of money income depicted by the preceding two paragraphs is contrasted with the behavior of prices of goods and services, which took opposite direction. I would illustrate the madness of rising prices by looking at two goods – diesel and water. A liter of diesel was six pounds (SSP6.0/liter), which was equivalent to USD2.0 in mid-December 2015. The liberalized rate of diesel is now SSP240.0/liter or USD0.71 (or 71US cent) in July 2020. The price of a liter of diesel has risen in terms of SSP by 3,900%. It has, however, declined in USD terms by 64.5%. The price of a small bottle of mineral water used to be one pound (i.e. SSP1.0), which was equivalent to USD0.34 (or 34 US cent) before the realignment of the exchange rate. The price of the same bottle of mineral water is now SSP70 (or 29 US cent), which is an increase of 7,000% (or decline of 14.7% in terms of USD).

The two examples I have given here are just to make our story simple. But, the overall picture is captured by the annual inflation rate, which stood at 700% at end-September 2016 and came down to 69% at the end of December 2019.

The severity of the impact, on the population, of a combination of drastic drop in money income by 99.7% and sharp increases in the prices of goods and services represented by an annual inflation rate of 700% could not be over emphasized. In a situation of rising inflation, the purchasing power of money income is normally protected through indexing income to inflation. But, this is not practical in an environment of weak institutions and a monthly double-digit inflation. There is, however, a simple and practical way of protecting the purchasing power of money income, which is being eroded daily by skyrocketing prices. But, let us return to policy management and the role leadership in steering the economy toward sustainable peace, growth, and poverty eradication.

The role of leadership is to adjust decision-making process in the light of Table 9.1 (i.e. CPIA index). This is because the fundamentals of economic growth (e.g. saving, investment, infrastructure, social cohesion, etc.) have been affected negatively by the type and nature of the mixture (or lubricants) of public policies. Let us examine the policies that would restore or create a culture of saving, investment, and social cohesion at all levels of government and society. The most appropriate grouping of these policies is the one provided by the CPIA index as specified in Table 9.1.

The narrative being conveyed by the CPIA as presented in Table 9.1 is consistent with what the people have said, through grassroots consultations, about the state of South Sudanese economy. Hence, the TCoS should embark on revitalizing the South Sudanese economy through: a) economic policy management; b) structural policies; c) social inclusion and equity policies; and d) policies for public sector management and institutions. That is, the economy requires urgent actions to turn it around, so that it could perform its core functions, of which one is the production of goods and services.

It is all about the question of how political necessities could be leveraged to assure a coherent and accountable governance to realize the pressing demands for state creation that would in turn allow the economy to perform its core functions. Hence, the role of leadership (i.e. TCoS) is imperative in economic policy management.

The propensity to save would then be restored through appropriate policy mix in the following three areas of economic policy management: a) fiscal policy; b) monetary and exchange rate policy; and c) debt policy. Figures in Table 9.1 show that economic policy management has been the lowest (worst) performing category for three years in a row since 2016 with CPIA score of 1.0 compared to 1.8 in 2012 (i.e. before conflict). The CPIA for Sub-Saharan Africa-IDA eligible countries was 3.1 in 2018. All the three elements of economic policy management scored each the same score of 1.0 since 2016.

It is the TCoS that will restore macroeconomic stability through urgent actions aimed at discipline and credibility of economic policy management. The starting point then is to mobilize resources, to put in place a robust Public Financial Management (PFM[127]) system, and to ensure effective coordination of fiscal and monetary policies. I am now more optimistic than before the courageous decision of 14 February 2020 by the Presidency to return the country to 10 States. This is because the TCoS will make use of this renewed courage in addressing the underlined crisis of economic mismanagement.

The intellectuals are now called upon to undertake their responsibilities by providing evidence-based scenarios and policy options from which the Presidency would make choices. They cannot continue to be armchair critics at the time when their critical thinking is urgently needed at two levels – analytical dissection of the challenges and opportunities facing the country; and formulation of appropriate strategies for tackling the changing circumstances. Moreover, policymakers must own the policy option they select from the menu that is provided by experts from their comfort zones at the research centers. I am, however, aware of the tendency to suppress the freedom of thought in

---

127 Honorable Salvatore Garang Mabiordit, Minister of Finance and Planning has constituted in April 2020 a governance structure for the PFM to implement the PFM reform strategy stipulated in Chapter IV of R-ARCSS. The governance structure consists of: a) PFM oversight committee co-chaired by the Minister with the U.S. Ambassador representing development partners; b) PFM technical committee chaired by the First Undersecretary, MoFP and with representatives of key ministries and commissions, Ebony Center, School of Economic and Social Studies of the University of Juba, the IMF, World Bank, UNDP, African Development Bank, EU and Troika; and c) PFM Secretariat. This is a significant development, which will contribute toward narrowing the credibility gap of not only the economic cluster, but more importantly of the Presidency.

our country, but the National Dialogue process has created some space for political and civic activities.

Let us now look at the components of economic policy management. There are three main elements of economic policy management, which are used to influence the behavior of the secondary drivers of economic growth. They are: a) fiscal policy; b) monetary and exchange rate policy; and c) debt policy.

Fiscal policy

Fiscal policy is essentially about how governments collect revenues (mostly taxes) and spend them for the provision of public goods and services, such as roads, schools, health care, and security. The provision, *inter alia*, of these public goods, depends on the volume of savings in the economy. It is, therefore, one of the key instruments through which the leadership of a country influences how an economy performs its core functions. In this regard, the credibility and integrity of budgeting process is imperative. This is because the government builds up its savings through strict adherence to the implementation of the annual budgets as approved.

In economics, net saving is considered to be today's investment in the future. For instance, if GRSS does not spend all its revenue, say from crude oil, the portion that is not spent (i.e. not consumed) would be used next year for infrastructure development and/or building of classrooms and/or new healthcare facilities. Our interest then should be on the potential sources of savings and fiscal policy instruments, which are employed to realize these potentials. Before looking at the potential sources of savings, I would like us to have an understanding of the fiscal space within the budgeting process.

Understanding Fiscal Space within the Framework of FY2017/2018

The point of departure here is to seek a common understanding of the fiscal space. In doing this, I would turn to Peter Heller who defines fiscal space as a:

… room in a government's budget that allows it to provide resources for a desired purpose without jeopardizing the sustainability of its financial position or the stability of the economy[128].

I would define fiscal space in the context of South Sudan as a windfall that occurs during the budget execution and which was not foreseen when the budget was approved. It is basically a "lottery," won after the annual budget has been approved and signed into law. For example, an increase in either oil prices or production will generate more revenues for the GRSS; revenues that were not anticipated at the time of budget preparation and approval. Table 9.2 below gives the benchmarks used in the preparation of the FY2017/2018 budget. These are compared to actual values/levels (e.g. changes in oil prices and daily production) that are obtained during the implementation of the budget.

Table 9.2: A Framework for Fiscal Space In FY2017/2018 Budget

Variable	Benchmark	Actual	Comments
1. Oil production	110,000 bbl./day Or 3,300,000 barrels/ month or 39.6 million barrels for FY2017/2018	127,000 bbl./day Or 3,810,000 barrels per month or 45,720,000 barrels for FY2017/2018	There is an increase of 17,000 bbl./day, which provides an important fiscal space (i.e. saving) that was not foreseen during the budget preparation
2. Price of Dar Crude	$45/bbl. of which Sudan takes $24.1/ bbl. in lieu of transport, transit, & processing fees of $9.1/bbl. and TFA of $15/bbl.	$54.19/bbl. during the first half of FY2017/2018 and of which Sudan takes $24.1/bbl. in lieu of transport, transit, & processing fees of $9.1/ bbl. and TFA of $15/bbl. The price for the second half of FY2017/2018 is on average likely to be $65/ barrel.	An increase of oil price by $9.19/bbl. gives additional revenues to the budget that was not foreseen at the time of budget preparation. Moreover, the government should renegotiate the transitional financial arrangement/assis- tance (TFA) of $15/ barrel being exported through Sudan and which was agreed

---

128 See Back to Basics -- Fiscal Space: What It Is and How to Get It, by Peter Heller, Finance and Development, A Quarterly Magazine of the IMF, June 2005, Volume 42, Number 2

Variable	Benchmark	Actual	Comments
2. Price of Dar Crude *(continued)*			upon at the time South Sudan was relatively better off compared to Sudan. South Sudan is now facing economic crisis and it would be mutually beneficial if the TFA were cancelled
3. Exchange Rate	SSP155/$1.0	SSP165/$1.0	Depreciation of the SSP against the US dollar by 6.5%; increases, other things remaining the same, the nominal income (i.e. oil revenues of the government, which are denominated in dollar) by the same percentage. It is, however, inflationary and reduces the purchasing power of those people with fixed income, since inflation-adjusted income and cost-inflation index are not used in South Sudan
4. GRSS share of oil production in barrels per day	42% of 110,000 bbl./ day is equal to 46,200 barrels of which Sudan takes 28,000 bbl./day, leaving 18,200 bbl./day for GRSS. That means Sudan gets 60.6% of GRSS' share of oil revenues, which is worse than 49% under the CPA. The oil revenue sharing formula stipulated in the Wealth Sharing Protocol of CPA talks of 50/50 after 2% payment to the oil producing States, which means it is 98% that is being divided 50/50 and hence my assertion of 49% to GONU and 49% to GoSS.	54% of 127,000 barrels per day is equal to 68,580 barrels per day of which Sudan takes 28,000 bbl./day and 40,580 bbl./day for GRSS. That means Sudan gets 40.8% of GRSS' share of oil revenues, which is closer to 49% under the CPA.	There is a positive correlation between oil production and government-take (i.e. share in profit-oil). That is, whenever oil production declines, cost-oil increases (or profit-oil declines) bearing in minds that government-take is from the profit-oil. Hence, an increase of 12% in the share of oil revenues for the government is a significant enhancement in the fiscal space, especially if used wisely.

Variable	Benchmark	Actual	Comments
5. GRSS share of oil revenues in FY2017/2018 budget	a) Gross oil revenues in FY2017/2018: $820,851,613 or SSP127.232 billion for FY2017/2018 b) Payment to Sudan in FY2017/2018: $453,600,000 c) Payment to Nilepet and suppliers of refined products in FY2017/2018: $182,625,806 d) Payment to oil producing States & communities in FY2017/2018: $18,361,290 e) Net oil revenues for GRSS to finance FY2017/2018: $166,264,517 or SSP25.771 billion	a) Gross oil revenues in FY2017/2018: $1,471,452,480 b) Payment to Sudan in FY2017/2018: $595,000,080 c) Payment to Nilepet and suppliers of refined products in FY2017/2018: $182,625,806 d) Payment to oil producing States & communities in FY2017/2018: $73,572,624 e) Net oil revenues for GRSS to finance FY2017/2018: $620,253,970 or SSP96.14 billion	i) When the benchmark price is $45/bbl. and daily production as 110,000 bbl./day, then Sudan takes 55.3% of GRSS share of oil revenues due to the infamous TFA of $15/bbl., which is a huge burden on the fiscal sustainability of our budget. Arrogance and ignorance have not allowed the GRSS to assemble South Sudanese with experience and scarce skills to renegotiate the TFA. ii) Fuel subsidy takes 22.25% of the total oil revenues for GRSS in FY2017/2018 when the benchmark price is $45/bbl. and daily production as 110,000 bbl./day iii) With improved oil production and prices, GRSS should be able to fully finance FY2017/2018 from its net oil revenues and will still have $319.6 million to finance arrears and service the debt
6. Total Expenditure	FY2017/2018: 46.6 billion South Sudanese pounds or $300,600,000	FY2017/2018: 49.6 billion South Sudanese pounds or $300,600,000	This should be constant throughout the FY2017/2018 if no adjustments are made to the wage bill or change in the benchmarks setout in the budget

Variable	Benchmark	Actual	Comments
7. Financing gap/surplus if FY2017/2018 is funded only through net oil revenues	There is a gap of $134,335,483 or SSP20.822 billion, which is closed through a combination of financing packages given under variable (parameter) 8 below	There is estimated surplus of $319,653,970	GRSS could then improve the purchasing power of public sector employees without necessarily undermining its fiscal sustainability and macroeconomic stability. This could be done through the dollarization of the wage bill
8. Balancing the FY2017/2018 budget	a) Non-oil revenues of GRSS: $90,967,742 or SSP14.1 billion	a) Non-oil revenues of GRSS: $90,967,742 or SSP14.1 billion	GRSS should keep these budgetary items/variables as given in the approved budget (i.e. constant). The room for maneuver should be through the oil windfall
	b) External grants: $2,645,161 or SSP410 million	b) External grants: $2,645,161 or SSP410 million	
	c) External project loans: $14,193,548 or SSP2.2 billion	c) External project loans: $14,193,548 or SSP2.2 billion	
	d) Treasury Bills: $4,468,085 or SSP840 million	d) Treasury Bills: $4,468,085 or SSP840 million	
	e) Advanced oil Sales: $22,060,947 or SSP3.42 billion	e) Advanced oil Sales: $22,060,947 or SSP3.42 billion	

Source: Constructed by the author from information contained in the Budget Speech of the Minister of Finance and from data provided by the Crude Oil Marketing Committee, Ministry of Petroleum, GRSS

The analytical framework for fiscal space in the FY2017/2018 budget gives about $320 million, which GRSS could have used to achieve desirable policy objectives "without jeopardizing the sustainability of its financial position or the stability of the economy." This would not be possible, however, given the nature and magnitude of indiscipline in the execution of the budget.

Subsequent budgets (i.e. FY2018/2019 and FY2019/2020) have witnessed windfalls during their implementation, but they were all squandered and no building up of savings ever made. In fact, wages and salaries continue to be in arrears for several months up to the time

I am writing this section of the book. I will come to this point later when discussing the expenditure side of the budget.

The key assumption of the framework for fiscal space is to hold constant the total public expenditure, while allowing variations on the revenue side of the budget equation. A culture of thrift and saving has been missing within the public sector of South Sudan, this is because the budget is not considered and respected as an important tool for saving for "a rainy day!" I have deliberately chosen the FY2017/2018 to illustrate how an opportunity for building up savings was squandered, and which has become a normal practice. When the Minister of Finance tried to impose discipline in the execution of the budget he was dismissed from the Cabinet in March 2018!

Potential sources for building up savings

There are four potential sources for saving that I have identified in my paper on fiscal space in the FY2017/2018 approved budget[129]. They are still relevant today, especially if they are appropriately addressed by the TCoS. The RTGoNU could start building our savings that would in turn be invested in driving the fundamental and proximate locomotives of economic growth. These are:

- *Ending the war and reaching peace agreement;*
- *Restoring discipline in the management of the approved budget;*
- *Managing the exchange rate (ER) regime; and*
- *Reorienting humanitarian assistance toward food security, livelihoods, and economic recovery.*

The Revitalized Agreement on the Resolution of Conflict in the Republic of South Sudan (R-ARCSS) creates an enabling environment for all the economic agents to begin building up their savings. The impact of violence on economic growth is now well documented. According to the World Bank, the security sector in South Sudan takes

---

129 See "Challenges and Opportunities for Fiscal Space in the FY2017/2018 Budget of Government of South Sudan," a paper presented by Lual A. Deng to the DPF/TAF discourse on 24 February 2018

60% of the total annual expenditure of the GRSS[130]. Ending the war is, therefore, a necessary, though not a sufficient condition for ensuring fiscal sustainability in the Republic of South Sudan. High spending on the security sector is necessitated by the conflict, but this is absolutely not fiscally sustainable, for it undermines efforts for the mobilization of resources and consequently our quest for sustained peace, economic growth, and poverty eradication. The potential sources of savings would become clearer in looking at the budgetary process.

The Budgetary Process

A budget is an estimation of government's revenues and spending in a given period of time, which is usually 12 months. It has four phases of preparation, which determine the integrity and credibility of the budget process. The financial/fiscal year (FY) for GRSS runs from July 1st to June 30th. For instance, the FY2019/2020 is from 1 July 2019 to 30 June 2020. Other countries, such as Sudan do base their FYs on a calendar year (i.e. from January 1 through December 31).

I consider budgeting of any kind and by any entity to be a process of wealth creation. In this sense, the public budget, which is about how resources of the country are mobilized and allocated by the government on behalf of the people to achieve desired public goods, is essentially a mirror of the social, political, and economic choices of the society. Moreover, the government (i.e. state) finances its budget through taxes collected on the various economic activities in an economy. That is, the people are themselves the taxpayers who hold, through their elected representatives, the government accountable in the efficient management of these taxes. Hence, the popular phrase of "*tax-payers money*" we often hear in the politics of "matured democracies!"

In our case, the GRSS finances its budget mainly through oil revenue and, therefore, does not pay much attention to what the people say, since it is not their "money" per se. That is, people's oversight is significantly diminished and/or nonexistence at all. I have over the years been worried

---

130 See Country Engagement Note (CEN) for the Republic of South Sudan, Report No. 120369-SS of The World Bank published on 7 November 2017

about the consequences of weak public oversight of the use of GRSS' oil revenues:

> South Sudan in her quest for wealth creation must guard against greed and selfishness on the one hand, and ignorance and arrogance on the other. This, however, assumes that there are efficient institutions of economic governance that would in turn ensure coherent public policy. That is, in an environment of weak institutions, predatory behaviors flourish[131].

The quoted passage, from some of my earlier analyses of previous budgets of GRSS, would contribute toward the search for the most effective methods for ensuring discipline in the execution of approved budgets. It would seem to me that the "invisible hands" of greed and selfishness driven partly by forces of ignorance and arrogance have created a huge hole in our treasury. Or what the Americans would say, this is "pouring our assets down the rat hole of unproductive government spending!"

I use the FY2019/2020 approved budget to illustrate the importance of discipline at every phase of the four phases of the budget cycle. I have already given in Chapter Seven of this book the four phases of the budget cycle (see Figure 7.1) and sources of risk of corruption (see Figure 7.2).

The search for effective methods of budgetary discipline would be augmented, in my view, by the scholarly work, which I have cited in the previous sections of the book, of Daniel Akec Thiong[132] on the "**politics of fear**," Majak D'Agoôt's[133] "**gun class**," and Alex

---

131 From "Challenges and Opportunities for Fiscal Space in the FY2017/2018 Budget of Government of South Sudan", a paper presented by Lual A. Deng to the DPF/TAF discourse on 24 February 2018

132 Thiong, Daniel Akech. 2018. "How The Politics Of Fear Generated Chaos In South Sudan." African Affairs, 1–23. Published by Oxford University Press on behalf of Royal African Society.

133 "Taming the Dominant Gun Class in South Sudan." Special Report No. 4: Envisioning A Stable South Sudan (May 29, 2018). See https://africacenter.org/spotlight/taming-the-dominant-gun-class-in-south-sudan/

de Waal's[134] **kleptocracy**. The Nuer concept of "*Hakuma mitoat*[135]," would also add value to our search for full explanatory variables of pervasive budgetary indiscipline in South Sudan.

The integrity of the budget is a function of the inherent fiscal discipline embedded in all its four phases. Most governments in the world derive their revenues from taxes, which they in turn spend to meet citizens' social, political, and economic choices. There are normally four types/sources of tax revenues: a) payroll taxes, which constitute about 36% of total resource envelope; b) individual income taxes, constituting half (50%) of total revenue; c) corporate income taxes (6%); and d) other taxes (e.g. excise taxes, estate & gift taxes, custom duties, remittances from central bank, miscellaneous fees and fines), which contributes about 8% of the total tax revenues of a country, such as the United States of America[136].

The share of oil revenues in the GRSS' resource envelope for FY2019/2020 approved budget is about 92.6%. It is, therefore, imperative that a robust system of transparency and accountability is put in place to manage the oil and gas sector of the South Sudanese economy. Efficient and effective management of the approved budget would on the one hand ensure timely implementation of the budget, and on the other building up savings through any windfall emanating from the oil revenue during the financial year. Let us now look at the four phases of the budget cycle.

Planning phase

This is the first and critical phase in which priority areas for spending are determined within the overall public policy objectives of the

---

134 de Waal, Alex. 2014. "When Kleptocracy Becomes Insolvent: Brute Causes of The Civil War In South Sudan." African Affairs, 113/452, 347–369. Published by Oxford University Press on behalf of Royal African Society

135 A government managed by a small group of smart individuals who understand each other very well and who have decided to use public resources for their own individual and collective welfare without regard to the rest of the society

136 I derived these percentages from 2018 Federal Budget of the United States of America, just for illustration purposes and not in anyway advocating for the adoption of the American budgeting system

government of the day. The Ministry of Finance and Planning (MoFP) would under ideal situation send out, at the beginning of the third quarter of the Fiscal Year (i.e. January in the case of GRSS), a circular to all the public sector spending units. The circular advises the spending units to begin preparation of the new budget within given parameters. The R-ARCSS and COVID-19 pandemic are good examples of some of the binding parameters that should be reflected in the preparation of the FY2020/2021 budget. The circular should have gone out as soon as the new cabinet of the RTGoNU was formed.

It would be recall that the overarching objectives of the FY2019/2020 budget were to **consolidate peace** and **stabilize the economy**. I would assume that they are the same for the FY2020/2021 budget. Budget planners are, therefore, expected to have had identified spending priorities with respect to consolidating peace on the one hand, and stabilizing the economy on the other. Spending priorities toward achieving these two objectives would be interlinked and reinforcing each other given their nature of being pre-conditions for sustainable peace, economic growth, and poverty eradication.

The Revitalized Agreement on the Resolution of Conflict in the Republic of South Sudan (R-ARCSS) is an important framework for identifying spending priorities, which would in turn constitute, in my view, what is called "mandatory spending." There is no, to the best of my knowledge, classification of the budget outlays of GRSS into **mandatory and discretionary spending**. There is now an opportunity, in my view, to introduce such a system in the light of R-ARCSS. The Collegial Presidency, and not the Council of Ministers, should determine the spending priorities for the FY2020/2021 budget. The role of the Council of Ministers is to translate into implementable programs, the policy directives and priorities of the Collegial Presidency.

The TNL could introduce a budget control bill that would enhance the role of the legislature in the budget process. The bill could initiate two key innovations with respect to budgeting in South Sudan, though such practices are the norms in many countries. The first is the preparation of the budget to begin on July 1, which is the very day the new fiscal year begins. The second is the new presentation of the outlays (i.e. total expenditure) by mandatory and discretionary spending. Moreover, this new presentation could either be by spending blocks as was practiced during the time of Hon. Aggrey Tisa Sabuni when he was Minister of Finance (2013 – 2015) or into the following:

- A Capital budget (i.e. PIP);
- A Core Staff budget for the essential functions of each government agency; and
- Annual operating budget for programs.

I have discussed the capital budget in the earlier part of fiscal policy. On the core staff, the thought would be to remove core staff from any discretionary activity and lock it in, as part of mandatory spending (i.e. entitlement arrangement)[137]. That is, like Social Security program in those countries, which have such a system. In this way, the core staff of the government is protected. They can still be dismissed, but their salaries are not in doubt and should be paid on time. With this endowment effect in place, it would be essential to index their salaries through a system of cost of living allowance (COLA). Then, in the operational (program) budget, GRSS could have staffing levels for those individuals necessary to carry out specific programs and initiatives.

The main purpose here is to figure out how to protect employees in the core "civil service," so that they make a commitment to the government in return for an obligation to them. What is needed is their devotion and commitment to the service of the people of South Sudan. It is hard to get that when they go for months without pay.

I would use this agreement (i.e. R-ARCSS) to identify what I think to be mandatory spending in the context of consolidating peace, which is a precondition for macroeconomic stability and delivery of basic services by the South Sudanese State. I present in Table 9.3 below the priority areas for mandatory spending, which could have guided the preparation (i.e. phase 2) of the FY2019/2020 budget. There is, nevertheless, an opportunity to use it in the preparation of the FY2020/2021 budget of the RTGoNU.

---

137 I am grateful to Professor Daniel W. Bromley of the University of Wisconsin-Madison for this paragraph in which he encouraged me to be forthright with some of my ideas on how to improve the budgeting process in South Sudan

Table 9.3: Suggested Priority Areas for Mandatory Spending in R-ARCSS

Chapter of R-ARCSS	Priority Area for Mandatory Spending
1. R–TgoNU	a) Expanded presidency b) Expanded Cabinet c) Expanded Transitional National Legislative Assembly (TNLA)
2. Permanent Ceasefire & Transitional Security Arrangement	a) Establishment of Cantonment/Assembly areas b) Reunification of forces c) DDR
3. Humanitarian Assistance & Reconstruction	a) Repatriation, Resettlement, Rehabilitation, Relief, & Re-integration (5Rs) of refugees, IDPs, & POCs b) Special Reconstruction Fund (SRF)
4. Resource, Economic and Financial Management Arrangements	a) Institutional Reform b) Fiscal and Financial Allocation Monitoring Commission (FFAMC) c) Economic and Financial Management Authority (EFMA)
5. Transitional Justice, Accountability, Reconciliation & Healing	a) Commission for Truth, Reconciliation and Healing (CTRH) b) Hybrid Court for South Sudan (HCSS)
6. Parameters for Permanent Constitution	**Discretionary spending**
7. JMEC	Funded by donors
8. Procedures for the amendment of R-ARCSS	**Discretionary spending (if any)**

The second overarching objective is to stabilize the economy. There are two critical spending priorities, toward this second objective, in the FY2019/2020 approved budget. These were provision of basic services (e.g. education, health, water, rule of law) and infrastructure. Provision of basic services, which are part of secondary drivers of economic growth, is premised on efficient and effective institutions (one of the fundamental causes of economic growth) that are managed by highly motivated and relatively well-remunerated employees (i.e. human capital, which is one of the proximate causes of economic growth). Wages and salaries of the public sector will have to be reviewed with the aim of improving the conditions of employees in this critical area of spending.

As for infrastructure (i.e. physical capital, which is one of the proximate causes of economic growth), the President has already identified roads and bridges as a top spending priority area in the FY2019/2020 budget. This is known as the capital budget or capital expenditure in the annual budget of a government. The budget planners must implement the directives of the President with respect to the infrastructure development within the framework of a medium-term strategy, which is the National Development Strategy (NDS, July 2018 – June 2021).

I would like to point out at this juncture that spending on infra-structure, which is an integral part of capital budget, is normally spread over a medium-term period of say, three years. Hence, the most appro-priate tool that the budget planners could use is Public Investment Program (PIP). This is especially relevant in the context of South Sudan National Development Strategy (July 2018 – June 2021). That is, the PIP is a critical instrument for determining spending priorities in the context of capital budget in which a certain rate of economic growth of the economy is targeted. A good example is the Juba-Rumbek 400-kilometer highway being constructed by a Chinese company and for which **USD 602.3 million** is being squeezed out of a single financial year.

This should not be the case, given other competing priorities brought about by R-ARCSS. Moreover, the Chinese construction company cannot complete the Juba-Rumbek highway by the end of the FY2019/2020. Evidence-based planning is imperative here. But, this is where resources have been squandered, since 2005, in the name of investment in public goods. This is where I fully agree with the framers of R-ARCSS in creating the infrastructure cluster to be headed by one of the five Vice Presidents in the newly established Collegial Presidency. The infrastructure cluster must ensure that there is a very high degree of discipline in the management of the approved budget for power generation (especially investment in hydro-power), railways, river transport, roads and bridges.

The conventional way of planning for capital budgeting is to look at the level of investment in the economy against desired rate of economic growth. This relationship is captured by capital–output ratio, which is the amount of capital required to produce a unit of output.

The most important factor here is the productivity of this capital. Hence, the starting point at the planning phase of the budget cycle is a simple equation: **I=S, which says saving and investment are equal in ex-ante as well as ex-post sense**. This simple equation should be qualified in the context of South Sudan where oil constitutes about two-thirds of the gross national product (GDP), 98% of exports, and 92.6% of total government revenues in the FY2019/2020. It is, therefore, assumed in this book that private investment is insignificant for now and what matters is government capital expenditure (i.e. investment). This assumption would be relaxed as the economy is stabilized and the quality of data is improved.

The next step is to decide on the rate of economic growth, which I denote as G. This is determined by another simple equation: **G=S/V**, where **S** is the propensity to save expressed as saving-output (i.e. income) ratio or total savings in the economy as a percentage of gross domestic product (GDP). And **V** is capita-output ration, which measures the productivity of investment. For developed economies a small amount of capital is required to produce one unit of output (i.e. GDP), while for developing economies where productivity of investment is low a large amount of capital is normally required. The capital-output ratio for developed economies is now empirically established to be three (3), which would normally guide budget planners in a developing economy setting.

I did, for the purposes of capital budget in the FY2019/2020, derive a capital-output ratio for South Sudan from the World Bank's Country Engagement Note on South Sudan issued in November 2017 (Annex 2 page 29). The World Bank projected then a growth rate of South Sudan's economy to be 1.2% in FY2018/19. Moreover, the average Gross Fixed Capital Formation (GFCF)[138] for South Sudan during the period 2008 – 2015 is given as 11.3% of GDP. The National Development Strategy (NDS) document (graph 1 page 37) gives an average of 10% during the period 2012 – 2015. I would use GFCF to represent saving-output ration (S) to get the capital-output ratio (V)

---

138 Gross fixed capital formation (GFCF) is a macroeconomic concept used in official national accounts. GFCF is a component of the expenditure on gross domestic product (GDP), and thus shows something about how much of the new value added in the economy is invested instead of being consumed. It is assumed in this book and for lack of accurate data that GFCF is equivalent to saving-output ratio (S) in our economy.

for South Sudan. It should be stated once more that the quality of data being used here is of low quality, but they provide important trends in our analysis of the planning process.

The calculation is: $G=S/V$ or $1.2=11.3/V$! Stated differently: $1.2V=11.3$, leading to $V=11.3/1.2$. The capital-output ratio for South Sudan is 9.4. Suppose the Ministry of Finance and Planning is targeting in the FY2020/2021 budget an economic growth rate (G) of 10%. This would require investment rate (or GFCF) of: $10=S/9.4=S=94\%$! This is not realistic for investment rate to be at such a high level, but it conveys a powerful message to policymakers in South Sudan that they will have to allocate more resources toward both physical and human capitals formation in order for the country to embark on the path to sustainable peace, economic growth, and poverty eradication.

The good news is that the Ministry of Finance and Planning was targeting an economic growth rate of 3.5% for the FY2019/2020. Maintaining this rate for the FY2020/2021, then we get the GFCF or investment rate of 33% derived as follows: $3.5=S/9.4$ or $S=3.5 \times 9.4=32.9\%$. A comparative look at the GFCF for Ethiopia during the period 2012 – 2015, shows an investment rate of 38% corresponding to a growth rate of 10.3% and a capital-output ratio of 3.7 or approximately 4.0.

Once spending priorities and plans for achieving them have been identified, the next step in the planning phase is to determine sources of funding. This is the stage at which the benchmark price and average daily production of crude oil are specified; tax rates are determined and could be raised and/or new taxes levied if the planners expect a resource gap. The final point at this planning phase is to provide indicative size of the resource envelope within which the identified spending priorities and associated plans will be funded.

Budgeting phase

Some analysts call this phase as the budget preparation phase. For the purposes of this book, budget preparation consists of two phases – planning and budgeting. The Ministry of Finance and Planning receives, at this phase, submissions from all the spending units/agencies, their estimated costs of their activities (i.e. total expenditure) for the fiscal year under consideration. My preference would be to allocate, at the planning phase, an indicative amount to each spending unit/agency within which it makes its proposal. This is because budgeting is the phase where the actual costing of public sector activities (capital and operating expenditures) is performed by each and every spending unit.

The budgeting phase is ideally a stage in which negotiations on respective allocations take place between the national planning authority (MoFP in the case of South Sudan) and those responsible for the budget and planning units in all the spending agencies of the government. In some countries, agencies are given indicative figure (i.e. money to spend) within which to determine their own spending priorities. This figure is normally based on historical patterns of spending by the agencies. The planning arm of MoFP coordinates budgeting process through various stages. Technical staff of the agencies drives the preparatory stage, while the negotiation point involves senior public sector personnel at the level of undersecretaries and agency heads.

I would like to illustrate here, for the sake of clarity for our policy-makers, using the federal government budget process of the United States of America. The MoFP is, with respect to budget preparation, analogous to the Office of Management and Budget (OMB) as shown in Box 9.2 below. I am not suggesting in any way that the MoFP should necessarily follow the budget process of the United States of America. The example is being given as by way of explaining the process of budgeting to the general public as well as policy community in the Republic of South Sudan. I would also think that the planning function, during the Transitional Period, be performed by the collegial presidency (or in my preferred option TCoS). The office of the VP in-charge of Economic Cluster could be tasked with the function of the process of budget preparation.

South Sudan has the opportunity to learn and adopt relevant best international practices in the area of public budgeting process. For instance, it is time to establish Assembly Budget Office (ABO) as a non-partisan body that would ensure transparency and integrity of the budget process through credible forecasts of proposals made during the preparation of the budget. The current practice gives the Executive unmatched power over the Legislature with respect to the budgeting process.

Box 9.2: The US Budget Process

The budget process lasts 18 months. Here's the schedule for the FY 2020 budget, the third one to be submitted by President Trump.

2018
- Early fall: Federal agencies submit budget requests to OMB.
- November: OMB sends its comments back to the agencies.
- December: Agencies submit the final budget request to OMB.

2019
- January: OMB submits the budget to president.
- February: President submits the budget to Congress. Trump did so in March.
- April 15: Congress prepares its Budget Resolution.
- June 10: Congress creates Appropriation Bills.
- June 30: House approves all bills and submits them to the President.
- September 30: All bills must be signed into law.

Source: https://www.thebalance.com/what-is-the-federal-budget-3306305

The initial drafts of the budget are subjected to the clusters of the Cabinet to deliberate upon. The Minister of Finance and Planning would then present what I call a "pooled draft" to the Council of Ministers, which should really be around April or May of every year. Once the Cabinet approves the draft, the Minister of Finance would then table it before the Transitional National Legislature (TNL) in what is known as the First Reading. The TNL should receive the draft budget in May in order for it to be approved by June 30th! The GRSS has, since independence, never presented the budget to the TNL before June 30th. For instance, the FY2019/2020 draft budget was presented to the TNL on Monday 8 July 2019. And the FY2020/2021 budget has not yet been presented to the Council of Ministers (we are in August)!

The government would have shut down if this were in other countries where it would be unconstitutional for a government to operate without approved budget or without "continuing resolution" by the TNL. But, this is South Sudan.

The key characteristic of the FY2019/2020 budget is the huge resource gap of **SSP77 billion (or USD497 million at the exchange rate of SSP155/USD1.0 as stipulated in the budget speech of the Minister of Finance and Planning).** The gap constitutes 37% of the approved FY2019/2020 budget. It is not normal, to the best of my knowledge, for an executive branch of government to present to the legislature a budget with such a huge resource gap without reasonable explanation on how to finance it. I would, therefore, venture into unpacking the abnormal nature of the decision of the executive or Council of Ministers in presenting the FY2019/2020 proposed budget to the TNL as it is!

The FY2019/2020 budget indicates total outlays of **SSP208.2** billion and a resource envelope (i.e. total revenues) of **SSP131.2 billion**. The difference between the total outlays and total revenues is what is being referred to here as the **resource gap**. I would show how the Transitional National Legislature (TNL) could have scrutinized the draft budget with the view to closing or eliminating all together the gap. The TNL has undisputed function of ensuring discipline in all phases of the budget cycle of which accurate calculation/determination of the resource gap and associated measures of closing it, are critical.

There are usually two broad ways of closing the resource gap. The first method is to reduce planned spending with the view to realigning expenditures with revenues, so that there is a balanced budget. The other approach would be either to raise revenues through borrowing from domestic and external sources or/and to increase taxes. Borrowing from domestic sources would mainly be from the Bank of South Sudan (BoSS) through what is known as deficit financing (i.e. printing more pounds), since South Sudan does not have a financial market from which GRSS can borrowing using government securities. We have seen in the previous sections the consequences of deficit financing, which has been inflationary and detrimental to macroeconomic stability as well as the living standards of the population.

I had provided alternative approach to closing the resource gap in the FY2019/2020 draft budget. First, I made use of the information that was given to the Economy, Development, and Finance Committee of the TNL. And secondly, I revisited the underlined key assumptions of the cost of Juba-Rumbek highway being constructed by a Chinese company.

The Minister of Petroleum together with the First Deputy Governor of Bank of South Sudan and their teams had aided this effort through credible information they provided to the Economy, Development, and Finance Committee of the TNL[139]. I did focus on GRSS' oil revenues, which constituted 92.6% of total revenues (i.e. resource envelope) in the FY2019/2020 budget. The share of GRSS in total oil production is derived from two types of crude oil – the Dar blend (from blocks 3 and 7) and Nile blend (from blocks 1, 2, and 4). The share of GRSS from the Dar blend was given as 44% and from the Nile blend was 39.5%. The share of **the Nilepet Corporation**, which is **8%**, was not part of the GRSS[140].

The total oil production was given in the budget to be 170,000 barrels per day (bpd). This figure was corrected by the Minister of Petroleum to be 173,000 bpd[141] **(130,000 from blocks 3 and 7; while 43,000 from blocks 1, 2, and 4)**. The share of GRSS from oil production in blocks 3 and 7 (i.e. the Dar blend) is, therefore, **57,200 bpd** (i.e. 0.44 x 130,000=57,200), which gives a projected total of **20,878,000 barrels (or bbl.)** in FY2019/2020. The share of GRSS from blocks 1, 2, and 4 (Nile blend) is 16,985 bpd (i.e. 0.395 x 43,000=16,985), which is **6,199,525 bbl.** in FY2019/2020. The combined total share of GRSS from the Dar and Nile blends is **27,077,525 bbl.,** which is higher than what has been given in the draft budget by **1,016,525 bbl.** It should now be obvious why transparency with respect to how cost-oil and profits-oil are calculated is imperative to have a correct size of the resource envelope.

---

139 This was on 15 August 2019

140 The Minister of Petroleum and his team have confirmed on 15 August 2019 before the Economy, Finance, and Development Committee of the TNL the authenticity of these percentages and arrangements, including the fact that NilePet gets its share from the operating companies and not from the government (GRSS) share

141 The Minister of Petroleum gave a figure of daily production ranging between 43,000 and 47,000 bpd, but I have decided to be conservative on these figures

The above facts are made use of, in our attempt to reduce the resource-gap. A careful examination of the following three items would enable us to show how the TNL could have pushed MoFP to revisit calculation of some elements of the resource envelope:

a) Savings from the amount that have been given to Nilepet in the draft budget;
b) Price differential, since the Nile blend is priced at the same price of London Brent, which is higher than the budget benchmark price of USD55/bbl. for Dar blend; and
c) Exchange rate differential of SSP85/bbl.

On the underlined key assumptions of the FY2019/2020 budget, I would turn to the amount allocated to Juba-Rumbek highway. The resource gap is heavily influenced by the assumption that **SSP93.4 billion will be spent on roads in the FY2019/2020**. This is, however, not true as I would show below.

I have challenged this assumption by using information obtained from the relevant agencies within the GRSS and in the private sector. Let us re-examine the budgeted spending on infrastructure. A careful look at the components of the budgeted capital expenditure would, however, reveal that there are serious issues with this allocation. One of these is that a Chinese construction company has been awarded a contract to build a **400-kilometer (km) long Juba-Rumbek highway** with the proceeds from the sales of **10,950,000 bbl. (or USD602.3 million)**. In fact, the Chinese construction company will not be able to complete the building of 400 km highway in the FY2019/2020.

Let us assume that the company would be able to construct 100 km during the FY2019/2020 at a cost of **USD1.8 mn/km** or a total cost of **USD180.0 million.** This means that the amount of **USD602.3 million** (i.e. SSP93.4 bn) appearing as spending for road in the total outlays of SSP208.3 billion should be, according to my calculations, **USD180.0 million (or SSP29.0 bn)**. Stated differently, the budgeted total outlays of SSP208.2 billion would now be, by my calculations, **SSP143.8 billion**. The transparency, demonstrated by senior officials from the Ministry of Petroleum and BoSS, in providing accurate information has also facilitated the recalculation of the share of GRSS's oil revenues. The recalculation has yielded projected total oil revenue to increase from SSP100.9 billion given in the FY2019/2020 budget to **SSP144.3 billion, which leads to a total GRSS' revenues of SSP174.2 billion** (i.e. 144.3 bn from oil revenues + 29.9 bn non-oil revenues).

Hence, the difference between total outlays and total revenues would, according to my calculations, yield a surplus of **SSP30.4 (i.e. 174.2 – 143.8) billion (or USD188.8 million at the exchange rate of SSP161/USD1.0)**. The TNL could have had allocated this amount of **SSP30.4 billion** to priority spending areas (e.g. public universities and other core institutions) that were left out in the budget. This surplus, in terms of crude oil, is equivalent to 10,000 bpd or 3,650,000 bbl. in the FY2019/2020.

I had the opportunity to express my opinion in writing to the joint Economic and Finance Committee of the TNL about the above figures in general, and on how to reallocate the amount budgeted for infrastructure development (i.e. roads) in particular. I had stated, "The point of departure for the TNL is a careful analysis of the infrastructure development fund, which has been allocated 30,000 bpd or 10,950,000 bbl. per year (i.e. USD602.3 million) in the draft budget. The GRSS should be commended for taking such a visionary step toward the development of South Sudan by creating such a facility[142]." I then made the following two recommendations: a) establishment of interest-earning escrow account, under the management of BoSS at a reputable international financial institution; and b) use part of this fund for the salaries of the public sector employees in the core institutions of the national government. My colleagues did not pay attention to these recommendations.

I would now like to revisit the above two recommendations, in addition to a third recommendation to allocate the balance of USD 422.3 million to the Special Reconstruction Fund (SRF) stipulated in the R-ARCSS (Article 3.2). This is in the light of the realistic figure of USD180 million for Juba-Rumbek highway in the FY2019/2020 budget.

---

142 "Reducing the Resource Gap in the FY2019/2020 Proposed Budget Through Transparency and Accountability in the Management of Oil Revenues." A presentation by Lual A. Deng to the DPF/TAF Discourse, Juba Grand Hotel, Juba, South Sudan, 10 August 2019

THE NATIONAL DIALOGUE

Budget execution phase

This is the third phase of the budget cycle in which rules and procedures for the implementation of the approved budget are paramount.
Law in the form of appropriation act governs the implementation of
the approved budget. That is, the appropriation bill is approved by the
legislature (i.e. TNL in our case) together with the budget, which is
then signed into law (Act) by the President. In this regard, any alter-
ation of approved budget items is a violation of law.

For instance, spending units that spend more than what have
been allocated to them in the approved budget; do in fact violate the
appropriation act. This violation of the appropriation act is known
as indiscipline in the jargon of public financial management (PFM).
There is, in fact, pervasive indiscipline with respect to budget execution
in South Sudan. This challenge is at the core of the public financial
management in the Republic of South Sudan.

I would like to illustrate this point by quoting one of the courageous Ministers of Finance of South Sudan, who gave an insider view
of some of the difficulties facing the execution of the budget:

> Rt. Hon. Speaker, indiscipline is still a feature of our budget management.
> We have weak procurement practices, expenditures are poorly priori-
> tized, and some agencies are able to disregard their budget while others
> receive nothing. The costs of indiscipline are immediate and real. When
> scarce resources are diverted to unplanned operating expenditures, we
> cannot pay salary and wages to about half a million employees on the
> government payroll.[143]

The Minister was presenting the FY2017/2018 draft budget in August
2017. He was subsequently proven right. For instance, salaries for
November 2017 of the members of the TNLA were paid in mid-Feb-
ruary 2018. And this was at the time when GRSS had received about
$150 million as windfall from half-year oil revenues that were not
anticipated at the time of the approval of FY2017/2018 budget!

---

143 From the FY2017/2018 Budget Speech to the Transitional National Legislature by Hon. Stephen Dhieu Dau, Minister of Finance and Planning, TGoNU

If the salaries of members of the National Legislature were three months behind (i.e. in arrears) what would be the situation for other spending units, including the states, counties, and Payams? But, what evidence do we need more than what the former Minister of Finance has provided in the above passage? The culture of fiscal indiscipline continues unabated.

Monitoring, reporting, and audit phase

This is the fourth and final phase of the budget cycle. The performance of the budget execution is assessed through quarterly reporting and annual audit reports. MoFP is required by law to send to the TNL quarterly reports on the implementation of the budget. The planning phase of the budget cycle would normally draw lessons of experience in the execution of the budget from reports generated here during the past fiscal years. But, it would seem to me that in the case of South Sudan, it is business as usual since the reports of the Auditor General (AG) of the Republic are not taken into account in the preparation of the annual budgets. Moreover, the policymakers would seem not to be interested in any system that restrain their own behavior, a point to which I turn for articulation to the same former Minister of Finance that I have quoted previously:

> Rt. Hon. Speaker, this fiscal year, I introduced measures to limit non-priority operating expenditures and improve our cash management. I established a Cash Management Committee, I cancelled outstanding cheques, I closed Government bank accounts held in commercial banks, and I placed limits on medical and travel claims. In doing so, I encountered considerable resistance from a number of quarters. Although everyone complains about the current economic situation, few people want to accept economic stabilization reforms that will limit their own individual opportunity to access State resources[144].

---

144 From the FY2017/2018 Budget Speech to the Transitional National Legislature by Hon. Stephen Dhieu Dau, minister of Finance and Planning, TGoNU

Minister Dau was dismissed from the Cabinet before he could complete the implementation of the FY2017/2018 at which he made the above cited passage. I am certain that people with legal training would deduce from this statement: *"In doing so, I encountered considerable resistance from a number of quarters,"* the people who have been instrumental in the dismissal of the minister. Resistance from a number of quarters has become another "unknown gunmen" in our Daniel Akec Thiong's **"politics of fear."** The quarters referred to by the Minister are the drivers of the **"politics of fear"** or the self-interested elites of Majak D'Agoôt's **"gun-class."**

Monetary Policy

Price stability is one of the key objectives of monetary policy in any economy. We have the Bank of South Sudan (BoSS), but I doubt if we have a coherent monetary policy in the pursuit of this cardinal objective, which is central to our macroeconomic stability. In fact, South Sudan has been, since January 2012, experiencing macroeconomic instability, evidenced by high inflation rates and volatility of the exchange rates. Yet, appropriate policy responses from our monetary authorities have not been in the horizon. Interest rate is, for instance, one of the instruments used to ensure price stability in general, and in turbulent times in particular. I am not aware if BoSS has ever used this important policy instrument.

But more importantly, the interest rate is used by the financial sector as a fundamental tool for building up domestic savings, which are in turn used as investible funds. Ray Dalio would seem to state the same point differently:

> Changes in the amount of buying (total $) typically have a much bigger impact on changes in economic activity and prices than do changes in the total amount of selling (total Q). That is because there is nothing that's easier to change than the supply of money and credit (total $)[145].

The recent response of a number of central banks to the global economic

---

145 Ray Dalio (2012) How the Economic Machine Works – Leveragings and Deleveragings

blowback of COVID-19 is, in my view, a powerful confirmation of the complementarity of the monetary policy to that of fiscal policy. When these two arms of macroeconomic policy are well coordinated in the event of crisis, the impact of economic management policy on changes in economic activity and prices would normally be positive.

Price stability, in the case of South Sudan, is essentially a function of the exchange rate regime. This is because South Sudan, as I have argued elsewhere, has been witnessing the "dollarization phenomenon." That is, empirical literature on dollarization suggests that *"in countries with high inflation, foreign currencies are first used as a store of value, then as a unit of account and finally as a medium of exchange.*[146]" This process is critically important if appropriate policy responses are to be pursued in the case of South Sudanese economy.

Let us look at the signs of a dollarized economy at two levels: a) international level where we could draw some lessons of experience from the rest of the world; and b) South Sudan level[147].

Socorro Heysen of the IMF had undertaken a comprehensive survey of countries in the world with a sign of dollarization[148]. The share of foreign currency deposits to total bank deposits during the period 1996 – 2001 is given in Table 9.4 below for 99 countries from 8 regions of the world

Table 9.4: Percent Share of Foreign Currency Deposits to Total Bank Deposits

Region	Number of Countries	1996	1997	1998	1999	2000	2001
South America	9	45.8	41.6	44.6	48.1	49.2	50.9

---

146 For more on this, see for instance - Adam Bennett (1999): Monetary Policy in Dollarized Economies; Impact of Dollarization; Kurt Schuler (2000): Some Theory and History of Dollarization; Bonga and Dhoro (2015): Currency Substitution, Dollarisation and Possibility of De-dollarisation in Zimbabwe; Myriam Quispe-Agnoli (2002): Costs and Benefits of Dollarization

147 This section is based on my paper: Protecting Purchasing Power From Skyrocketing Prices In South Sudan Through Partial Dollarization, by Lual A. Deng (2016)

148 See Dollarization: Back to Basics, published in Finance & Development, March 2005, IMF/World Bank

Transition Economies	26	37.3	38.9	43.5	44.3	46.9	47.7
Middle East	7	36.5	37.2	37.7	37.5	38.2	41.9
Africa	14	27.9	27.3	27.8	28.9	32.7	33.2
Asia	13	24.9	28.0	26.8	28.8	28.7	28.2
Central America	6	23.2	23.4	24.7	24.8	25.2	27.3
Caribbean	10	6.3	7.6	6.8	6.7	6.1	6.2
Developed Economies	14	7.4	7.5	7.5	6.7	7.0	6.6

Source: From Socorro Heysen (2005) - International Financial Statistics, the IMF's Economic Data Sharing System, and statistical publications by various central banks.

Two categories of countries – Caribbean and developed economies - from Table 9.4 above, have less than 10% share of foreign currency deposits in total bank deposits and would not therefore be of interest to our analysis at this point in time. Highly dollarized countries constitute 75% of all the countries of the dollarization regime. All the fourteen (14) African countries had moved from a moderate dollarization in 1996 to a highly dollarized status by 2001. I had already discussed the case of Zimbabwe, as an African story of a country that had at one point officially adopted USD as a legal tender.

The case of Latin American countries should be of great interest, for this is where dollarization was popularized in the 1990s when they (countries) were experiencing high inflation rates. The quest for dollarization in Latin America is articulated by Georgios Karras[149]:

> Despite cautious comments by the previous U.S. Treasury Secretary (Summers, 1999), enthusiasm for "dollarization," the replacement of national currencies in the Americas by the U.S. dollar, is spreading fast and for a growing number of countries. In fact, dollarization has been endorsed by both academic economists (Barro, 1999) and the business community (Wall Street Journal, 1999a, 1999b; Financial Times, 1999).

Moreover, Myriam Quispe-Agnoli) in a survey of the extent of dollarization of seventeen (17) Latin American countries found the following:

---

149 See Costs and Benefits of Dollarization: Evidence from North, Central, and South America, Journal of Economic Integration 17(3), September 2002; 502-516

1. *Three countries were fully dollarized – Panama (1904), Ecuador (2000), and El Salvador (2001) have adopted United States dollar (USD) as a legal tender;*
2. *Seven countries were highly dollarized (i.e. partial dollarization);*
3. *One, which is Honduras moderately dollarized (28%); and*
4. *Six with share of foreign currency deposits in the money supply below 10%.*

Signs of a dollarized South Sudan economy

The first sign is explained, in my view, by the following four general characteristics: a) regulatory environment (e.g. allowing foreign banks to operate in the country and South Sudanese to have foreign currency accounts); b) share of oil in the gross domestic product (i.e. about 66% of GDP); c) share of oil in total export (about 99%); and d) share of oil in the annual total government revenues (i.e. 98%). I have already discussed these characteristics in the preceding sections and which have confirmed that the economy of South Sudan is highly dollarized. What follows then is a brief highlight of each of these characteristics.

The regulatory environment provided a free entry of foreign banks to the economy of South Sudan, which are allowed to conduct transactions in the SSP and foreign currencies, especially the United States of America dollar. It would seem to me then that our economic policymakers misunderstood the meaning of a market economy (free market economy), for even in the United States of America (considered as the mother of capitalism) inter-state banking system is regulated.

The second sign of dollarization phenomenon is the high ratio of foreign currency deposits in the total bank deposits (i.e. combined local currency and foreign currencies, which are mostly dominated by USD). Table 9.5 below gives this ratio for 26 out of 29 commercial banks operating in South Sudan. The other indicator of the extent of dollarization is the share of foreign currency deposits in the money supply (or total liquidity, which includes foreign currency deposits).

Table 9.5: Share of USD in Total Bank Deposits in The Banking Sector in South Sudan

Name of Financial Institution	SSP (000)	USD (000)	Total Deposit (SSP & USD (000)	Deposits % USD in total Bank deposits
1. AfriLand First Bank	104,201.7	36,604.7	140,806.4	26.0
2. Alpha Bank	86,366.1	582.904.3	669,270.4	87.1
3. Buffalo Commercial Bank	187,008.8	34,029.3	221,038.6	15.4
4. CfC Stanbic Bank	443,533.0	2,147,181.9	2,590,714.9	82.9
5. Charter One Bank	258,074.0	186,980.0	3,987,094.8	46.0
6. Co-operative Bank	377,965.4	1785.7	5,119.5	35.0
7. Ebony National Bank	56,476.3	5,174	61,650.4	8.4
8. Eco Bank	181,823.2	1,343,412.4	1,525,235.6	88.1
9. Eden Commercial Bank	239,206.2	164,467.3	403,673.5	40.7
10. Ethiopian Commercial Bank	193,589.2	207,438.5	401,027.7	69.8
11. Equity Bank	1,541,507.6	3,566,459.8	5,107,967.4	69.8
12. International Commercial Bank	49,639.4	22,690.9	72,330.3	31.4
13. Ivory Bank	1,630,242.0	249,657.2	1,879,899.2	13.3
14. Kenya Commercial Bank	3,299,031.0	7,846,736.0	11,145,767.4	70.4
15. Kush Bank	169,894.4	86,273.4	256,167.8	34.0
16. Liberty Commercial Bank	168,006.0	3,621.8	171,627.8	2.1
17. Mountain Trade and development Bank	36,175.0	20,649.2	56,824.2	36.3
18. National Credit Bank	37,469.4	12,471.4	49,940.7	25.0
19. Nile Commercial Bank	122,642.4	18,994.2	141,636.6	13.4
20. Opportunity Bank	15,384.2	1,987.2	17,371.5	11.4
21. Orbit Bank	3,592.1	11.2	3,603.2	0.3
22. Phoenix Commercial Bank	139,119.5	4,880.1	143,999.6	3.4
23. Qatar National Bank (QNB)	2,154,674.0	1,832,420.8	3,987,094.8	46.0
24. Regent Bank	33,33.8	1,785.7	5,119.5	35.0
25. Royal Express Bank	7,885.6	7.0	7,892.6	0.09
26. South Sudan Commercial Bank	83,757.0	67,434.0	151,191.0	44.6
Total	11,590,597.3	18,721,379.9	30,311,977.2	61.8

Source: Constructed by the author from data obtained from the banking sector

It is obvious from Table 9.5 above that 12 commercial banks are highly dollarized. Their share of foreign currency deposits in total bank deposits ranges between 31.4% and 88.1%. Table 9.5 shows that the foreign currency deposits in the money supply is about 61.8% (or 62%), which confirms that South Sudan economy falls within the category of economies that are highly dollarized. Such a picture has serious implications to the design, application, and management of monetary policy. This is because SSP, on which monetary policy in South Sudan is based, constitutes only 38% of the total bank deposits.

It is, however, possible that policymakers in general, and monetary authorities in particular might not have been aware of this phenomenon. This is evidenced by the liberal way USD was allocated, during the first six months of independence, to commercial banks and forex bureaus. For instance, the Bank of South Sudan used, during that period, to sell weekly about USD75 million to commercial banks (e.g. a commercial bank was allocated up to USD5.0 million) and forex bureaus – a forex was able to buy up to USD2.5 million). There was clearly no strategy to build foreign reserves for rainy days ahead. The result is the widening gap; we are witnessing today, in the USD/SSP exchange rate between the official market (SSP165/$1.0) and parallel market (SSP330/$1.0)!

The third and final sign, which shows that South Sudan economy is experiencing the phenomenon of dollarization, is the behavior of economic agents. It is now established fact that this behavior of economic agents in South Sudan is consistent with theory and empirical literature on dollarization. People think in terms of "foreign currency, which is dollar" and **prices in domestic currency are indexed to the exchange rate**." They (i.e. economic agents) now think in terms of USD as by way of protecting their money income and assets.

I took in 2016 a quick survey of four categories of businesses **(hotels, travel agencies, restaurants, and retailers)** in Juba, and found that they all index their prices to the daily SSP/USD exchange rate prevailing in the parallel market for foreign exchange. In this regard, the erratic behavior of inflation in South Sudan is essentially driven by the exchange rate volatility. Hence, South Sudan has an opportunity to avoid the Zimbabwean track if it could embark now on a process of partial dollarization as by way of restoring, on the one hand the purchasing power of money income, and on the other economic stability and growth to the economy.

There is, however, a very strong resistance on such a policy approach from policymakers and from some powerful elites who are benefiting from the status quo. Even the technically simple issue of the realignment of the parallel market and official exchange rates was opposed in 2013. It should be pointed out here that the real exchange rate is that determined by the parallel market (popularly known as black market), while the nominal exchange rate is the one determined by BoSS.

The authorities eventually adopted in December 2015, the realignment policy. It was, however, applied inappropriately and against the advice of a number of seasoned South Sudanese economists. The failure of December 2015 realignment venture is being cited widely as being the reason for opposing any innovation with respect to exchange rate regime. This point might be comprehendible if we look at the following passage from Socorro Heysen:

> Institutional factors play an important role in determining why some countries with a history of macroeconomic instability are dollarized and others are not. Some countries may seek to contain the decline in savings that can result from inflation by authorizing the use of a foreign currency; others may try to resist dollarization by promoting financial indexation schemes or resorting to capital controls. That said, the lack of deep financial markets to support a liquid market for indexed instruments and the simplicity, transparency, and credibility of dollar instruments may tilt the balance in favor of partial dollarization in some countries.[150]

Debt policy

There are two important sources from which governments borrow to finance budgetary shortfalls. The first is external borrowing, which is usually from three sources: a) multilateral creditors, such as the World Bank, International Monetary Fund (IMF), African Development Bank, etc.; b) bilateral creditors, such as Qatar, China, USA, UK, Norway; and c) commercial banks and private financial firms. The

---

150 From Socorro Heysen (2005) - International Financial Statistics, the IMF's Economic Data Sharing System, and statistical publications by various central banks

second source is from domestic sources, such as the central bank (e.g. BoSS) and commercial banks.

GRSS does not have established and coherent debt policy. It has not made use of concessional loans for multilateral creditors and instead it has been involved in very expensive loans from shady sources, advanced sales of crude oil as well as oil-collateralized loans. The COVID-19 pandemic provides an opportunity for GRSS to benefit from the Rapid Credit Facility (RCF) of the IMF and Development Policy Operations (DPO) of the World Bank. Credits from the multi-lateral institutions will go toward financing physical capital (e.g. roads & bridges, power generation) and human capital (e.g. education & healthcare). These credits/loans are, however, difficult to be diverted by the kleptocracy to their private and personal use, and they are therefore not given priority.

On domestic borrowing, Governments influence economic activity through the use of government securities, such as the treasury bills (TBs), treasury notes, treasury bonds, savings bonds, and so forth. GRSS issued treasury bills in 2013 to meet budgetary challenges arising from the shutdown of oil production in January 2012. The commercial banks responded enthusiastically by purchasing these TBs, but the GRSS has since then defaulted. Hence, government securities are not currently in use in South Sudan. It is nevertheless, time for the GRSS to formulate a coherent debt policy as part of the overall strategy of consolidating peace, stabilizing the economy, and combating COVID-19.

CHAPTER TEN

REVITALIZING THE ECONOMY: INVESTING IN BROAD CAPITAL FORMATION

◆

The central premise of endogenous growth theory is that broad capital accumulation (physical and human) does not experience diminishing returns.[151]

I have added social capital to be the third component of broad capital, which is articulated by Brian Snowdon and Howard R. Vane in the above passage. South Sudan has the resources to initiate a program of investment in a broad capital accumulation. I provide in the rest of this chapter some ideas in this regard.

Infrastructure Development Fund (IDF)

GRSS has allocated in the FY2019/2020 budget 30,000 barrels of crude oil per day for road construction. The current arrangement is that proceeds from the sales of the allocation of daily 30,000 bbl. from daily production are deposited into a *zero-interest earning account at*

---

151 Brian Snowdon and Howard R. Vane. 2005. Modern Macroeconomics: Its origins, Development and Current state. Edward Elgar: Cheltenham, UK and Northampton, MA, USA

a Chinese bank! This is problematic from the perspective of the PFM and it would be appropriate as well as good public policy if these proceeds were used in establishing an Infrastructure Development Fund (IDF). Moreover, the proceeds are to be deposited monthly into interest-earning account at one of the international investment banks. Alternatively, MoFP could seek the services of an independent transaction adviser to provide options for the utilization of resources made available under this noble initiative of establishing the IDF. The Government of Norway could also assist in the management of the IDF. I had sought in the course of preparing my written position to the TNL an expert opinion from Dr. Peter J. Middlebrook, CEO, Geopolicity Inc. His initial views are presented in Table 10.1 below, which he had also shared with Dr. David Nailo Mayo, Chairman of the Economy, Development, and Finance Committee, Transitional National Legislative Assembly (TNLA). Dr. Middlebrook stated his views in the following long passage:

A transaction advisory firm would normally seek to (i) put in place the most optimal terms and conditions for the deal including contract term, procurement arrangements (i.e. local content), oil price fluctuations, risks and mitigation measures (ii) establish cost benefit calculations including net present value and rate of return analysis (iii) undertake market testing (iv) outline the best options for ringfencing the infrastructure investment perhaps as a Special Purpose Vehicle (SPV) to improve performance monitoring and value for money (v) and establish key performance indicators for the procurement process. The contract should be pegged to the USD given ongoing devaluation and the infrastructure to be built, must be planned and overseen by sector Ministries. Ideally, a joint procurement committee has oversight of all procurement under the contract, to maximize the benefits to local works, services and technical assistance providers. Feasibility studies would be undertaken, independently, to secure optimal investment mixes (i.e. roads, power, fiber optic, water, storage etc.)[152].

---

152 From: South Sudan / China – Oil Sales Transaction Advisory

Table 10.1: Options for the use of resources allocated to infrastructure development

Base Option	Optimal Options
• Assess and Improve Terms and Conditions (i.e. local content, performance monitoring, feasibility design)	• Calculate Net Present Value of the Deal • Undertake Feasibility Studies including VfM • Appoint Independent Transaction Advisors • Identify Alternative Structures (SPV, KPIs, VfM)
• Strengthen Local Content Arrangements (i.e. 60% local contractors and labor)	
• Asset evaluation / contractor taxation	•
• Appoint Independent Transaction Advisor and identify most optimal options from an economic standpoint, including market testing, for YR1, YR3, YR5 timeframe	• Market testing to identify alternative VfM options • Appoint Independent Transaction Advisors
• Consider market-based sales and sovereign management and contracting	• Establish joint Government / Partner Special Purpose Vehicle to manage project.
• Establish Five Year Infrastructure Investment plan, around which investments (anchor, ancillary and spinoff are made)	• Establish options for hedging against exchange, oil price and other risks. • Links to ancillary investments (Special Economic Zones) and Small to Medium
• Explore SPV and matching infrastructure with donor funds	Enterprises. • Consider Joint Ventures
• Support competitive procurement and transparent award	• Explore options for leveraging
• Build in operations and maintenance financing to sustain.	

The IDF can finance the following projects/program, which have been recommended by the National Dialogue:

Hydro-electricity: Memorandum of Understanding (MoU) was signed in February 2012 with China Gezhouba Group, for 540mw Bedden Dam project at estimated cost of USD1.4bn. Other proposed schemes were 42mw Fula Rapids; 890mw Grand Fula; 410mw Laki, and 230mw Shukoli. None of these schemes has materialized, which would have provided over 2,000mw to the economy of South Sudan, especially in the development of agro-industries. It is therefore imperative that these projects be restarted, using the build, operate, own, and transfer (BOOT) system.

Roads: The Ministry of Roads and Bridges announced in January 2012 a 10-year plan to build 12,640km of roads. Actual road construction during 2005- 2019 is limited to some roads in Juba town, plus construction of US-funded 192-km Juba-Nimule road. A Japanese-funded project to build a second bridge over the Nile in Juba was launched in 2011; disruption of the project by the current conflict means it will now be completed, (other things remaining the same), in mid-2021. The IDF should give priority to roads that strengthen the supply chain of the agricultural sector.

River transport: Rehabilitate navigation routes from Juba to Kosti, in Sudan and encourage the private sector to operate boats to carry passengers and goods.

Railways: Rehabilitate, in cooperation with Sudan, Wau-Aweil-Babanusa railway line and extend this line to Kaya, on the border with Uganda, through Wau-Tambura-Yambio – Yei route. Construction of a railway line from Juba to Djibouti port via Akobo-Addis Ababa. And another from Malakal via Melut-Palodge – Pagak -Addis Ababa -Djibouti port.

I would add to the above list of projects/programs, construction of dykes in areas, such as Jonglei that are frequently flooded.

Improving the living conditions of core public sector employees

Efficient public sector is a necessary, though not sufficient step toward human capital formation. This is because affective allocation to health and education in the annual budget depends on a vibrant public service. Hence, restoring discipline and integrity to the public budget requires effective and efficient public service, which is managed by highly motivated and well-remunerated staff. This calls for a critical appraisal of living conditions of public sector employees who are critical elements in the revitalization of the economy of South Sudan. There was an opportunity to do this during the FY2019/2020 budget preparation, by considering indexing wages and salaries of public sector employees to inflation. That is, cost-of-living allowance (COLA) is the conventional way of indexing wages/salaries to inflation so as to protect their purchasing power, during high-inflation periods. South Sudan has been through periods of high inflation since the failed attempts in December 2015 to realign the official and parallel market exchange rates.

There are, however, genuine practical difficulties in applying indexation of wages and salaries to what is clearly exchange rate-induced inflation. Lack of technical capacity is one of the elements underpinning such genuine difficulties in South Sudan. However, these difficulties could be overcome if we were to adopt a simpler and practical method for protecting the purchasing power of the wages and salaries of the public sector employees.

I have been advocating, though in vain, for an alternative type of indexation, which I believe would not only protect the purchasing power of the wages and salaries of public sector employees, but also stabilize the economy of South Sudan. This alternative is **the exchange rate indexation**. This is on the argument that the economy of South Sudan is highly dollarized by IMF standard. That is, our economy is at the stage in which economic agents think in terms of United States of America dollar (USD) and prices in South Sudanese pound (SSP) are indexed to the daily SSP/USD exchange rate.

I would like to revisit the idea of indexing wages and salaries to the U.S. dollar. It should be stated here that indexing does not mean abandoning the SSP as the legal tender in the country. A recent decision by the Board of Directors of BoSS would seem to me that leaders of our monetary authority have misunderstood the concept of dollarization. Hence, South Sudanese policymakers in general and members of the TNL in particular should invest time and efforts to understand when does the unofficial dollarization take place. The following long passage from Kurt Schuler could enhance such an understanding:

> Unofficial dollarization often occurs in stages that correspond to the textbook functions of money as a store of value, means of payment, and unit of account. In the first stage, which economists sometimes call "asset substitution," people hold foreign bonds and deposits abroad as stores of value. They do so because they want to protect against losing wealth through inflation in the domestic currency or through the outright confiscations that some countries have made. In the second stage of unofficial dollarization, which economists sometimes call "currency substitution,"

people hold large amounts of foreign-currency deposits in the domestic banking system (if permitted), and later foreign notes, both as a means of payment and as stores of value. Wages, taxes, and everyday expenses such as groceries and electric bills continue to be paid in domestic currency, but expensive items such as automobiles and houses are often paid in foreign currency. In the final stage of unofficial dollarization, people think in terms of foreign currency, and prices in domestic currency become indexed to the exchange rate[153].

How do we quantitatively measure the phenomenon of unofficial dollarization described in the passage quoted above? The literature on dollarization gives two indicators[154]: **a) share of foreign currency deposits in the money supply (or total liquidity, which includes foreign currency deposits)**; and **b) share of foreign currency deposits in total bank deposits**. I assume, in the case of South Sudan economy and for ease of analysis, total money supply to be more or less equal to total bank deposits. According to the IMF an economy is considered highly dollarized if the share of foreign currency deposits in the money supply is equal to or greater than 30% and moderately dollarized if it is below 30%, but more than 16.4%. It is on the basis of these indicators that researchers have been able to determine the extent to which countries have dollarized, partially or fully (or officially and unofficially). Countries that allow a foreign currency to circulate together with a local currency are considered to be in what is called a "dual monetary system!"

I would like, in the context of restoring discipline to the budgeting process, to identify three core institutions that could have had benefited from USD422.3 million in the FY2019/2020 budget. These are: a) the public universities; b) the TNL; and c) national civil service. I have provided in Table 10.2 below what could have been done at this phase of the budgeting process of the FY2019/2020 budget.

---

153 See Kurt Schuler (2000): Basics of Dollarization - Global Policy Forum

154 For more on this, see for instance - Adam Bennett (1999): Monetary Policy in Dollarized Economies; Impact of Dollarization; Kurt Schuler (2005): Some Theory and History of Dollarization; Bonga and Dhoro (2015): Currency Substitution, Dollarisation and Possibility of De-dollarisation in Zimbabwe; Myriam Quispe-Agnoli (2002): Costs and Benefits of Dollarization

Table 10.2: Improving the living conditions through exchange rate indexing of wages and salaries for staff of core institutions

Category	Number of persons	Amount in USD based on exchange rate of SSP161/USD1.0 used in the FY2019/2020 budget	Comment
1. Public Universities	Details about the number of the staff (academic and non-academic) are with the administration of these universities	58.4 million	The Cabinet approved pay raise for a total cost of **SSP9.4 billion** after the budget was presented to the TNL. This should not wait for supplementary budget, since this raise was within total outlays of the FY2019/2020 draft budget
2. National Legislature	1,000 persons	12.0 million	This figure is for members of the two houses and their staff. The assumption here is that the payroll of the national legislature is about USD1.0/month, which would make the TNL more efficient and effective in performing its oversight role of the budget process
3. Core Institutions	12,000 persons	144.0 million	It is assumed here that 12,000 highly qualified South Sudanese in the civil service would each be paid USD1,000/month. For instance, the capacity of the Presidency would be enhanced through reassignment of 36 highly qualified South Sudanese as follows: 10 staff to the office of the President, 6 staff to the office of FVP, and 5 staff to each of the four VPs. The head count of the

Category	Number of persons	Amount in USD based on exchange rate of SSP161/USD1.0 used in the FY2019/2020 budget	Comment
			total number of central government employees is given to be 15,000. This figure does not include the organized forces, states and local government employees
			This amount is about 50% of the realized savings of USD422.3 million from 30,000 bopd for road construction.
Total estimated cost		214.4 million	

The average monthly cost of improving the living conditions of core staff is about USD17.9 million. I had recommended, during the preparation of the FY2019/2020 budget that this amount be paid in U.S. dollar, so as to prevent hyperinflation. Two questions are often asked: a) where will GRSS get the dollars? And b) is it not going to lead to a Zimbabwean scenario?

The answer to the first question should now be obvious in the light of the analysis of the budget of GRSS. We have shown earlier that oil revenue, which is paid in dollars, accruing to the GRSS constitutes 92.6% of its total revenues for the FY2019/2020 budget. That is, the GRSS gets more than 90% of its total revenues in the U.S. dollars.

It should be stated at this point that the overall objective of partial dollarization is to restore economic stability and growth to an economy facing macroeconomic instability characterized by high inflation. This objective should guide our analysis of costs and benefits of dollarization. Empirical literature shows beyond doubt that the benefits of dollarization outweigh its costs. What is discussed here, however, in the case of South Sudan is partial dollarization and not a full one. That is, South Sudan could adopt a partially dollarized system as a temporary measure, while building resilient institutions and capacities for economic policy management. Let us briefly discuss costs and benefits of dollarization; bearing in mind that what is being proposed for South Sudan is a partial dollarization.

I would like to present the benefits of dollarization in Table 10.3 for ease of discussion.

Table 10.3: General Benefits of Dollarization

Benefit	General Comment
1. Stability & growth	Protection of money income and assets is achieved through reduction in inflation. This is because the "risk of depreciation of domestic currency is reduced," especially when exchange rate volatility is a key driver of high inflation rates as is the case in South Sudan.
2. Development of sound financial sector/ system	A stable capital market would emerge, which could reduce capital outflows and ensure "balance of payments that is less prone to crisis."
3. Credibility of economic policy	"**Political will**" is a scarce commodity in many countries that experience persistent macroeconomic instability, which is under-pinned by deficit-financing (or inflationary-financing). And when policymakers accept the key objective of monetary policy, which is price stability, they are essentially accepting discipline in fiscal policy that would in turn enhance confidence in economic policy formulation & execution.
4. Conducive environment for investment	Economic climate is more credible and foreign direct investment (FDI) would flow smoothly, which in turn contributes toward closing the saving-gap facing the domestic economy. Development partners will also be supportive in the light of reduced credibility gap of our policymakers.

There are only two main costs of full dollarization. The first is the loss of power for printing money to finance fiscal deficit. The second is when the country gives up its "national monetary autonomy and seigniorage as well as an effective lender of last resort for domestic banks[155]." These would not, however, be applicable in the case of a partially dollarized system envisaged for South Sudan. The Bank of South Sudan will continue to have the full functions of a national monetary authority and the SSP will continue as our legal tender. Moreover, people are currently free to have bank account in the USD and they are also allowed to carry USD notes.

---

155 See Dollarization: Pros and Cons, by Benjamin J. Cohen (2000), http://www.polsci.ucsb.edu/faculty/cohen

Let us now turn to the case of Zimbabwe in which policymakers abandoned the local currency and fully adopted USD as the legal tender in 2009. They would not have been forced to do this had they responded with appropriate policy measures at the beginning of the economic crisis. Moreover, the case of Zimbabwe is unusual according to Bonga and Dhoro:

> The process of dollarization in Zimbabwe was peculiar in that it was not backed by international reserves, as is normally the case with countries that have dollarized. The only foreign currency that the government had was from taxation after full dollarisation[156].

Why did Zimbabwe fully dollarize in 2009? This question would be answered by looking at the trends of the inflation rate during the period 1998 – 2008. I have heavily relied on a table given by Bonga and Dhoro, which provides the inflation rates since 1980. My choice of the year 1998 is because that was the time the Zimbabwean economy began to experience persistent high inflation rates (see Table 10.4 below).

Table 10.4: Zimbabwean Inflation Rates During the period 1998 – 2008

Year	Inflation Rate (%)
1998	48
1999	56.9
2000	55.27
2001	112.1
2002	198.93
2003	598.75
2004	132.75
2005	585.84
2006	1,281.11
2007	66,212.3
2008 – July	231,150,888.87
2008 – August	471,000,000,000
2008 – September	3,840,000,000,000,000
2008 – Mid-November	89,700,000,000,000,000,000

Source: From a table given by Bongo and Dhoro (2015:31)

---

156 Bonga and Dhoro (2015): Currency Substitution, Dollarisation and Possibility of De-dollarisation in Zimbabwe, Journal of Economics and Finance (IOSR-JEF) e-ISSN: 2321-5933, p-ISSN: 2321-5925.Volume 6, Issue 1.Ver. I (Jan.-Feb. 2015), PP 30-38 www.iosrjournals.org

The picture depicted by the inflation rates in Table 10.4 above would appear to be counter intuitive, that is beyond imagination and comprehension under normal circumstances. This is the picture that has been misunderstood by many South Sudanese analysts and policy-makers alike. But, this is what forced the Zimbabwean policymakers to abandon their local currency and went for full dollarization. It was not the consequence of dollarization. It was the result of inaction to reverse the worsening economic situation, which eventually forced Zimbabwe to do what our policymakers are resisting to do before it is too late.

The simplest way for understanding the Zimbabwean scenario is to go back to basics of the demand for money. People demand money, as stated earlier, for store of value, medium of exchange, and unit of account. In the light of these functions, the Zimbabwean national currency (also called dollar) would undoubtedly not have performed them when the inflation rate reached 231 million percent in July 2008. As if the message was not sufficiently internalized by both policy-makers and economic agents in Zimbabwe, the inflation rate reached 471 billion percent just within a month and trillions by September 2008. The demand function of the Zimbabwean national currency was now sufficiently altered and currency substitution began in earnest.

I would like to present the same drama conveyed by Table 10.4, in a graphic form (see Figure 10.1).

Inflation in Zimbabwe, 1998-2008

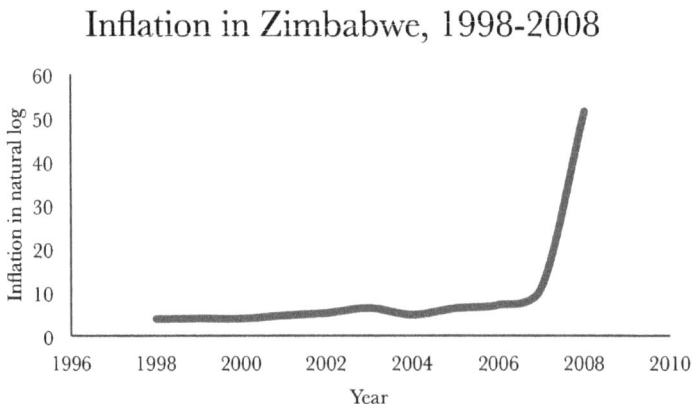

Figure 10.1: Inflation in Zimbabwe During the Period 1998 - 2008

The graph shown in Figure 10.1 above clearly demonstrates beyond doubt the point at which Milton Friedman's cardinal principle that "inflation is always and everywhere a monetary phenomenon," is observed. The national currency lost to perform all the three functions of the demand for money as a result of hyperinflation. A new currency that could meet the demand for money functions was therefore imperative so as to ensure normal operation of the economy. Bonga and Dhoro have captured vividly the drama of the "disappearance" of the Zimbabwean national currency. They pointed out that the Reserve Bank of Zimbabwe (i.e. central bank) was: "unable to convert domestic money balances of the banking system" and "could not provide the lender of last resort function." Hence, Zimbabwe was forced to officially adopt the United States of America dollar as a legal tender.

The central objective of paying the salaries of the public sector employees in dollars is to protect the value of SSP by creating an effective demand for it. That is, the GRSS is the major employer in the economy of South Sudan and when its employees are paid in dollars, they would in turn buy the SSP from the banking sector and thereby raising the price of the pound (i.e. the value of pound will increase, other things being equal, against the dollar). It is analogous to paying employees in-kind with a commodity called dollar, which the payees would in turn sell to the banking sector in exchange for the SSP. This commodity is earned through another commodity called crude oil, which is priced internationally in the United States of America dollar (USD). **Simply put, if the GRSS does not have dollars, then it does not have a budget.**

It would be recalled that the budget is nothing, but a statement of government's income (revenue) and expenditure. And this income, in the case of South Sudan, is mainly (92.6%) from the sales of crude oil, which is denominated in the U.S. dollar. In the case of Zimbabwe, the government's income was mainly from taxes. The recent drastic decline in the price of crude oil due to the Saudi-Russia price war could strengthen the argument against paying public sector employees in dollars. Nevertheless, I would maintain my argument in favor of partial dollarization.

The simple way, in my view, is for South Sudan's policymakers as well as the general public to be guided by best practices in economic policy management. Empirical evidence on the success of dollarization, instead of COLA, as a way of protecting the purchasing power of money income is now easily accessible and economic policymakers should make use of it in fixing the economy of South Sudan.

Investing in Social Capital Accumulation

Poverty is a fundamental constraint to social capital formation. The problem of poverty dominated the deliberations of the SPLM economic team during the second half of 2004. It was also the time the Joint Assessment Mission (JAM), which was co-led by the World Bank and UN, was in progress. The World Bank and UN staff were using the phrase "**poverty reduction or poverty alleviation.**" Dr. John Garang did not like these terms, so he called us to brainstorm on the best way to combat poverty as the second objective of the liberation struggle. He began by challenging us that the term poverty reduction is already a recognition of the failure to defeat the enemy. After days of deliberations the consensus was to always use poverty eradication in all the SPLM policy documents.

I subsequently developed a framework for poverty eradication comprising of three phases[157]. The first phase concerns poverty alleviation in the short-term through efforts, such as humanitarian assistance and emergency relief supplies. About two-thirds (63.8%) of the population of South Sudan is food insecure[158]. I have excluded, in calculating the percentage of food insecurity, Internally Displaced Persons (IDPs who are about 1.9 million persons) and refugees (2.4 million people), from the total population of South Sudan, which is estimated to be 12.3 million people. The UN agencies and Non-governmental Organizations (NGOs) provide "life-saving food assistance and emergency livelihoods support to 5.1 million South Sudanese[159]" or 63.8% (i.e. 5.1/8) of the total population without

---

157 See my book (2013), The Power of Creative Reasoning: The Ideas and Vision of John Garang
158 See Humanitarian Bulletin. Issue No. 02 of February 20, 2018
159 Ditto

IDPs and refugees. The humanitarian relief supplies are not taxed and therefore reduce the amount of non-oil revenues to GRSS that would have accrued to the treasury. Hence, the full implementation of R-ARCSS will redirect humanitarian assistance toward enhanced food security and livelihoods, which would in turn increase savings for investment in broad capital formation in general, and social capital in particular.

The second phase is poverty reduction, which focuses on medium-term measures. There are two cluster of policies for social capital formation in the medium-term. They are: social inclusion and equity policies and public sector management and institutions.

Social Inclusion and equity policies

The cluster has five components with CPIA score ranging between 1.0 for environmental sustainability and 2.5 for building human resources. The components are (with scores for 2019): a) gender equity (2.0); b) equity of public resource use (2.0); iii) building human resources (2.5); iv) social protection and labor (1.5); and v) environmental sustainability (1.0). The National Dialogue Steering Committee has recommended the following:

1. *Operationalize the women enterprise development fund (Article 4.15.1.5 of R-ARCSS) as a window of SSRDF and which will be used to enhance women economic empowerment;*

2. *Operationalize the youth enterprise development fund (Article 4.15.6.4) as a window of SSRDF for youth empowerment scheme (YES);*

3. *Initiate environmental audit of the oil producing areas and take immediate actions to ameliorate the environmental damages that have been caused;*

4. *Ensure the effectiveness of the South Sudan Pension Fund; and*

5. *Operationalize the Future Generation Fund as by way of ensuring inter-generational equity.*

Policies for public sector management and institutions

The Public Sector Management and Institutions Cluster has been the second poorly performing cluster during the period 2012 – 2019. There are five components: a) property rights and rule-based governance (1.5); b) quality of budgetary and financial management (1.0), which is the lowest performing in this cluster; c) efficiency of revenue mobilization (2.0); d) quality of public administration (1.5); and e) transparency, accountability, and corruption in the public sector (1.5). The following six points were identified through grassroots consultations as main causes for the poor performance of this cluster:

1. *Nepotism affects access to business and job opportunities;*
2. *Multiple taxes at several checkpoints;*
3. *Land issues, especially in Greater Equatoria also reported under governance and security clusters;*
4. *Awarding of letters of credit (LCs) to briefcase companies owned by politicians and generals;*
5. *Involvement of constitutional post holders and generals in business contracts;* and
6. *Money laundering and repatriation of money by foreigners back to their countries.*

In the light of the above six points, the Steering Committee has made the following five recommendations:

1. *Resolve communal land issues and formulate the most appropriate land tenure system consistent with our basic principles of social inclusion and equity;*
2. *Strengthen systems of transparency and accountability in the management of public resources;*
3. *Develop and implement a comprehensive PFM Reforms Strategy as recommended by the IMF to re-establish PFM System, Institutions, and Fiscal Reporting;*
4. *Promote adherence and enforce compliance with all PFM laws; and*
5. *Undertake various forms of capacity building activities in key PFM areas, and develop retention and succession plans for staff with key PFM skills.*

The RTGoNU has now embarked on the PFM reform strategy. The Minister of Finance and Planning established on 17 April 2020 the governance structure for the PFM. This was in response to various recommendations of the IMF since 2012 and to Chapter IV of R-ARCSS, specifically Article 4.1.4, which states that:

> The RTGoNU shall establish a high-level, competent and effective oversight mechanism that shall control revenues collection, budgeting, revenue allocation and expenditure. The oversight mechanism may solicit technical and advisory resources on economic governance from regional and international community. The mechanism shall be guided by principles of mutual consent in accountability[160].

The governance structure consists of three bodies: a) PFM Oversight Committee; b) PFM Technical Committee; and c) PFM Secretariat. This was a bold and significant move on the part of the Minister of Finance and Planning; a move that has in turn enabled the IMF and the World Bank to launch two virtual PFM missions to South Sudan in June and July 2020 respectively. Let us first look at the composition of the governance of the PFM-Oversight Committee (PFM-OC) and PFM Technical Committee (PFM-TC) before examining the recommendations of the IMF. **Membership of the PFM-OC comprises of the following**:

1. Minister of Finance and Planning, Co-Chair;
2. A representative of the Development Partners, Co-Chair;
3. Minister of Petroleum, Deputy Co-Chair;
4. Minister of Labor, Secretary;
5. Minister of Justice and Constitutional Affairs, member;
6. Minister of Public Service and Human Resource Development, member;
7. Minister of Gender and Child Welfare, member;
8. Minister of Federal Affairs, Member;
9. Governor of the Bank of South Sudan, member;
10. Chairperson of Public Accounts Committee (PAC), RTNLA, member;

---

160 See page 46 of R-ARCSS document

11. Auditor General, member;
12. Commissioner General of the National Revenue Authority, member;
13. Chair of the Anti-Corruption Commission, member;
14. Head of the Procurement Authority, member; and
15. A representative of Civil Society Organizations, member

The PFM-TC comprises of the following members:

1. First Undersecretary, Ministry of Finance and Planning, Chair
2. Undersecretary of Planning, Ministry of Finance and Planning, Deputy Chair
3. Undersecretary, Ministry of Petroleum, Secretary
4. Undersecretary, Ministry of Labor, Deputy Secretary
5. Undersecretary, Ministry of Justice and Constitutional Affairs, member
6. Undersecretary, Ministry of Public Service and Human Resource Development, member
7. Chief Administrator/Undersecretary, Ministry for Presidential Affairs, member
8. DG of Capital Markets, Bank of South Sudan, member
9. DG of the National Revenue Authority, member
10. Deputy Auditor General, National Audit Chamber, member
11. Executive Director/Commissioner Anti-corruption Commission, member
12. National Bureau of Statistics, member
13. Fiscal and Financial Allocation and Monitoring Commission, member
14. Civil Society Representative, member
15. Financial Intelligence Unit, NSS, member
16. DG of Procurement, member
17. A representative of Ebony Center for Strategic Studies, member
18. A representative of the School of Economic & Social Studies, University of Juba, member
19. One representative each from World Bank, IMF, AfDB, UNDP, IGAD, EU, and Troika, members

The Ministry of Finance and Planning, had identified, with technical backstopping from the Ebony Center for Strategic Studies, eleven PFM reform priorities. These priorities were the focus of the two virtual PFM missions of the IMF and World Bank. They are:

1. Implementation of a Treasury Single Account (TSA);
2. Strengthening of cash management;
3. Relocation of the Loan Committee to MoFP;
4. Review, verification, and clearance of all arrears;
5. Review and verification of loans and contracts collateralized or guaranteed against crude oil;
6. Strengthening of the Anti-corruption Commission and the Audit Chamber;
7. Establishment of a Public Procurement and Asset Disposal Authority (PPADA);
8. Rolling out of electronic payroll using biometric system;
9. Strengthening of Fiscal and Financial Allocation Monitoring Commission;
10. Strengthening of macro-fiscal framework (MFF); and
11. Strengthening of the budget process and budget credibility.

The PFM virtual mission of the IMF focussed on priorities 1, 2, 4, and 10 from the above list and the remaining 7 priorities were addressed by the World Bank. Priority number 3 (relocation of the Loan Committee to MoFP) has already been implemented, which is one of the key indicators of **political will** to undertake PFM reforms as stipulated in Chapter IV of R-ARCSS. There is really a huge credibility gap, which South Sudanese political leaders must strive to eliminate before they are fully trusted by the people of South Sudan as well as our development partners.

The IMF PFM virtual mission made the following key recommendations for implementation in 2020:

Table[161] 10.5: Key Recommendations for Implementation
in 2020

PFMRS

1.1 Strengthen leadership and governance arrangements of the PFMRS:
- Arrange at least monthly meetings of the Oversight Committee to discuss and provide leadership on key PFM issues.
- Appoint the Technical Committee, and a Secretariat headed by a full-time Coordinator.
- Initiate discussions with key DPs on financial and technical support for the PFMRS.
- Build initial contacts with CSOs and the parliament.

1.2. Identify the core PFM areas for improvement and start the rollout of the PFMRS:
- Develop a Concept Note on the PFMRS, which is approved by the Cabinet.
- Keep the strategy simple and focused and allow plenty of time for implementation.

Macro-Fiscal Framework

2.1 Simplify the current MFF to focus on the collection, analysis and forecasting of the most critical parameters, using more streamlined forecasting techniques:
- Include real and nominal GDP, oil production, prices and revenue, non-oil revenue, the CPI, and exchange rates within the core of the MFF.
- Collect and analyze historical data and make forecasts for critical parameters.

Hibernate non-essential elements of the framework.

2.2 Address institutional blockages that impede the provision of data for the MFF, particularly by operationalizing the existing MOU on Macroeconomic Management

---

161 It is Table 1 of the IMF document - South Sudan: Public Financial Management Reform Priorities, Technical Report, July 2020

- Assign responsibility to the Oversight Committee as a standing agenda item.
- Develop protocols of data sharing and assign responsibilities under the MOU.
- Establish timelines for the regular production and reporting of data to the MoFP.

TSA, Cash Management and Arrears

3.1 Initiate implementation of the TSA:

- Assign full-time responsibility within the Treasury for managing banking arrangements.
- Issue a template to MDAs and banks for completing an inventory of all bank accounts.
- Compile a full inventory of bank accounts.
- Prepare short term action plan (10 largest MDA bank accounts) for incorporation in the TSA.
- Initiate discussions with BoSS to agree on aggregation and pooling arrangements.

3.2 Strengthen cash management:

- Engage cash management staff with MPD to help update cash flow forecasts.
- Formally establish a full-time CMU and appoint staff.
- Reinstate cash flow forecasting and prepare consolidated forecasts.

3.3 Initiate the implementation of an arrears management strategy:

- Notify the MDAs of reduced spending limits for FY2021.
- Update the IFMIS allotment controls to record cash limits as approved by the CMC.
- Issue a template of all unpaid invoices both within and outside the IFMIS.
- Prepare consolidated quarterly reports of arrears.

- Develop and approve an Arrears Management Strategy under the OC leadership.
- Upgrade the IFMIS to record all unpaid invoices and the original incurrence date.

Source: Table 1. of The South Sudan: Public Financial Management Reform Priorities

The key recommendations given in Table 10.5 will be implemented given the leadership and current composition of the PFM-OC. I have the privilege to observe the deliberations of the PFM-OC and if this culture of debating the reform strategy continues, which is essentially public policy at its best, then the country would begin to regain its binding narrative, on 9 July 2011, of triumph and freedom. Here public policy, as an instrument, is the engine (or locomotive) is driven by leadership. The status of this engine is a function of a robust PFM pursued by the leadership of a country.

And the third phase is poverty eradication in the long-run, where there will be no South Sudanese citizen living below the universal poverty line. This is because structural policies would have been put in place to diversify the economy of South Sudan.

Structural policies

This group (or cluster) of policies has been the best performing one for South Sudan. It has, nevertheless, been affected by conflict in that the CPIA score dropped from 2.3 in 2012 to 1.8 in 2019. This cluster is comprised of three sectors (or components) with each scoring 1.8 in 2019. The components are: a) trade; b) financial sector; and c) business environment. There is a general perception that foreigners have taken over the business sector of our economy. Here is a summary of the views from the grassroots consultations during the National Dialogue process on the sources of economic problems in South Sudan:

1. *The market is being controlled by foreigners;*
2. *Lack of regulation of price of items and market generally;*

3. *South Sudan has opened its borders to everyone; and*
4. *Lack of diversification of the economy.*

The Steering Committee of the National Dialogue subsequently recommended for consideration of the National Dialogue Conference the following recommendations with respect to trade and business regulation:

1. *Foreigners should not be allowed to engage in retail and micro businesses and foreign companies should be limited to large scale investment and trade;*
2. *Foreign banks operating in South Sudan should be encouraged to give 50% of their loans to local businesses;*
3. *All companies operating in South Sudan should exercise corporate social responsibility;*
4. *The Government should ensure that the water-tankers business is controlled and owned by South Sudanese; and*
5. *The GRSS should combine the Special Reconstruction Fund (SRF) stipulated in Chapter III (Article 3.2) of R-ARCSS with Health Care Support Fund (Article 4.6.1.5), Students Support Fund (Article 4.6.1.6) and Enterprise Development Funds (Article 4.15) stipulated in Chapter IV of R-ARCSS into a South Sudan Reconstruction and Development Fund (SSRDF) with all these proposed funds as its windows.*

There is urgency to understand the structure of the South Sudanese economy in order to recommend structural policies that would in turn lead the process of economic revitalization. I would focus on four sectors: a) primary (or extraction); b) secondary (or manufacturing); c) tertiary (or service); and d) quaternary (or knowledge). It should be obvious from this list that the people of South Sudan at the grassroots level have correctly diagnosed the lack of diversity to be one of root causes of our economic problems. So, to diversify the economy is the first step toward its revitalization. Our economy is dependent on oil, which is a subsector of the primary sector.

The challenge then is how to get out of the dependency on a single commodity to a more diversified economy. This called for the identification of key economic agents/players in tandem with the sectors of the economy. I would then construct a policy matrix (see Table 10.6

below) on how to move beyond oil to the sectors of the real economy of South Sudan. I would try to make some suggestions for revitalizing the economy in this policy matrix, with the main purpose of triggering a debate on economic diversification. Moreover, the matrix assumes there is a right mix of economic management (i.e. fiscal, monetary, exchange rate, and debt) policies in place.

Table 10.6: Some Ideas on How to Diversify the South Sudanese Economy

Required Institutional Strategy/Action from economic agents/players	Four Sectors of the Economy of South Sudan			
	Primary Sector:	Secondary Sector	Tertiary Sector	Quaternary Sector
	Extraction of raw materials, e.g. agriculture, mining, fishing, wildlife	Manufacturing, e.g. construction, power generation, canning, breweries, water bottling	Services, e.g. retail, hotels, restaurants, banking, tourism, entertainment, healthcare, transport	Knowledge, e.g. education, R&D, IT, public sector entities, communications
1. Government	- Making agriculture the engine of growth of the economy - Use oil to fuel the engine of economic growth - Regulatory frameworks for extraction activities that respect the environment & society - Property rights, including land tenure system	- Roads & bridges connecting surplus areas with deficit ones, railways - Power generation from hydro, crude oil, solar & wind sources - Joint Venture (JV) with private sector on agro-industries, e.g. Mongalla sugar scheme, Melut sugar scheme, Nzara industrial complex, Gold refinery, oil refineries, petro-chemical industries	- Robust regulatory frameworks - Capitalize South Sudan Agricultural Bank - Strengthen BoSS by ensuring its professional leadership - Pooled all the funds stiplulated in Chapters III & IV of R-ARCSS into a single body, such South Sudan Reconstruction & Development Fund (SSRDF), with the main function of project preparation and development, e.g. physical infrastructure, agro-industries, etc.	- Leadership and overall vision for economic & social transformation - Free & compulsory primary education - Primary healthcare - National Research Council with specialized councils, such as agricultural research council, economic & social research council, medical research council, engineering research council - Public universities & centers of excellence - National Laboratory for human & animal diseases

Required Institutional Strategy/Action from economic agents/players	Four Sectors of the Economy of South Sudan			
	Primary Sector:	Secondary Sector	Tertiary Sector	Quaternary Sector
2. Households	- Crop farming - Dairy farming - Ranching - Fishing	- Labor & land to the manufacturing activities	- Labor to the service sector - Cooperatives for production and consumption activities	- Contribution to human capital formation - Nurturing ethics & moral values of hard working, integrity and tolerance
3. Corporate	- Large-scale commercial farming, dairy, fishing, & ranching - Exploration & production of oil & gas, gold and other minerals	-JV on Agro-industries, e.g. Mongalla sugar scheme, Melut sugar scheme, Nzara industrial complex, Gold refinery, oil refineries, petro-chemical industries - Construction of housing & commercial buildings Furniture making, carpentry, brick-laying, leather, fruit canning, food processing, breweries, water bottling, - Light industry, e.g. manufac-turing of clothes, shoes, paper making, consumer electronics and home appliances	- Retail, hotels, restaurants, banking, tourism, entertainment, healthcare, transport	- Research & Development (R&D) - Private univer-sities and centers of learning - Business leadership and new techniques of production and management
4.Development Partners	- Technical assistance & grants to agriculture	- Providing loans & grants for infrastructure development	- Grants for social safety nets for vulnerable house-holds	- Technical assis-tance & grants to education & healthcare
5. NGOs	- Provide seeds, tools, and extension services to farming house-holds	- Monitor social & environmental impact of devel-opment projects & industries	- Provide social safety nets to vulnerable house-holds	- Contribute toward human capital formation

How is it then the National Dialogue is a framework for poverty eradi-cation? If the ten objectives of the National Dialogue were met, then it would be such a framework. I have reproduced below the ten objec-tives of the National Dialogue, which were stated in the Introduction Chapter of this book:

1. *End all forms of violence in the country;*
2. *Redefine and re-establish stronger national unity;*
3. *Strengthen social contract between the citizens and their state;*
4. *Address issues of diversity;*
5. *Agree on a mechanism for allocating and sharing of resources;*
6. *Settle historical disputes and sources of conflict among communities;*
7. *Set a stage for an integrated and inclusive national development strategy;*
8. *Agree on steps and guarantees to ensure safe, free, fair and peaceful elections and post transition in 2018;*
9. *Agree on a strategy to return internally displaced persons and refugees to their homes; and*
10. *Develop a framework for national peace, healing, and reconciliation.*

Social cohesion underpinned all the above ten objectives. This particular point has been articulated by the reports of the grassroots consulta-tions. Our people at the grassroots level have made eight groups of recommendations that will, in my view, lead to the restoration of a binding narrative of triumph and freedom. Such a restoration would in turn lead to social cohesion and poverty eradication. The eight groups of recommendations are given below.

Grassroots recommendations on Repentance, Healing and Reconciliation

This group consists of the following nine recommendations, which have been summarized from the fifteen reports of the Subcommittees of the Steering Committee:

1. **Repentance, Forgiveness and Reconciliation:** People need **to forgive one** another and avoid revenge attitudes. Forgiveness is

very important for the people who have been in conflict for so long.

2. **Repentance and Confession of guilt before God:** the people of South Sudan should go back to God in their different religions so that God can help them achieve peace by his grace.

3. **National Peace, Reconciliation and Healing Process:** There should be a process of peace, **reconciliation and healing** beginning from the top political leaders to the citizens for genuine forgiveness in South Sudan. **Politicians should forgive and reconcile** with each other to save the country from the recurrent violent conflicts. They highlighted the importance of politicians uniting their ranks and file to forge a way forward.

4. **Apology for atrocities:** All parties in conflict that have committed atrocities to come back to the people and apologize.

5. **Establish healing & reconciliation centers all over the country.**

6. **Respect of Human Dignity and Tolerance:** There should be respect for human dignity and tolerance of one another.

7. **Promote dialogue among communities:** Initiate community dialogue and awareness about the consequences of the 2013 war and its effects on the children and their future, including women and elderly who had no connection to what was done in Juba. Such inclusive dialogue should reach out to all the grassroots.

8. **Confidence building between nationalities (tribes) of Upper Nile State:** The grassroots urge the people to embrace each other in unity and harmony in order to foster the future of this young nation.

9. **Review of the Recommendations of Wunlit Conference** should be revisited so that Dinka and Nuer stop being the cause of problems in the country.

Grassroots recommendations on crimes committed against human dignity

There are two recommendations under this group:

1. **Strengthen accountability and justice institutions in South**

Sudan: Court cases against the perpetrators of murder and rape and other atrocities as a commitment that never again shall such things happen in the Republic of South Sudan.

2. **Child Abduction should be criminalized** all over the country.

Grassroots recommendations on Problems caused by the Pastoralists

The following are recommendations from grassroots consultations under this group:

1. **Recovering stolen cattle:** The government should intervene to recover cattle raided from hiding in the host communities e.g. from Kajo Keji because the raiders are well known even to the Government.
2. **Remove the cattle from the IDP land:** Thousands of refugees say they will not come home unless the cattle are driven out of their Land.
3. **Pastoralists and IDPs should evacuate** the Madi land immediately to enable the Madi community to return to their ancestral land.
4. **Regulate cattle movement** by law and conduct comprehensive disarmament of civilians. **Voluntary or force return of cattle** to their original areas and Government should regulate their movement by law.
5. **Enforcement of t**he order of the President for cattle to be returned to the state of origin should be enforced without favor. Cattle owning Communities to go back to traditional consultations and agreements on cattle grazing areas.

Grassroots recommendations on Educational Policies on Social Cohesion

The following are the recommendations under this group:

1. **National Education Program**: There is need for an aggressive education program with clear targets over the next ten years because the cause of the current conflicts is due to ignorance and very low levels of education and community awareness.
2. **Public Education Program on Nationalism:** There should be intensive social awareness on nationalism, patriotism and sense of belonging to promote love, acceptance of our diversity in order to develop common identity.
3. **Reintroduce boarding schools** in order to **cultivate nationalism**, unity and sense of diversity between the various South Sudanese ethnic groups.
4. **Nationalism and Patriotism** and clear history of the liberation struggle of the people of South Sudan for freedom and independence should be part of school curriculum to fight tribalism, corruption, and nepotism.
5. **Fighting illiteracy through Education**: Communities should be mobilized to reject cattle raiding and cattle wealth acquired through it. Enhancement of development in educational sector by complete educational policy reform to fight illiteracy among the communities.
6. **Cultural Program on the South Sudan Broadcasting Corporation (SSBC)**: Play our cultures and images on the national Television in Juba.

Grassroots Recommendations on Land, Border disputes, and IDPs

The following are the recommendations from the grassroots consultations of this group:

1. **Plots and Land grabbed:** should be returned to the rightful owners through intervention of law enforcement agents.
2. **Review land policies and Laws that govern land ownership,** such as the policy of land belong to the community.
3. **Equitable land distributions & application of laws. Conservation of cultural heritage**, historic places and slave

trade relics in Uyu Juku (Deim Zuber), Rodom park.

4. **Boundary Committees:** Formation of internal boundary committee to address the land disputes between states, counties, **Payams** and other administrative units.
5. **Restoration of 1956 borders** between communities, which served justice for all the citizens.
6. **Local Government Administrators (LGAs):** The LGAs Should be deployed by the government all over South Sudan in areas other than their own.
7. **Reconsider the division of states to promote peaceful coexistence** among the communities and tribes; the states should not be created on the basis of tribes.
8. **Participation of the rebels** in the subcommittees to ensure success of the National Dialogue process.
9. **Repatriation of internally displaced persons (IDPs)** across the nation.

Grassroots Recommendations on Security of the civilians

The following are the recommendations under this group identified through the grassroots consultations:

1. **Disarmament of Civilians:** The youth and women recommended the removal of arms from the hands of illegal users and improve on the national army. This calls for disarmament across the country to ensure the viability of peace for innocent civil population in South Sudan.
2. **Disarmament** should start with the organized forces and all the civil populations should be disarmed in the same following manner: (a) voluntary disarmament through persuasion; (b) government should come with a project of buying guns from the people; and (c) forceful disarmament where necessary.
3. **Army Barracks far from Civilian population:** The army barracks be relocated to places far away from civilian settlements.

Grassroots Recommendations on the Traditional Authority

The following are recommendations concerning this group of issues:

1. **Traditional Authority to Settle the Disputes:** The local communities through chiefs be given a chance to discuss among themselves to bring peace and harmony.
2. **Empowering the local traditional authority** to exercise their influence on how to bring peace in the country.
3. **Formation of South Sudan Elders forum.**

Grassroots recommendations on Compensations

The following are recommendations from the grassroots consultations on this group of issues:

1. **Formulate criteria and procedures for the compensation for the innocent deaths.**
2. **Compensation** funds should be directed towards community development and national benefit rather than individuals.
3. **Enforcement of Anti-tribal laws:** The people of South Sudan need to abandon tribalism through establishment and enforcement of anti-tribalism laws, intermarriages, promotion of patriotism and nationalism in schools, military colleges and other communal settings.
4. **Encourage Intermarriages:** Intermarriages should be encouraged amongst the youth of all tribes Government to prioritize education because ignorance and negative cultures promote violence.

We now have sufficient information about the thinking of our people at the grassroots level. The eight groups of recommendations with respect to social cohesion and by extension, poverty eradication are consistent, as I have stated in the previous chapters, with the thinking of three African thinkers – Chinua Achebe, Julius Nyerere, and Francis

Mading Deng. Things started to fall apart since 6 August 2005, which is the day we laid to rest John Garang de Mabior. It is the day we, the elites of the SPLM, started to walk away from the promise of the payback time for our people as envisioned by Dr. John Garang and as articulated by Julius Nyerere's African traditional society in which *"we were individuals within a community. We took care of the community, and the community took care of us. We neither needed nor wished to exploit our fellow men[162]."*

The National Dialogue has shown beyond doubt, where, when, and why the ruling elites have abandoned the vision of the liberation struggle, which is the establishment of a viable South Sudanese state at peace within itself and with its neighbors. It has also recommended how to get back to the path of building this viable state underpinned by coherent governance, whose foundation is faith, rule of law, and institutions.

Faith is based on trust and this is where social capital is imperative. It is also a function of political morality of the ruling elites, which the framers of R-ARCSS have articulated in Article 4.1.3 as follows:

> The RTGoNU shall develop a code of ethics and integrity for public officials emphasizing the values of honesty and integrity. In addition, it shall expand the curriculum in the educational system to inculcate the spirit of nationalism and promote the values of honesty, integrity and respect for public property[163].

The above Article is a powerful one, which, if fully implemented, would go a long way to address most of the social ills that have undermined the cohesiveness of our communities and societies. Reconciliation and healing through intra- and inter-communal dialogue would alleviate poverty in the short-term. This is because reconciliation and healing will in turn enhance social mobility and sharing of common resources and services, such as pasture land, water points, schools, healthcare facilities, security, markets, veterinary services, and so forth.

------

162 Julius K. Nyerere. 1962. Ujamaa: The basis of African Socialism, Dar es Salam, April 1962

163 From Chapter IV of Revitalized Agreement on The Resolution of Conflict in the Republic of South Sudan (R-ARCSS), Addis Ababa, Ethiopia, 12 September 2018

A complementary action for alleviating poverty is the establishment of the Hybrid Court for South Sudan (HCSS) as stipulated in Chapter V of R-ARCSS. Article 5.3.1.1 states:

> There shall be established an independent hybrid judicial court, the Hybrid Court for South Sudan (HCSS). The Court shall be established by the African Union Commission to investigate and where necessary prosecute individuals bearing responsibility for violations of international law and/or applicable South Sudanese law, committed from 15th December 2013 through the end of the Transitional Period[164].

That would be, in the eyes of ordinary South Sudanese people, the beginning of the application of the rule of law and administration of justice at all levels of governance in the country. There is a clear synergy between the National Dialogue and R-ARCSS with respect to the call for transitional justice, accountability, national reconciliation and healing. Moreover, Article 4.1.2 of R-ARCSS states:

> Political leaders and stakeholders shall establish effective leadership and commitment in the fight against corruption. Any leader found to have condoned or engaged in corrupt practices shall be held accountable and barred from holding public office in accordance with this Agreement and the law[165].

The framers of R-ARCSS meant by "effective leadership," the Collegial Presidency. Effective leadership is, however, a function of institutions by:

> which authority in a country is exercised. This includes (1) the process by which governments are selected, monitored and replaced, (2) the capacity of the government to effectively formulate and implement sound policies, and (3) the respect of citizens and the state for the institutions that govern economic and social interactions among them[166].

---

164 Ibid

165 Ibid

166 See htt://www.worldbank.org/wbi/governance/Kaufmann

It is obvious from the above paragraph that institutions are needed at all phases of the strategy to combating poverty. That is, resilient institutions will lead to poverty eradication through effective governance in the long-term, when the current crop of leadership would have retired and replaced by Dr. John's "**Seeds of the Nation**" generation.

Selected Bibliography

Acemoglu, Daron. *Introduction to modern economic growth*. Princeton NJ: Princeton University Press, 2009.

Acemoglu, Daron, Simon Johnson and James A. Robinson. *Why Nations Fail: The Origins of Power, Prosperity, and Poverty*. New York: Crown Publishing Group, 2016.

Allison, Graham. "Lee Kuan Yew: Lessons for leaders from Asia's 'Grand Master." Special CNN Updated 1817 GMT (0217 HKT) March 28, 2015.

Arvanitidis, Paschalis, George Petrakos and Sotiris Pavleas. "On the Dynamics of Economic Growth: An Expert Survey." Political Economy 29, no.1 (2010): 59-86.

Barro, Robert J. 1991. "Economic growth in a cross-section of countries." *Quarterly Journal of Economics* 106, no.2 (1991): 407-443.

Bennett, Adam. *Monetary Policy in Dollarized Economies; Impact of Dollarization*. Washington D.C: IMF, 1999.

Besley, Timothy, and Torsten Persson. *Pillars of Prosperity: The Political Economics of Development Clusters*. Princeton, NJ: Princeton University Press, 2001.

Besouw, B.V., E. Ansink, and B.V. Bavel. "The economics of violence in natural states". *Journal of Economic Behavior & Organization* 132 (2016):139 -156.

Bromley, Daniel W. *South Sudan: Institutional Environment for Service Delivery*. Ebony Policy Brief: EPB #2019/2. Juba, South Sudan: Ebony Center, 2019.

− − *South Sudan: Country Policy and Institutional Environment*. Policy Brief, EPB#2019/1. Juba, South Sudan: Ebony Center for Strategic Studies, 2019.

Charap, J. and Harm, C. "Institutionalized Corruption and the Kleptocratic State." *IMF* Working Paper, WP/99/91. Washington: International Monetary Fund, 1999.

Cohen, Benjamin J. *Dollarization: Pros and Cons*. Santa Barbara, CA: UCSB, 2000.

Cohen, Roger. "The New Middle East of a Post-Sectarian Generation: America is gone. Regional leaders have concluded Trump is all hat and no camel, a pawn of Saudi Arabia." The New York Times, Opinion. November 8, 2019. https://www.nytimes.com/2019/11/08/opinion/lebanon-pro-tests.html

Commission on Growth and Development. *The Growth Report: Strategies for Sustained Growth and Inclusive Development*. Washington, DC: International Bank for Reconstruction and Development and the World Bank, 2008.

Commons, John R. Institutional Economics: Its Place in Political Economy. *Madison*: University of Wisconsin Press, 1959.

Chomsky, Noam. 2002. Understanding Power: The Indispensable Chomsky

D'Agoôt, Majak. *Taming the Dominant Gun Class in South Sudan: Special Report No. 4: Envisioning A Stable South Sudan*. May 29, 2018, https://africacenter.org/spotlight/taming-the-dominant-gun-class-in-south-sudan.

Deng, Lual A et al. "A Conceptual Framework for Resolving the Crisis of Governance and Leadership in South Sudan." Paper presented to *the Development Policy Forum (DPF)*, 19 July 2014, Juba Grand Hotel, Juba, Republic of South Sudan. https://paanluelwel.com/2014/08/01/a-conceptual-framework-for-resolving-the-crisis-of-governance-and-leadership-in-south-sudan-2/ Deng, Lual A. *Protecting Purchasing Power From Skyrocketing Prices In South Sudan Through Partial Dollarization*. Juba, Sourth Sudan" Ebony Center for Strategic Studies, 2016.

De Waal, Alex. "When Kleptocracy Becomes Insolvent: Brute Causes of The Civil War In South Sudan." *African Affairs*, 113 no.452 (2014): 347–369.

Dimant, Eugen and Tosato, Guglielmo.(1 January 2017). "Causes and Effects of Corruption: What Has Past Decade's Empirical Research Taught Us? A Survey." *Journal of Economic Surveys* 32, no.2 (2017): 335–356.

FFP. 2011. "Failed States Index 2011." *Fund for Peace (FFP)*. June 18, 2011, https://www.pucsp.br/ecopolitica/downloads/failed_states_index_2011.pdf

FRGFO. National Dialogue Handbook: A Guide for Practitioners. Berlin: Berghof Foundation, 2017.

Garang de Mabior, John. Address at the Signing Ceremony of Comprehensive Peace Agreement (CPA).

THE NATIONAL DIALOGUE

Speech, Nairobi, Kenya , January 9, 2005.

Geda, Alemayehu and Steve Kayizzi-Mugerwa. "Sudan: A Macroeconomic Framework for Negotiation and Cooperation between North and South Sudan." IAES Working Paper Series No. A02/2012, 2012.

Gelbard, E., and Deléchat Corinne. "Building Resilience in Fragile States in Sub-Saharan Africa." Building Resilience in Sub-Saharan Africa's Fragile States 11-14. Washington, D.C.: International Monetary Fund, 2015.

Goodwin, Doris Kearns. Leadership: In Turbulent Times. 1st Ed. New York: Simon and Schuster, 2018.

Heller, Peter. "Back to Basics -- Fiscal Space: What It Is and How to Get It." Finance and Development 42, no.2 (2005).

Intergovernmental Authority on Development. Signed Revitalized Agreement On The Resolution Of The Conflict In South Sudan. R-ARCSS. Addis Ababa, Ethiopia, 12 September 2018.

Jones, Benjamin F. and Benjamin A. Olken. "Do Leaders Matter? National Leadership and Growth Since World War II." The Quarterly Journal of Economics 120, no.3 (2005): 835–864.

Jones, Jamin F. National Leadership and Economic Growth. Northwestern University, New Palgrave Dictionary of Economics, 2008.

Karras, Georgios. "Costs and Benefits of Dollarization: Evidence from North, Central, and South America." Journal of Economic Integration 17, no.3 (2005): 502-516.

Kauffman, Daniel, Aart Kraay and Massimo Mastruzzi. Governance Matters VI: Aggregate and Individual Governance Indicators 1996-2006. Washington D.C: World Bank, 2007.

Keynes, John Maynard. "The Great Slump of 1930." The Nation & Athenæum 1.no1 (1930): 1

Klitgaard, Robert. Controlling Corruption. Berkeley, CA: University of California Press, 1998

Kuznets, Simon. 1971. "Modern Economic Growth: Findings and Reflections: Nobel Memorial Lecture" in Kuznets, Simon, Population, Capital, and Growth: Selected Essays. London: Heinemann, 2007. 165-184

Lewis, W. Arthur. "Economic Development with Unlimited Supplies of Labor." The Manchester School. 22 (1954) 139–191.

Lowe, A. "The Classical Theory of Economic Growth." Social Research 21, no. 1 (1954): 127-158.

Mayardit, Salva Kiir. "Concept Note of South Sudan National Dialogue." December, 2016.

Nielsen, K. and B. Johnson. "New Perspectives on Markets, Firms and Technology." In E. Elgar, ed., Institutions and Economic Change. London: Edward Elgar Publishing, 1998.

Nkurunziza, J. D. and R. H. Gates. "Political Institutions and Economic Growth in Africa". The Center for the Study of African Economies. Working Paper No. 185, 2008.

Noam Chomsky.

North, D. C. Institutions, Institutional Change, and Economic Performance. New York, NY & Cambridge: Cambridge University Press, 1990.

Nyerere, Julius K. Ujamaa: "The Basis of African Socialism." Ujamaa – Essays on Socialism. Oxford: Oxford University Press, 1973

OECD. States of Fragility 2015: Meeting Post-2015 Ambitions. OECD Publishing, Paris, 2015. Republic of South Sudan Ministry of Petroleum and Mining. MPM Marketing Reports, Volume 1A. Juba, South Sudan, 2011.

Putnam, Robert D. Bowling Alone: The Collapse and Revival of American Community. New York: Simon and Schuster, 2001

Rodrik, Dani, Arvind Subramanian, and Francesco Trebbi. "Institutions Rule: The Primacy of Institutions over Geography and Integration in Economic Development". IMF Working Paper WP/02/189. Washington D.C: IMF, 2002.

Rodrik, Dani. "An African Growth Miracle?" Journal of African Economies 27, no.1 (2016): 1–18.

— "The Why and How of Growth Diagnostics". SSS. IAS.EDU. 10 September 2013. https://www.sss.ias.edu/files/pdfs/Rodrik/Presentations/Growth-diagnostics.pdf.

Romer, Paul M. 1990. "Endogenous Technological Change." The Journal of Political Economy 98, No.5, Part 2 (1990): S71- S102.

Rostow, Walt W. Stages of Economic Growth: A Non-communist Manifesto. Cambridge: Cambridge University Press, 1960.

Smith, Adam. An Inquiry into the Nature and Causes of the Wealth of Nations, Vol.3. London: Adam Smith, 1776.

Smith, Adam. "On the Need for peace, easy taxes, and a tolerable administration of justice (1755)." Liberty Fund.org.12 January 2009. https://oll.libertyfund.org/quotes/436

Snowdon, Brian and Howard R. Vane. Modern Macroeconomics: Its origins, Development and Current State. Cheltenham, UK and Northampton, MA, USA: Edward Elgar, 2005.

South Sudan Council of Churches. Implementation of Church Action Plan for Sustainable Peace and Reconciliation in South Sudan. Juba, South Sudan: SSCC, 2016.

SSND. Communiqué of The Bahr El Ghazal Regional Conference. 25 June 2019. https://www.ssnationaldialogue.org/resource/communique-bahr-el-ghazal-regionalconference//.

SSNC. *Communiqué of the Business Community Conference.* 25 November 2019. https://www.ssnationaldialogue.org/resource/communique-business-community-conference-juba-south-sudan-21st-22nd-november-2019/

Stigant, Susan and Elizabeth Murray. "National Dialogue: A Tool for Conflict Transformation?" *A Peace Brief number 194.* Washington D.C: United States Institute of Peace (USIP), 2015.

Thiong, Daniel Akech. "How The Politics Of Fear Generated Chaos In South Sudan." *African Affairs* 1, no.23 (2018): 613-635.

UNDP. 1998. "Capacity Assessment and Development in a System and Strategic Management Context." Technical Advisory Paper for *Management Development and Governance Division, Bureau for Development Policy.* New York: UNDP, 1998.

Vito, Tanzi. "Corruption: Arm's-length Relationships and Markets." *The Economics of Organised Crime.* Ed. Fiorentini, G. i Pelzman, S.M. Cambridge: Cambridge University Press, 1995 Weber, Max. *The Protestant Ethic and the Spirit of Capitalism.* Crown Nest Australia: Allen and Unwin, 1930.

World Bank. "Building Institutions for Markets". *World Development Report 2002.* Oxford: Oxford University Press, 2002.

Van Sant, Jerry. "A Composite Framework for Assessing the Capacity of Development Organizations." *USAID.* Washington D.C: USAID, 2000.

INDEX

INDEX OF NAMES

www.ingramcontent.com/pod-product-compliance
Lightning Source LLC
Chambersburg PA
CBHW052011030426
42334CB00029BA/3169